LEARN TO CODE BY SOLVING PROBLEMS

A Python Programming Primer

by Daniel Zingaro

**no starch
press**

San Francisco

Printed in the United States of America

26 25 24 23 22   2 3 4 5 6

ISBN-13: 978-1-7185-0132-4 (print)
ISBN-13: 978-1-7185-0133-1 (ebook)

Publisher: Bill Pollock
Executive Editor: Barbara Yien
Production Manager: Rachel Monaghan
Production Editor: Kassie Andreadis
Developmental Editor: Alex Freed
Interior and Cover Design: Octopod Studios
Cover Illustrator: Rob Gale
Technical Reviewer: Luke Sawczak
Copyeditor: Kim Wimpsett
Proofreader: Emelie Battaglia
Indexer: Sanjiv Kumar Sinha

For information on distributions, bulk sales, corporate sales, or translations, contact No Starch Press, Inc. directly at info@nostarch.com or:

No Starch Press, Inc.
245 8th Street, San Francisco, CA 94103
phone: 1.415.863.9900
www.nostarch.com

Library of Congress Cataloging-in-Publication Data
Names: Zingaro, Daniel, author.
Title: Learn to code by solving problems : a Python programming primer / by
    Daniel Zingaro.
Description: San Francisco, CA : No Starch Press, [2021] | Includes index.
Identifiers: LCCN 2021011082 (print) | LCCN 2021011083 (ebook) | ISBN
    9781718501324 (print) | ISBN 9781718501331 (ebook)
Subjects: LCSH: Python (Computer program language) | Computer programming.
Classification: LCC QA76.73.P98 Z55 2021 (print) | LCC QA76.73.P98
    (ebook) | DDC 005.13/3--dc23
LC record available at https://lccn.loc.gov/2021011082
LC ebook record available at https://lccn.loc.gov/2021011083

[S]

To Dad,
for the computer code

and

To Mom,
for the teacher code

About the Author

Dr. Daniel Zingaro is an associate teaching professor of computer science and award-winning teacher at the University of Toronto. His main area of research is computer science education, where he studies how students learn (and sometimes don't learn) computer science material. He is the author of *Algorithmic Thinking* (No Starch Press, 2021), a book that helps learners understand and use algorithms and data structures.

About the Technical Reviewer

Luke Sawczak is a frequent freelance editor and hobby programmer; his favorite projects include a prose-to-poetry converter, a visual aid for cutting the right number of slices of cake, and a version of Boggle that uses numbers made for math tutors. He currently teaches French and English on the outskirts of Toronto. He also writes poetry and composes for the piano, which he would do for a living if he could. He can be found online at *https://sawczak.com/*.

BRIEF CONTENTS

CONTENTS IN DETAIL

2
MAKING DECISIONS

5

ORGANIZING VALUES USING LISTS

7
READING AND WRITING FILES

ACKNOWLEDGMENTS

For real? I got to work with the No Starch Press people again? Barbara Yien brought me aboard. Bill Pollock and Barbara trusted me with the pedagogical approach of the book. Alex Freed, my developmental editor, was careful, kind, and timely. I thank all those involved in the production of the book, including my copyeditor Kim Wimpsett, production editor Kassie Andreadis, and cover designer Rob Gale. I'm very lucky.

I thank the University of Toronto for offering me the time and space to write. I thank Luke Sawczak, my technical reviewer, for his careful review of the manuscript.

I thank everyone who contributed to the problems that I used in this book and to competitive programming in general. I thank the DMOJ administrators for their support of my work.

I thank my parents for handling everything—*everything*. All they asked me to do was learn.

I thank Doyali, my partner, for giving more of our time to a book and for modeling the care it takes to write.

Finally, I thank all of you for reading this book and wanting to learn.

INTRODUCTION

We use computers to accomplish tasks and to solve problems. For example, perhaps you've used a word processor to write an essay or letter. Perhaps you've used a spreadsheet program to organize your finances. Perhaps you've used an image editor to touch up a picture. It's hard to imagine doing these things these days without a computer. We get a lot of mileage out of our word processors and spreadsheet programs and image editors.

Those programs are written as general-purpose tools to accomplish a wide variety of tasks. Ultimately, though, they're programs written by others, not by us. What do we do when an off-the-shelf program doesn't quite do what we need?

In this book, our goal is to learn how to take control of our computer by going beyond what can be done by an end user using preexisting programs. We're going to write our own programs. We won't write a word processor or a spreadsheet or an image editor. Those are huge tasks that, fortunately, people have already done. Rather, we're going to learn how to write small programs to solve problems that we otherwise wouldn't be able to solve. I want to help you learn to communicate instructions to a computer; these instructions will tell the computer how to carry out your plan for solving a problem.

To give instructions to a computer, we write code in a *programming language*. A programming language specifies the rules for the code we write and dictates what the computer does in response to that code.

We're going to learn to program in the Python programming language. That's a concrete skill that you'll take away from this book, one that you can put on your résumé. More than Python, though, you'll learn the type of thinking required to solve problems using a computer. Programming languages come and go. The way that we solve problems does not. I hope that this book helps you on your way from end user to programmer and that you have fun exploring what's possible.

Online Resources

Supplementary resources for the book, including downloadable code and additional exercises, are available at *https://nostarch.com/learn-code-solving -problems/*.

Who This Book Is For

This book is for anyone who wants to learn how to write computer programs to solve problems. I have three particular types of people in mind.

First, you may have heard about the Python programming language and want to learn how to write code in Python. I'll explain in the next section why Python is a great choice as a first programming language to learn. You'll learn a lot about Python in this book, and you'll be in a position to read more advanced books on Python if that's your next step.

Second, if you haven't heard of Python or just want to learn what programming is all about, don't worry: this book is for you, too! This book will teach you how to think about programming. Programmers have particular ways of breaking down problems into manageable pieces and expressing solutions to those pieces in code. At this level, it doesn't matter what programming language is being used, because the way that programmers think is not tied to a particular language.

Finally, you may be interested in learning some other programming language such as C++, Java, Go, or Rust. Much of what you learn as a byproduct of learning Python will be useful when you study those other programming languages. Plus, Python is certainly worth learning in its own right. Let's turn to why next.

Why Learn Python?

Years of teaching introductory programming have demonstrated to me that Python is a great choice for a first programming language. Compared to other languages, Python code is often more structured and readable. Once you get used to it, you might agree that parts of it almost read like English!

Python also comes with many features that are not available in other languages, including powerful tools to manipulate and store data. We'll use many of these features throughout the book.

Not only is Python an excellent teaching language, but it's also one of the most in-demand programming languages in the world. Programmers use it to write web applications, games, visualizations, machine learning software, and more.

There we have it: a language well-suited for teaching that also carries a professional advantage for you. I can't ask for any more than that!

Installing Python

Before we can program in Python, we need to install it. Let's do that now.

There are two major versions of Python: Python 2 and Python 3. Python 2 is an older version of Python and is no longer supported. In this book, we use Python 3, so you'll need to install Python 3 on your computer.

Python 3 was a major evolution from Python 2, but Python continues to change even within version 3. The first version of Python 3 was Python 3.0. Then Python 3.1 was released, then Python 3.2, and so on. At the time of writing, the latest version of Python 3 is Python 3.10. Versions as old as Python 3.6 will suffice for this book, but I encourage you to install and work with the latest version of Python.

Follow these steps for your operating system to install Python.

Windows

Windows doesn't come with Python by default. To install it, go to *https://www.python.org/* and click **Downloads**. This should offer you the option of downloading the latest version of Python for Windows. Click the link to download Python and then run the installer. On one of the first screens in the installation process, click either **Add Python 3.10 to PATH** or **Add Python to environment variables**; this makes running Python much easier. (If upgrading Python, you may need to click "Customize installation" to find this option.)

macOS

macOS doesn't come with Python 3 by default. To install it, go to *https://www.python.org/* and click **Downloads**. This should offer you the option of downloading the latest version of Python for macOS. Click the link to download Python and then run the installer.

Linux

Linux comes with Python 3, but it may be an older version of Python 3. Installation instructions will vary depending on which Linux distribution you're using, but you should be able to install the newest version of Python using your favorite package manager.

How to Read This Book

Reading this book from cover to cover in one sitting is likely to teach you very little. It would be like trying to learn piano by inviting someone into your house to play piano for a few hours and then kicking them out, lowering the lights, and serenading. That's not how a practice-based skill is learned.

Here is my advice for making your way through the book:

Space out your work.   Massing your practice into a small number of sessions is far less effective than spacing your practice out. When you feel tired, take a break. No one can tell you how much time to work before taking a break. No one can tell you how long it should take you to finish the book. It's up to your own mind and body.

Pause to test your understanding.   Reading about something can give us the illusion that we understand it better than we do. Applying the material forces what we know and what we think we know into alignment. For that reason, at key points in each chapter, I've included multiple-choice "concept check" questions that ask you to make a prediction. Take these seriously! Read each question and commit to a response without checking anything using your computer. Then, read my answer and explanation. This is an opportunity to confirm that you're on the right track. If you answer incorrectly or answer correctly but for the wrong reason, take time to remedy your understanding before continuing. This could involve playing around a little more with the relevant Python feature being discussed, rereading material from the book, or searching for additional explanations and examples online.

Practice programming.   Making predictions while you read will help solidify your understanding of key concepts. But you need more than that to become an adept problem-solver and programmer. You need to practice using Python to solve new problems, whose solutions you haven't read about in the book. Each chapter concludes with a list of practice exercises. Please work through as many of these exercises as you can.

Learning how to program takes time. Don't be discouraged if you progress slowly or make a lot of mistakes. Don't be intimidated by any blustering peacocks that you might encounter online. Surround yourself with people and resources that can help you learn.

Using Programming Judges

I've decided to structure this book around problems from *programming judge* websites. A programming judge website offers a repository of programming problems that can be solved by programmers around the world. You submit your solution—your Python code—and the site runs tests on your code. If your code produces the correct answer for each test case, then it's likely that your solution is correct. If instead your code produces the wrong answer for one or more test cases, then your code is incorrect, and revisions are required.

There are several reasons why I think programming judges are particularly suitable sites for learning programming:

Rapid feedback   Rapid, targeted feedback is crucial in the early stages of learning to program. Programming judges provide feedback as soon as you submit your code.

High-quality problems   I find the problems on programming judges to be high quality. Many problems are originally from competitive programming contests. Other problems are written by individuals who are associated with a programming judge or simply want to help others learn. See the Problem Credits appendix for the source of each problem that we'll study.

Quantity of problems   The programming judges contain hundreds of problems. I've selected only a small number for this book. If you need more practice, trust me: the programming judges can provide it.

Community features   The programming judges enable users to read and respond to comments. If you're stuck on a problem, browse the comments for hints dropped there by others. If you're still stuck, consider posting a comment of your own asking for help. Once you've successfully solved a problem, your learning is not done! Many programming judges allow you to view the code that others have submitted. Dig through a few such submissions to see how they compare to yours. There are always multiple ways to solve a problem. Perhaps your way is most intuitive to you right now, but opening yourself to other possibilities is an important step toward programming mastery.

Making Your Programming Judge Accounts

We'll use several programming judge websites throughout the book. That's because each programming judge hosts some problems that are not found on other programming judges; we need multiple programming judges to cover all of the problems that I've chosen.

Here are the programming judges that we'll use:

Judge	URL
DMOJ	https://dmoj.ca/
Timus	https://acm.timus.ru/
USACO	http://usaco.org/

Each programming judge requires that you create an account before you can submit code. Let's go through the process of creating your accounts now and learn a little about the judges while we're at it.

The DMOJ Judge

The DMOJ judge is the judge we'll use most often in the book. More than for any other judge, it's worth your time exploring the DMOJ website and learning about what the judge offers.

To create an account on the DMOJ judge, go to *https://dmoj.ca/* and click **Sign up**. On the registration page that comes up, enter your username, password, and email address. This page also allows you to set your default programming language. We'll exclusively be using the Python programming language in this book, so I suggest clicking **Python 3** here. Click **Register!** to create your account. Once registered, you can use your username and password to log in to DMOJ.

Each problem in the book begins by indicating the judge website where the problem can be found and the problem code that you should use to access it. For example, the first problem that we'll work on in Chapter 1 is found on DMOJ and is problem dmopc15c7p2. To find this problem on DMOJ, click **Problems**, type **dmopc15c7p2** in the search box, and click **Go**. You should see the problem as the only result. If you click the problem title, you should see the problem itself.

When you're ready to submit Python code for a problem, find the problem and click **Submit solution**. On the resulting page, paste your Python code into the text box and click **Submit!**. Your code will then be judged and the results shown.

The Timus Judge

To create an account on the Timus judge, go to *https://acm.timus.ru/* and click **Register**. On the registration page that comes up, enter your name, password, email address, and other requested information. Click **Register** to create your account. Then, check your email for a message from Timus containing your judge ID. You'll need your judge ID whenever you submit Python code.

There's currently no way to set your default programming language, so be sure to choose the available version of Python 3 whenever you submit Python code.

We use the Timus judge only once, in Chapter 6, so I won't say any more about it here.

The USACO Judge

To create an account on the USACO judge, go to *http://usaco.org/* and click **Register for New Account**. On the registration page that comes up, enter your username, email address, and other requested information. Click **Submit** to create your account. Then, check your email for a message from USACO containing your password. Once you have your password, you can use your username and password to log in to USACO.

There's currently no way to set your default programming language, so be sure to choose the available version of Python 3 whenever you submit Python code. You'll also need to choose the file containing your Python code rather than paste your code into a text box.

We won't be using the USACO judge until Chapter 7, so I won't say any more about it here.

About This Book

Each chapter in the book is driven by two or three problems from a programming judge website. In fact, I start each chapter by posing our first problem, before teaching any new Python at all! My goal in doing this is to motivate you to want to learn the Python features that we need to solve the problem. Don't worry if you're not sure how to solve a problem after reading its description. (If you can't solve the problem yet, then you're reading the right book!) If you understand what the problem is asking you to do, then you're all set. We're going to learn Python and solve the problem together. Subsequent problems in the chapter may introduce further Python features or ask us to extend what we learned in the first problem. Each chapter concludes with exercises that you should solve on your own to practice what you just learned.

Here's a rundown of what we'll learn in each chapter:

Chapter 1: Getting Started   There are quite a few introductory concepts that we'll need to learn before we can solve any problems with Python. In this chapter, we'll learn these concepts, including entering Python code, working with strings and numbers, using variables, reading input, and writing output.

Chapter 2: Making Decisions   In this chapter, we'll learn about if statements, which allow our programs to decide what to do based on whether specific conditions are true or false.

Chapter 3: Repeating Code: Definite Loops   Many programs continue running as long as there is work to do. In this chapter, we'll learn about the for loop, which lets our programs process each piece of input until the job is done.

Chapter 4: Repeating Code: Indefinite Loops   Sometimes we don't know in advance how many times our program should repeat some specified behavior. for loops are not appropriate for these kinds of problems. In this chapter, we'll learn about the while loop, which repeats code as long as a specific condition is true.

Chapter 5: Organizing Values Using Lists   A Python list allows us to use a single name to refer to a whole sequence of data. Using a list helps us organize our data and leverage the powerful list operations (such as sorting and searching) that Python provides. In this chapter, we'll learn all about lists.

Chapter 6: Designing Programs with Functions   A large program, with lots of code, can become unwieldy if we don't organize it well. In this chapter, we'll learn about functions, which help us design programs composed of small, self-contained chunks of code. Using functions leads to programs that are much easier to understand and modify. We'll also learn about top-down design, an approach to designing programs with functions.

Chapter 7: Reading and Writing Files   Files are convenient for providing data to our programs or obtaining data from our programs. In this chapter, we'll learn how to read data from and write data to files.

Chapter 8: Organizing Values Using Sets and Dictionaries   As we begin to solve increasingly challenging problems, it's important that we think about how our data is stored. In this chapter, we'll learn about two new ways to store data using Python: using a set and using a dictionary.

Chapter 9: Designing Algorithms with Complete Search   Programmers don't start from scratch for each problem they solve. Instead, they think about whether a general solution pattern—a type of *algorithm*—can be used to solve it. In this chapter, we'll learn about complete-search algorithms, which can be used to solve a wide range of problems.

Chapter 10: Big O and Program Efficiency   Sometimes we'll manage to write a program that does the right thing but does so too slowly to be useful in practice. In this chapter, we'll learn how to communicate about the efficiency of programs, and we'll learn about tools we can use to write more efficient code.

1

GETTING STARTED

Programming involves writing code to solve a problem. As such, I want to solve problems with you from the outset. That is, rather than learning Python concept by concept and then solving a problem, we're going to use a problem to dictate the concepts we need to learn.

In this chapter, we'll solve two problems: determining the number of words in a line (like the word-count feature in a word processor) and calculating the volume of a cone. Solving these problems requires a tour of quite a few Python concepts. You may feel that you need more details to fully understand some of what I introduce here and how it all fits together in the design of a Python program. Don't worry: we'll revisit and elaborate on the most important concepts in later chapters.

What We'll Be Doing

As described in the introduction, we'll be solving competitive programming problems using the Python programming language. The competitive programming problems can each be found on an online judge website. I assume that you've followed the instructions in the introduction to install Python and make your judge accounts.

For each problem, we'll write a program to solve it. Each problem specifies the kind of *input* that our program will be provided, and the kind of *output* (or result) that is expected. Our program correctly solves the problem if it can take any valid input and produce the correct output.

In general, there will be millions or billions of possible inputs. Each such input is referred to as a *problem instance*. For example, in the first problem that we'll solve, the input is a line of text, like `hello there` or `bbaabbb aa abab`. Our task will be to output the number of words in the line. One of the most powerful ideas in programming is that often a small amount of general-purpose code can solve a seemingly endless number of problem instances. Whether the line has 2 words or 3 or 50, it won't matter. Our program will get it right every time.

Our programs will perform three tasks:

Read input   We need to determine the specific instance of the problem that we're solving, so we first read the provided input.

Process   We process the input to determine the correct output.

Write output   Having solved the problem, we produce the desired output.

The boundaries between these steps may not always be crisp—we might have to interleave some processing with producing some output, for example—but it will be helpful to keep these three broad steps in mind.

You likely use programs on a daily basis that follow this input-process-output model. Consider a calculator program: you type in a formula (the input), the program crunches your numbers (process), and the program displays the answer (output). Or consider a web search engine: you type in a search query (input), the search engine determines the most relevant results (process), and it displays them (output).

Contrast these kinds of programs with *interactive* programs, which fuse input, processing, and output. For example, I'm typing this book using a text editor. When I type a character, the editor responds by adding that character to my document. It doesn't wait for me to type the entire document before displaying it to me; it interactively displays it as I build it. We won't be writing interactive programs in this book. If you're interested in writing such programs after studying this book, you'll be happy to hear that Python is certainly up for the task.

The text for each problem is found both here and on the online judge. However, the text won't match, because I've rewritten it for purposes of consistency throughout the book. Don't worry: what I've written conveys the same information as the official problem statement.

The Python Shell

For each problem in the book, we want to write a program and save it in a file. But that assumes we know what program to write! For many of the problems in the book, we'll need to learn some new Python features before we can solve the problem.

The best way to experiment with Python features is by using the Python shell. It's an interactive environment where you type some Python code and press ENTER, and Python shows you the result. Once we learn enough to solve the current problem, we'll stop using the shell and start typing our solution in a text file instead.

To begin, create a new folder on your desktop called *programming*. We'll use that folder to store all of the work that we do for this book.

Now, we'll navigate to this *programming* folder and launch the Python shell. Follow these steps for your operating system whenever you'd like to start the Python shell.

Windows

On Windows, do the following:

1. Hold down SHIFT and right-click your **programming** folder.

2. From the resulting menu, click **Open PowerShell window here**. If that choice isn't there, click **Open command window here**.

3. At the bottom of the resulting window, you'll see a line that ends with a greater-than sign (>). This is your operating system *prompt*, and it's waiting for you to type a command. You type operating system commands here, *not* Python code. Be sure to press ENTER after each command.

4. You're now in your *programming* folder. You can type `dir` (for *directory*) if you'd like to see what's there. You shouldn't see any files yet, because we haven't created any.

5. Now, enter `python` to start the Python shell.

When you start the Python shell, you should see something like this:

```
Python 3.10.1 (tags/v3.10.1:2cd268a, Dec  6 2021, 19:10:37)
[MSC v.1929 64 bit (AMD64)] on win32
Type "help", "copyright", "credits" or "license" for more information.
>>>
```

What's important here is that you see a Python version of at least 3.6 in the first line. If you have an older version, especially 2.*x*, or if Python doesn't load at all, please install a recent version of Python following the instructions in the introduction.

At the bottom of this window, you'll see a >>> Python prompt. This is where you type Python code. Never type the >>> symbols yourself. Once you're done programming, you can press CTRL-Z and then press ENTER to quit.

macOS

On macOS, do the following:

1. Open Terminal. You can do that by pressing COMMAND-spacebar, typing **terminal**, and then double-clicking the result.

2. In the resulting window, you'll see a line that ends with a dollar symbol ($). This is your operating system *prompt*, and it's waiting for you to type a command. You type operating system commands here, *not* Python code. Be sure to press ENTER after each command.

3. You can enter the `ls` command to obtain a list of what's in the current folder. Your *Desktop* should be listed there.

4. Enter `cd Desktop` to navigate to your *Desktop* folder. The `cd` command stands for *change directory*; *directory* is another name for folder.

5. Enter `cd programming` to navigate to your *programming* folder.

6. Now, enter `python3` to start the Python shell. (You could also try entering `python`, without the 3, but that might start up an older version of Python 2. Python 2 is not suitable for working through this book.)

When you start the Python shell, you should see something like this:

```
Python 3.10.1 (v3.10.1:2cd268a3a9, Dec  6 2021, 14:28:59)
[Clang 13.0.0 (clang-1300.0.29.3)] on darwin
Type "help", "copyright", "credits" or "license" for more information.
>>>
```

What's important here is that you see a Python version of at least 3.6 in the first line. If you have an older version, especially 2.*x*, or if Python doesn't load at all, please install a recent version of Python following the instructions in the introduction.

At the bottom of this window, you'll see a >>> Python prompt. This is where you type Python code. Never type the >>> symbols yourself. Once you're done programming, you can press CTRL-D to quit.

Linux

On Linux, do the following:

1. Right-click your *programming* folder.

2. In the resulting menu, click *Open in Terminal*. (You can also open the terminal and navigate to your *programming* folder if you're more comfortable with that.)

3. At the bottom of the resulting window, you'll see a line that ends with a dollar sign ($). This is your operating system *prompt*, and it's waiting for you to type a command. You type operating system commands here, *not* Python code. Be sure to press ENTER after each command.

4. You're now in your *programming* folder. You can type ls if you'd like to see what's there. You shouldn't see any files yet, because we haven't created any.

5. Now, enter **python3** to start the Python shell. (You could also try entering python, without the 3, but that might start up an older version of Python 2. Python 2 is not suitable for working through this book.)

When you start the Python shell, you should see something like this:

```
Python 3.10.1 (main, Dec 21 2021, 18:59:49)
[GCC 7.5.0] on linux
Type "help", "copyright", "credits" or "license" for more information.
>>>
```

What's important here is that you see a Python version of at least 3.6 in the first line. If you have an older version, especially 2.*x*, or if Python doesn't load at all, please install a recent version of Python following the instructions in the introduction.

At the bottom of this window, you'll see a >>> Python prompt. This is where you type Python code. Never type the >>> symbols yourself. Once you're done programming, you can press CTRL-D to quit.

Problem #1: Word Count

Now it's time for our first problem! We're going to use Python to write a little word-count program. We'll learn how to read input from the user, process the input to solve the problem, and output the result. We'll also learn how to manipulate text and numbers in our programs, make use of built-in Python operations, and store intermediate results on our way to the solution.

This is DMOJ problem dmopc15c7p2.

The Challenge

Count the number of words provided. For this problem, a *word* is any sequence of lowercase letters. For example, hello is a word, but so are non-English "words" like bbaabbb.

Input

The input is one line of text, consisting of lowercase letters and spaces. There is exactly one space between each pair of words, and there are no spaces before the first word or after the last word.

The maximum length of the line is 80 characters.

Output

Output the number of words in the input line.

Strings

Values are a fundamental building block of Python programs. Each value has a *type*, and the type determines the operations that can be performed on the value. In the Word Count problem, we're working with a line of text. Text is stored as a string value in Python, so we'll need to learn about strings. To solve the problem, we output the number of words in the text, so we also need to learn about numeric values. Let's begin with strings.

Representing Strings

A *string* is the Python type that's used to store and manipulate text. To write a string value, we place its characters between single quotes. Follow along in the Python shell:

```
>>> 'hello'
'hello'
>>> 'a bunch of words'
'a bunch of words'
```

The Python shell echoes each string that I've typed.

What happens when our string contains a single quote as one of its characters?

```
>>> 'don't say that'
  File "<stdin>", line 1
    'don't say that'
         ^
SyntaxError: invalid syntax
```

The single quote in the word don't terminates the string. The rest of the line, t say that', therefore doesn't make sense, and that's what generates the syntax error. A *syntax error* means that we have violated the rules of Python and have not written valid Python code.

To fix this, we can take advantage of the fact that double quotes can also be used to delimit strings:

```
>>> "don't say that"
"don't say that"
```

Unless the string in question has a single quote, I won't use double quotes in this book.

String Operators

We can use a string to hold the text whose words we want to count. To count the words—or to do anything else with strings—we need to learn how to work with strings.

Strings come with a rich variety of operations that we can perform. Some of them use special symbols between their operands. For example, the + operator is used for string concatenation:

```
>>> 'hello' + 'there'
'hellothere'
```

Oops—we need a space between those two words. Let's add one to the end of the first string:

```
>>> 'hello ' + 'there'
'hello there'
```

There's also the * operator, which replicates a string a specified number of times:

```
>>> '-' * 30
'------------------------------'
```

That 30 there is an integer value. I'll have more to say about integers shortly.

CONCEPT CHECK

What is the output of the following code?

```
>>> '' * 3
```

A. ''''''

B. ''

C. This code produces a syntax error (invalid Python code)

Answer: B. '' is the empty string—a string of zero characters. Repeating an empty string three times is still an empty string!

String Methods

A *method* is an operation specific to a type of value. Strings have a large number of methods. For example, there's a method called upper, which produces the uppercase version of a string:

```
>>> 'hello'.upper()
'HELLO'
```

The information we get back from a method is known as the method's *return value*. For example, we could say for the previous example that upper returned the string 'HELLO'.

Performing a method on a value is known as *calling* the method. Calling a method involves placing the *dot operator* (.) between the value and the method name. It also requires parentheses after the method name. For some methods, we leave those parentheses empty, as when calling upper.

For other methods, we can optionally include information there. Still other methods require information and won't work at all without it. Information we include when calling a method is referred to as the method's *arguments*.

For example, strings have a strip method. If called with no arguments, strip removes all leading and trailing spaces from a string:

```
>>> '   abc'.strip()
'abc'
>>> '   abc      '.strip()
'abc'
>>> 'abc'.strip()
'abc'
```

But we can also call it with a string as the argument. If we do, that argument determines which characters are stripped from the beginning and the end:

```
>>> 'abc'.strip('a')
'bc'
>>> 'abca'.strip('a')
'bc'
>>> 'abca'.strip('ac')
'b'
```

Let's talk about one more string method: count. We pass it a string argument, and it tells us how many occurrences of that argument are found in our string:

```
>>> 'abc'.count('a')
1
>>> 'abc'.count('q')
0
```

```
>>> 'aaabcaa'.count('a')
5
>>> 'aaabcaa'.count('ab')
1
```

If occurrences of the argument overlap, only the first counts:

```
>>> 'ababa'.count('aba')
1
```

Unlike the other methods I've described, count is directly useful to our Word Count problem.

Think of a string like 'this is a string with a few words'. Notice that a space comes after each word. In fact, if you had to count the number of words by hand, you might use the spaces to tell you where each word ends. What if we count the number of spaces in a string? To do that, we can pass a string consisting of a single space character to count. It looks like this:

```
>>> 'this is a string with a few words'.count(' ')
7
```

We get a value of 7. That's not quite the number of words—the string has eight words—but we're close. Why are we getting 7 instead of 8?

The reason is that each word has a space after it except the last word. Counting the spaces therefore fails to account for the final word. To remedy that, we need to learn how to handle numbers.

Integer and Floating-Point Numbers

An *expression* is made up of values and operators. We'll now see how to write numeric values and combine them with operators.

There are two different Python types that represent numbers: integers (with no decimal part) and floating-point numbers (with a decimal part).

We write integer values as numbers with no decimal point. Here are some examples:

```
>>> 30
30
>>> 7
7
>>> 1000000
1000000
>>> -9
-9
```

A value on its own is the simplest kind of expression.

The familiar mathematical operators work on integers. We have + for addition, - for subtraction, and * for multiplication. We can use these operators to write more complicated expressions.

```
>>> 8 + 10
18
>>> 8 - 10
-2
>>> 8 * 10
80
```

Notice the spaces around the operators. While 8+10 and 8 + 10 are the same as far as Python is concerned, the latter makes the expression easier for us humans to read.

Python has two division operators, not one! The // operator performs integer division, which throws away any remainder and rounds the result down:

```
>>> 8 // 2
4
>>> 9 // 5
1
>>> -9 // 5
-2
```

If you want the remainder of the division, use the mod operator, written as %. For example, dividing 8 by 2 leaves no remainder:

```
>>> 8 % 2
0
```

Dividing 8 by 3 leaves a remainder of 2:

```
>>> 8 % 3
2
```

The / operator, in contrast to //, doesn't do any rounding:

```
>>> 8 / 2
4.0
>>> 9 / 5
1.8
>>> -9 / 5
-1.8
```

These result values are not integers! They have a decimal point and belong to a different Python type called *float* (for "floating-point numbers"). You can write float values by including a decimal point:

```
>>> 12.5 * 2
25.0
```

We'll focus on integers for now and return to floating-point numbers when we solve Cone Volume later in this chapter.

When we use multiple operators in an expression, Python uses precedence rules to determine the order that operators are applied. Each operator has a precedence. Just like when we evaluate a mathematical expression on paper, Python performs multiplications and divisions (higher precedence) before additions and subtractions (lower precedence):

```
>>> 50 + 10 * 2
70
```

Again, like on paper, operations inside parentheses have the highest precedence. We can use this to force Python to perform operations in our desired order:

```
>>> (50 + 10) * 2
120
```

Programmers often add parentheses even when not technically required. That's because Python has many operators, as we'll see, and keeping track of their precedence is error-prone and not something that programmers typically do.

If you're wondering whether integer values and float values have methods, just like strings, they do! But they aren't all that useful. For example, there's a method that tells us how much of the computer's memory is taken up by an integer. The bigger the integer, the more memory it requires:

```
>>> (5).bit_length()
3
>>> (100).bit_length()
7
>>> (99999).bit_length()
17
```

We need the parentheses around the integers; otherwise, the dot operator gets confused with a decimal point, and we get a syntax error.

Variables

We now know how to write string and numeric values. We'll also find it valuable to be able to store them so we can access them later. In Word Count, it would be convenient to be able to store the line of words somewhere and then count the number of words.

Assignment Statement

A *variable* is a name that refers to a value. Whenever we later use a variable's name, it gets substituted by what that variable refers to. To make a variable refer to a value, we use the *assignment statement*. An assignment statement consists of a variable, an equal sign (=), and an expression. Python evaluates the expression and makes the variable refer to the result. Here's an example assignment statement:

```
>>> dollars = 250
```

Now, dollars is substituted by 250 whenever we use it:

```
>>> dollars
250
>>> dollars + 10
260
>>> dollars
250
```

A variable refers to only one value at a time. Once we use an assignment statement to make a variable refer to another value, it no longer refers to the old value:

```
>>> dollars = 250
>>> dollars
250
>>> dollars = 300
>>> dollars
300
```

We can have as many variables as we like. Large programs typically use hundreds of variables. Here's an example of using two variables:

```
>>> purchase_price1 = 58
>>> purchase_price2 = 9
>>> purchase_price1 + purchase_price2
67
```

Notice that I've chosen variable names that give some sense of what they're storing. These two variables, for example, have to do with the prices of two purchases. Using variable names p1 and p2 would be easier to type, but in a few days we'd probably forget what the names mean!

We can make variables refer to strings, too:

```
>>> start = 'Monday'
>>> end = 'Friday'
>>> start
'Monday'
>>> end
'Friday'
```

As with variables that refer to numbers, we can use these in larger expressions:

```
>>> start + '-' + end
'Monday-Friday'
```

Python variable names should start with a lowercase letter and then can contain additional letters, underscores to separate words, and numbers.

Changing Variable Values

Suppose we have a variable `dollars` that refers to value 250:

```
>>> dollars = 250
```

Now we want to increase the value so that `dollars` refers to 251. This won't work:

```
>>> dollars + 1
251
```

The result is 251, but that value is gone, not stored anywhere:

```
>>> dollars
250
```

What we need is an assignment statement that captures the result of `dollars + 1`:

```
>>> dollars = dollars + 1
>>> dollars
251
>>> dollars = dollars + 1
>>> dollars
252
```

It's common for learners to think of the assignment symbol = as equality. But don't do that! The assignment statement is a command to make a variable refer to the value of an expression, not a claim that two entities are equal.

CONCEPT CHECK

What is the value of y after the execution of the following code?

(continued)

```
>>> x = 37
>>> y = x + 2
>>> x = 20
```

A. 39

B. 22

C. 35

D. 20

E. 18

Answer: A. There's only one assignment to y, and it makes y refer to the value 39. The x = 20 assignment statement changes what x refers to, from 37 to 20, but this has no impact on the value referred to by y.

Counting the Words Using a Variable

Let's take stock of our progress toward solving the Word Count problem:

- We know about strings, and we can use a string to store the line of words.

- We know about the string count method, which we can use to count the number of spaces in the line of words. That gives us one less than the output value that we need.

- We know about integers, whose + operator we can use to add 1 to a number.

- We know about variables and the assignment statement, which help us hold on to values so that we don't lose them.

Putting all of this together, we can make a variable refer to a string and then count the number of words:

```
>>> line = 'this is a string with a few words'
>>> total_words = line.count(' ') + 1
>>> total_words
8
```

The line and total_words variables aren't required here; here's how we could do it without them:

```
>>> 'this is a string with a few words'.count(' ') + 1
8
```

But using variables to capture intermediate results is a good practice for keeping code readable. Once our programs get longer than a few lines, variables will be indispensable.

Reading Input

One problem with the code that we've written is that it works only on the particular string that we've typed in. It tells us that there are eight words in `'this is a string with a few words'`, but that's all it can do. If we want to know how many words are in a different string, we'll have to replace the current string with a new one. To solve Word Count, though, we need our program to work on *any* string provided as input to our program.

To read a line of input, we use the `input` function. A *function* is similar to a method: we call it, perhaps with some arguments, and it returns a value to us. One difference between a method and a function is that a function does not use the dot operator. All information passed to functions is through arguments.

Here's an example of calling the `input` function and then typing some input—in this case, the word testing:

```
>>> input()
testing
'testing'
```

When you type `input()` and press ENTER, you don't get a `>>>` prompt back. Instead, Python waits for you to type something on the keyboard and press ENTER. The `input` function then returns the string you typed. As usual, if we don't store that string anywhere, then it's lost. Let's use an assignment statement to store what we type:

```
>>> result = input()
testing
>>> result
'testing'
>>> result.upper()
'TESTING'
```

Notice in the last line that I've used the `upper` method on the value returned by `input`. This is allowed because `input` returns a string, and `upper` is a string method.

Writing Output

You've seen that typing expressions at the Python shell causes their values to be displayed:

```
>>> 'abc'
'abc'
>>> 'abc'.upper()
```

```
'ABC'
>>> 45 + 9
54
```

That's just a convenience provided by the Python shell. It assumes that if you type an expression, then you probably want to see its value. But when running a Python program outside of the Python shell, this convenience is gone. Instead, we must explicitly use the print function whenever we want to output something. The print function works from the shell, too:

```
>>> print('abc')
abc
>>> print('abc'.upper())
ABC
>>> print(45 + 9)
54
```

Notice that strings output by print don't have quotes around them. That's good—we probably don't want to include quotes when communicating with users of our programs anyway!

One nice feature of print is that you can supply as many arguments as you like, and they all get output with separating spaces:

```
>>> print('abc', 45 + 9)
abc 54
```

Solving the Problem: A Complete Python Program

We're now ready to solve Word Count by writing a complete Python program. Exit the Python shell and you'll be back at your operating system command prompt.

Launching a Text Editor

We'll use a text editor to write our code. Follow the steps for your operating system.

Windows

On Windows, we'll use Notepad, a bare-bones text editor. At the operating system command prompt, navigate to your *programming* folder if you're not already there. Then type notepad word_count.py and press ENTER. Since the *word_count.py* file doesn't exist, Notepad will ask you whether you'd like to create a new *word_count.py* file. Click **Yes** and you'll be ready to type your Python program.

macOS

On macOS, you can use whichever text editor you like. One editor that you likely already have installed is TextEdit. At the operating system command prompt, navigate to your *programming* folder if you're not already there. Then type the following two commands, pressing ENTER after each one:

```
$ touch word_count.py
$ open -a TextEdit word_count.py
```

The touch command creates an empty file so that your text editor can open it. Now you're ready to type your Python program.

Linux

On Linux, you can use whichever text editor you like. One editor that you likely already have installed is gedit. At the operating system command prompt, navigate to your *programming* folder if you're not already there. Then type gedit word_count.py and press ENTER. Now you're ready to type your Python program.

The Program

With your text editor loaded, you can type the code of our Python program. The code is in Listing 1-1.

```
❶ line = input()
❷ total_words = line.count(' ') + 1
❸ print(total_words)
```

Listing 1-1: Solving Word Count

When entering that code, don't enter the ❶, ❷, or ❸. Those are there to help us walk through the code and are not part of the code itself.

We begin by acquiring the line of text from the input and assigning it to a variable ❶. That gives us a string, on which we can use the count method. We add 1 to the count of spaces to account for the final word in the string, and we use the variable total_words to refer to that result ❷. The last thing to do is output the value referred to by total_words ❸.

Be sure to save the file once you've finished typing the code.

Running the Program

To run the program, we'll use the python command from our operating system command prompt. As we've seen, entering python by itself runs the Python shell, but we don't want that this time. Instead, we want to tell Python to run the program in *word_count.py*. To do that, navigate to your *programming* folder, and enter python word_count.py. Here and throughout the book, please use the python3 command instead of the python command if needed.

Your program is now waiting at the input prompt for you to type something. Type a few words, press ENTER, and you should see our program working correctly. For example, type the following:

```
this is my first python program
```

You should see the program produce 6 as the output.

If instead you see a Python error, go back over the code and make sure you've typed it in exactly. Python requires precision. Even a missing parenthesis or single quote will lead to an error.

Don't be frustrated if it takes you some time to get this program to run. Getting a first program to run can require a lot of work. We have to be able to type a program into a file, invoke Python to run that program, and fix any errors resulting from an incorrect program. But the procedure for running programs doesn't change, no matter how complex the program, so time you spend here will be well worth it as you work through the rest of the book.

Submitting to the Judge

Congratulations! I hope it was satisfying to run your first Python program on your computer. But how do we know this program is correct? Does it work for all possible strings? We can test it on a few more strings, but the way we'll gain even more confidence in the correctness of our code is by submitting it to the online judge. The judge automatically runs a bunch of tests on our code and tells us whether we passed the tests or if something is wrong.

Go to *https://dmoj.ca/* and log in. (If you don't have a DMOJ account, please create one following the instructions in the introduction.) Click **Problems**, and search for the Word Count problem code dmopc15c7p2. Click the search result to load the problem—it's called Not a Wall of Text rather than Word Count.

You should then see the text of the problem, as written by the problem author. Click **Submit Solution**, and paste our code into the text area. Be sure to select Python 3 as the programming language. Finally, click the **Submit** button.

DMOJ runs tests on our code and shows us the results. For each test case, you'll see a status code. *AC* stands for *accepted* and is what you want to see for each test case. Other codes include *WA* (*wrong answer*) and *TLE* (*time limit exceeded*). If you see one of these, double-check the code that you pasted, making sure it exactly matches the code from your text editor.

Assuming all test cases are accepted, we should see that our score is 100/100 and that we've earned 3 points for our work.

For each problem, we'll follow the approach that we used to solve Word Count. First, we'll explore using the Python shell, learning new Python features as needed. Then, we'll write a program that solves the problem. We'll test that program on our computer by supplying our own test cases. Finally, we'll submit the code to the judge. If any test cases fail, we'll look over our code again and fix the problem.

Problem #2: Cone Volume

In Word Count, we needed to read a string from the input. In this problem, we'll need to read integers from the input. Doing so requires an extra step to produce an integer from a string. We'll also learn a little more about doing math in Python.

This is DMOJ problem dmopc14c5p1.

The Challenge

Calculate the volume of a right circular cone.

Input

The input consists of two lines of text. The first line contains integer r, the radius of the cone. The second line contains integer h, the height of the cone. Both r and h are between 1 and 100. (That is, the minimum value for r and h is 1, and the maximum value is 100.)

Output

Output the volume of the right circular cone with radius r and height h. The formula to calculate the volume is $(\pi r^2 h)/3$.

More Math in Python

Say we have r and h variables referring to a radius and height, respectively:

```
>>> r = 4
>>> h = 6
```

Now we want to evaluate $(\pi r^2 h)/3$. Substituting a radius of 4 and height of 6, we have $(\pi * 4^2 * 6)/3$. Using a value of 3.14159 for π, a calculator gives a result of 100.531. How can we do this in Python?

Accessing Pi

To access the value of π, we'll use a suitable variable. Here's an assignment statement to PI with a lot of accuracy in its value:

```
PI = 3.141592653589793
```

This is more a *constant* than a variable, since we'll never want to change the value of PI in our code. It's Python convention to use uppercase letters for such variables, as I've done here.

Exponents

Looking back at our formula, $(\pi r^2 h)/3$, the only thing we haven't talked about yet is how to perform the r^2 part. Since r^2 is the same as $r * r$, we can use multiplication rather than exponentiation.

```
>>> r
4
>>> r * r
16
```

But it's more transparent to use exponentiation directly. We always want to write code that's as clear as possible. Besides, one day you might have to calculate larger exponents, where repeated multiplication becomes increasingly unwieldy. Python's exponentiation operator is **:

```
>>> r ** 2
16
```

Here's the complete formula:

```
>>> (PI * r ** 2 * h) / 3
100.53096491487338
```

Great—that's close to the 100.531 result we expected!

Notice that we're producing a floating-point number here. As we discussed in "Integer and Floating-Point Numbers" in this chapter, the / division operator produces a floating-point result.

Converting Between Strings and Integers

We're ultimately going to have to read the radius and height as input. We'll then use those values to calculate the volume. Let's give it a try:

```
>>> r = input()
4
>>> h = input()
6
```

The input function always returns a string, even if the user types an integer:

```
>>> r
'4'
>>> h
'6'
```

The single quotes confirm that these values are strings. Strings cannot be used to perform mathematical calculations. If we try, we get an error:

```
>>> (PI * r ** 2 * h) / 3
Traceback (most recent call last):
  File "<stdin>", line 1, in <module>
TypeError: unsupported operand type(s) for ** or pow(): 'str' and 'int'
```

A `TypeError` is generated when we use values of the wrong type. Python is objecting to us using the ** operator on the string referred to by r and the integer 2. The ** operator is purely mathematical and has no meaning when used with strings.

To convert our strings to integers, we can use Python's `int` function:

```
>>> r
'4'
>>> h
'6'
>>> r = int(r)
>>> h = int(h)
>>> r
4
>>> h
6
```

Now we can once again use these values in our formula:

```
>>> (PI * r ** 2 * h) / 3
100.53096491487338
```

Whenever you have a string whose characters represent an integer, you can use the `int` function to convert it to a value whose type is integer. It can cope with leading and trailing spaces, but not non-numeric characters:

```
>>> int('  12  ')
12
>>> int('12x')
Traceback (most recent call last):
  File "<stdin>", line 1, in <module>
ValueError: invalid literal for int() with base 10: '12x'
```

When converting a string returned by `input` to an integer, we can take it in two steps, first assigning the return value of `input` to a variable and then converting that value to an integer:

```
>>> num = input()
82
>>> num = int(num)
>>> num
82
```

Or we can combine the `input` and `int` calls:

```
>>> num = int(input())
82
>>> num
82
```

Here, the argument passed to int is the string returned by input. The int function takes this string and returns it as an integer.

If we ever need to convert the other way, from an integer to a string, we can do that with the str function:

```
>>> num = 82
>>> 'my number is ' + num
Traceback (most recent call last):
  File "<stdin>", line 1, in <module>
TypeError: can only concatenate str (not "int") to str
>>> str(num)
'82'
>>> 'my number is ' + str(num)
'my number is 82'
```

We can't concatenate a string and an integer. The str function returns '82' from 82 so that it can be used in a string concatenation.

Solving the Problem

We're ready to solve Cone Volume. Create a text file called *cone_volume.py* and type the code in Listing 1-2.

```
❶ PI = 3.141592653589793


❷ radius = int(input())
❸ height = int(input())

❹ volume = (PI * radius ** 2 * height) / 3

❺ print(volume)
```

Listing 1-2: Solving Cone Volume

I've included blank lines to separate the code into its logical pieces. Python ignores these blank lines, but such blank lines can make it easier for us to read and chunk the code.

Notice that I've used descriptive variable names: radius instead of r, height instead of h, and volume. Single-letter variable names are the norm in math formulas, but when writing code, we can use variable names that convey more information.

We begin by making a variable called PI refer to an approximation of pi ❶. We then read the radius ❷ and height ❸ from the input, converting both from strings to integers. We use the formula for the volume of a right circular cone to compute the volume ❹. Lastly, we output the volume ❺.

Save your *cone_volume.py* file.

Run your program by typing `python cone_volume.py` and then type a value for the radius and a value for the height. Use a calculator to verify that your program produces the correct output!

What happens if you type garbage for the radius or height? For example, run your program and type the following:

```
xyz
```

You should see an error:

```
Traceback (most recent call last):
  File "cone_volume.py", line 3, in <module>
    radius = int(input())
ValueError: invalid literal for int() with base 10: 'xyz'
```

It is not user-friendly at all, that's for sure. But for purposes of learning to program, we won't worry about this. All of the test cases on the judge will be valid according to the problem's input specification, so we'll never have to worry about what to do with invalid input.

Speaking of the judge, DMOJ owes us three points, because we've finished writing correct code for this problem. Go ahead and submit your work!

Summary

And we're off! We've just solved our first two problems by writing Python code. We learned about the fundamentals of programming, including values, types, strings, integers, methods, variables, the assignment statement, and input and output.

Once you're comfortable with this material—perhaps by working on some of the following exercises—it's on to Chapter 2. There, we'll learn how our programs can make decisions. We'll no longer be writing programs that invariably run from top to bottom. They'll be more flexible, doing what's needed for the specific problem instance being solved.

Chapter Exercises

Each chapter ends with some exercises for you to try. I encourage you to complete as many exercises as you can.

Some exercises may take you a long time. You might get frustrated with repeated Python errors. Like with any skill worth learning, focused practice is needed. When you're starting to work on an exercise, I recommend solving a few examples by hand. That way you know what the problem is asking and what your program is supposed to do. Otherwise, you might be writing code without a plan, contending both with organizing your thoughts and with writing the program at the same time.

If your code isn't working, ask: what, precisely, is the behavior that you want? What are the lines of code that are likely culprits for the error that you're getting? Is there another, perhaps simpler, approach you could try?

I've included solutions to the exercises on the book website (*https://nostarch.com/learn-code-solving-problems/*). But don't peek at those until you've given your chosen exercise an honest try. Or two. Or three. If you do look at a solution and learn how one might solve the problem, take a break and then try solving it yourself from scratch. There's often more than one way to solve a problem. If your solution does the right thing but is different from mine, it doesn't mean that one of us is wrong. Rather, it serves as an opportunity for you to compare your code to mine, perhaps learning alternate techniques in the process.

1. DMOJ problem wc16c1j1, A Spooky Season
2. DMOJ problem wc15c2j1, A New Hope
3. DMOJ problem ccc13j1, Next in Line
4. DMOJ problem wc17c1j2, How's the Weather? (Be careful with the direction of conversion!)
5. DMOJ problem wc18c3j1, An Honest Day's Work (Hint: how can you determine the number of bottle caps and the total paint required by those bottle caps?)

Notes

Word Count is originally from the DMOPC '15 April Contest. Cone Volume is originally from the DMOPC '14 March Contest.

2

MAKING DECISIONS

Most programs that we use on a daily basis behave differently depending on what happens during their execution. For example, when a word processor asks us whether we want to save our work, it makes a decision based on our response: saving our work if we answer "yes" and not saving our work if we answer "no." In this chapter, we'll learn about if statements, which let our programs make decisions.

We'll solve two problems: determining the result of a basketball game and determining whether a phone number belongs to a telemarketer.

Problem #3: Winning Team

In this problem, we'll need to output a message that depends on the outcome of a basketball game. To do that, we'll learn all about if statements. We'll also learn how we can store and manipulate true and false values in our programs.

This is DMOJ problem ccc19j1.

The Challenge

In basketball, three plays score points: a three-point shot, a two-point shot, and a one-point free throw.

You just watched a basketball game between the Apples and Bananas and recorded the number of successful three-point, two-point, and one-point plays for each team. Indicate whether the game was won by the Apples, the game was won by the Bananas, or the game was a tie.

Input

There are six lines of input. The first three give the scoring for the Apples, and the latter three give the scoring for the Bananas.

- The first line gives the number of successful three-point shots for the Apples.

- The second line gives the number of successful two-point shots for the Apples.

- The third line gives the number of successful one-point free throws for the Apples.

- The fourth line gives the number of successful three-point shots for the Bananas.

- The fifth line gives the number of successful two-point shots for the Bananas.

- The sixth line gives the number of successful one-point free throws for the Bananas.

Each number is an integer between 0 and 100.

Output

The output is a single character.

- If the Apples scored more points than the Bananas, output A (*A* for Apples).

- If the Bananas scored more points than the Apples, output B (*B* for Bananas).

- If the Apples and Bananas scored the same number of points, output T (*T* for Tie).

Conditional Execution

We can make a lot of headway here by using what we learned in Chapter 1. We can use input and int to read each of the six integers from the input. We can use variables to hang on to those values. We can multiply the number of successful three-point shots by 3 and the number of successful two-point shots by 2. We can use print to output an A, B, or T.

What we haven't learned yet is how our programs can make a decision about the outcome of the game. I can demonstrate why we need this through two test cases.

First, consider this test case:

```
5
1
3
1
1
1
```

The Apples scored 5 * 3 + 1 * 2 + 3 = 20 points, and the Bananas scored 1 * 3 + 1 * 2 + 1 = 6 points. The Apples won the game, so this is the correct output:

```
A
```

Second, consider this test case, where the Apples' and Bananas' scores have been swapped:

```
1
1
1
5
1
3
```

This time, the Bananas won the game, so this is the correct output:

```
B
```

Our program must be able to compare the total points scored by the Apples and the total points scored by the Bananas and use the result of that comparison to choose whether to output A, B, or T.

We can use Python's if statement to make these kinds of decisions. A *condition* is an expression that's true or false, and an if statement uses conditions to determine what to do. if statements lead to *conditional execution*, so named because the execution of our program is influenced by conditions.

We'll first learn about a new type that lets us represent true or false values, and how we can build expressions of this type. Then, we'll use such expressions to write if statements.

The Boolean Type

Pass an expression to Python's type function, and it'll tell you the type of the expression's value:

```
>>> type(14)
<class 'int'>
```

```
>>> type(9.5)
<class 'float'>
>>> type('hello')
<class 'str'>
>>> type(12 + 15)
<class 'int'>
```

One Python type we haven't met yet is the Boolean (bool) type. Unlike integers, strings, and floats, which have billions of possible values, there are only two Boolean values: True and False. These are exactly the values we need to represent the result of a condition.

```
>>> True
True
>>> False
False
>>> type(True)
<class 'bool'>
>>> type(False)
<class 'bool'>
```

What can we do with these values? With numbers, we had mathematical operators like + and - that let us combine values into more complex expressions. We'll need a new set of operators that work with Boolean values.

Relational Operators

Is 5 greater than 2? Is 4 less than 1? We can make such comparisons using Python's *relational operators*. They produce True or False and are therefore used to write *Boolean expressions*.

The > operator takes two operands and returns True if the first is greater than the second, and False otherwise:

```
>>> 5 > 2
True
>>> 9 > 10
False
```

Similarly, we have the < operator for less-than:

```
>>> 4 < 1
False
>>> -2 < 0
True
```

There's >= for greater-than-or-equal-to, and <= for less-than-or-equal-to:

```
>>> 4 >= 2
True
>>> 4 >= 4
```

```
True
>>> 4 >= 5
False
>>> 8 <= 6
False
```

To determine equality, we use the == operator. That's two equal signs, not one. Remember that one equal sign (=) is used in an assignment statement; it has nothing to do with checking equality.

```
>>> 5 == 5
True
>>> 15 == 10
False
```

For inequality, we use the != operator. It returns True if the operands are not equal and False if they are equal:

```
>>> 5 != 5
False
>>> 15 != 10
True
```

Real programs wouldn't evaluate expressions whose values we already know. We don't need Python to tell us that 15 doesn't equal 10. More typically, we'd use variables in these kinds of expressions. For example, number != 10 is an expression whose value depends on what number refers to.

The relational operators also work on strings. When checking equality, case matters:

```
>>> 'hello' == 'hello'
True
>>> 'Hello' == 'hello'
False
```

One string is less than another if it comes first in alphabetical order:

```
>>> 'brave' < 'cave'
True
>>> 'cave' < 'cavern'
True
>>> 'orange' < 'apple'
False
```

But things can be surprising when lowercase and uppercase characters are both involved:

```
>>> 'apple' < 'Banana'
False
```

Weird, right? It has to do with the way that characters are stored internally in a computer. Generally, uppercase characters come alphabetically before lowercase characters. And check this out:

```
>>> '10' < '4'
True
```

If these were numbers, then the result would be False. But strings are compared character by character from left to right. Python compares the '1' and '4', and because '1' is smaller, the < operator returns True. Be sure that your values have the types you think they have!

One relational operator that works on strings but not numbers is in. It returns True if the first string occurs at least once in the second, and False otherwise:

```
>>> 'ppl' in 'apple'
True
>>> 'ale' in 'apple'
False
```

CONCEPT CHECK

What is the output of the following code?

```
a = 3
b = (a != 3)
print(b)
```

A. True

B. False

C. 3

D. This code produces a syntax error

Answer: B. The expression a != 3 evaluates to False; b is then made to refer to this False value.

The if Statement

We'll now explore several variations of Python's if statement.

if by Itself

Suppose we have our final scores in two variables, `apple_total` and `banana _total`, and we want to output A if `apple_total` is greater than `banana_total`. Here's how we can do that:

```
>>> apple_total = 20
>>> banana_total = 6
>>> if apple_total > banana_total:
...     print('A')
...
A
```

Python outputs A, as we'd expect.

An if statement starts with the keyword `if`. A *keyword* is a word that has special meaning to Python and cannot be used as a variable name. The keyword `if` is followed by a Boolean expression, followed by a colon, followed by one or more indented statements. The indented statements are often referred to as the *block* of the if statement. The block executes if the Boolean expression is `True` and is skipped if the Boolean expression is `False`.

Notice that the prompt changes from >>> to .... That's a reminder that we're inside the block of the if statement and must indent the code. I've chosen to indent by four spaces, so to indent the code, press the spacebar four times. Some Python programmers press the TAB key to indent, but we'll exclusively use spaces in this book.

Once you type `print('A')` and hit ENTER, you should see another ... prompt. Since we don't have anything else to put in this if statement, press ENTER again to dismiss this prompt and return to the >>> prompt. This extra press of ENTER is a quirk of the Python shell; such blank lines are not required when we write a Python program in a file.

Let's see an example of putting two statements in the block of an if statement:

```
>>> apple_total = 20
>>> banana_total = 6
>>> if apple_total > banana_total:
...     print('A')
...     print('Apples win!')
...
A
Apples win!
```

Both print calls execute, producing two lines of output.

Let's try another if statement, this one with a Boolean expression that's False:

```
>>> apple_total = 6
>>> banana_total = 20
```

```
>>> if apple_total > banana_total:
...     print('A')
...
```

The print function is *not* called this time: apple_total > banana_total is False, so the block of the if statement is skipped.

if with elif

Let's use three successive if statements to print A if the Apples win, B if the Bananas win, and T if it's a tie:

```
>>> apple_total = 6
>>> banana_total = 6
>>> if apple_total > banana_total:
...     print('A')
...
>>> if banana_total > apple_total:
...     print('B')
...
>>> if apple_total == banana_total:
...     print('T')
...
T
```

The blocks of the first two if statements are skipped, because their Boolean expressions are False. But the block of the third if statement executes, producing the T.

When you put one if statement after another, they're independent. Each Boolean expression is evaluated, regardless of whether the previous Boolean expressions were True or False.

For any given values of apple_total and banana_total, only one of our if statements can run. For example, if apple_total > banana_total is True, then the first if statement will run, but the other two will not. It's possible to write the code to highlight that only one block of code is allowed to run. Here's how we can do that:

```
❶ >>> if apple_total > banana_total:
  ...     print('A')
❷ ... elif banana_total > apple_total:
  ...     print('B')
  ... elif apple_total == banana_total:
  ...     print('T')
  ...
  T
```

This is now a single if statement, not three separate if statements. For this reason, don't press ENTER at the ... prompt; instead, type the elif line.

To execute this if statement, Python begins by evaluating the first Boolean expression ❶. If it's True, then A is output, and the rest of the elifs are skipped. If it's False, Python continues, evaluating the second Boolean expression ❷. If it's True, then B is output, and the remaining elif is skipped. If it's False, Python continues, evaluating the third Boolean expression ❸. If it's True, then T is output.

The keyword elif stands for "else-if." Use this as a reminder that an elif expression is checked only if nothing "else" before it in the if statement was executed.

This version of the code is equivalent to the previous code where we used three separate if statements. Had we wanted to allow the possibility of executing more than one block, we'd have to use three separate if statements, not a single if statement with elif blocks.

if with else

We can use the else keyword to run code if all the Boolean expressions in the if statement are False. Here's an example:

```
>>> if apple_total > banana_total:
...     print('A')
... elif banana_total > apple_total:
...     print('B')
... else:
...     print('T')
...
T
```

Python evaluates the Boolean expressions from top to bottom. If any of them is True, Python runs the associated block and skips the rest of the if statement. If all the Boolean expressions are False, Python executes the else block.

Notice that there is no longer a test for apple_total == banana_total. The only way to get to the else part of the if statement is if apple_total > banana _total is False and banana_total > apple_total is False, that is, if the values are equal.

Should you use separate if statements? An if statement with elifs? An if statement with an else? It often comes down to preference. Use a chain of elifs if you want at most one block of code to execute. An else can help make the code clearer and removes the need to write a catchall Boolean expression. What's far more important than the precise styling of an if statement is writing correct logic!

What is the value of x after the following code runs?

```
x = 5
if x > 2:
    x = -3
if x > 1:
    x = 1
else:
    x = 3
```

A. -3

B. 1

C. 2

D. 3

E. 5

Answer: D. Because x > 2 is True, the block of the first if statement executes. The assignment x = -3 makes x refer to -3. Now for the second if statement. Here, x > 1 is False, so the else block runs, and x = 3 makes x refer to 3. I'd suggest changing if x > 1 to elif x > 1 and observing how the behavior of the program changes!

Do the following two snippets of code do exactly the same thing? Assume that temperature already refers to a number.

Snippet 1:

```
if temperature > 0:
    print('warm')
elif temperature == 0:
    print('zero')
else:
    print('cold')
```

Snippet 2:

```
if temperature > 0:
    print('warm')
elif temperature == 0:
    print('zero')
print('cold')
```

A. Yes

B. No

Answer: B. Snippet 2 *always* prints cold as its final line of output, because print('cold') is not indented! It is not associated with any if statement.

Solving the Problem

It's time to solve Winning Team. In this book, I'll generally present the full code and then discuss it. But as our solution here is longer than those in Chapter 1, I've decided in this case to present the code in three pieces before presenting it as a whole.

First, we need to read the input. This requires six calls of input, because we have two teams and three pieces of information for each team. We also need to convert each piece of input to an integer. Here's the code:

```
apple_three = int(input())
apple_two = int(input())
apple_one = int(input())

banana_three = int(input())
banana_two = int(input())
banana_one = int(input())
```

Second, we need to determine the number of points scored by the Apples and the Bananas. For each team, we add the points from three-point, two-point, and one-point plays. We can do that as follows:

```
apple_total = apple_three * 3 + apple_two * 2 + apple_one
banana_total = banana_three * 3 + banana_two * 2 + banana_one
```

Third, we produce the output. If the Apples win, we output A; if the Bananas win, we output B; otherwise, we know that the game is a tie, so we output T. We use an if statement to do this, as follows:

```
if apple_total > banana_total:
    print('A')
```

```
elif banana_total > apple_total:
    print('B')
else:
    print('T')
```

That's all the code we need. See Listing 2-1 for the complete solution.

```
apple_three = int(input())
apple_two = int(input())
apple_one = int(input())

banana_three = int(input())
banana_two = int(input())
banana_one = int(input())

apple_total = apple_three * 3 + apple_two * 2 + apple_one
banana_total = banana_three * 3 + banana_two * 2 + banana_one

if apple_total > banana_total:
    print('A')
elif banana_total > apple_total:
    print('B')
else:
    print('T')
```

Listing 2-1: Solving Winning Team

If you submit our code to the judge, you should see that all test cases pass.

> **CONCEPT CHECK**
>
> Does the following version of the code correctly solve the problem?
>
> ```
> apple_three = int(input())
> apple_two = int(input())
> apple_one = int(input())
>
> banana_three = int(input())
> banana_two = int(input())
> banana_one = int(input())
>
> apple_total = apple_three * 3 + apple_two * 2 + apple_one
> banana_total = banana_three * 3 + banana_two * 2 + banana_one
>
> if apple_total < banana_total:
>     print('B')
> ```

```
elif apple_total > banana_total:
    print('A')
else:
    print('T')
```

A. Yes

B. No

Answer: A. The operators and order of the code are different, but the code is still correct. If the Apples lose, we output B (because the Bananas win); if the Apples win, we output A; otherwise, we know that the game is a tie, so we output T.

Before continuing, you might like to try solving exercise 1 from "Chapter Exercises" on page 45.

Problem #4: Telemarketers

Sometimes we need to encode more complex Boolean expressions than those that we have seen so far. In this problem, we'll learn about Boolean operators that help us do this.

This is DMOJ problem ccc18j1.

The Challenge

In this problem, we'll assume that phone numbers are four digits. A phone number belongs to a telemarketer if its four digits satisfy all three of the following properties:

• The first digit is 8 or 9.

• The fourth digit is 8 or 9.

• The second and third digits are the same.

For example, a phone number whose four digits are 8119 belongs to a telemarketer.

Determine whether a phone number belongs to a telemarketer, and indicate whether we should answer the phone or ignore it.

Input

There are four lines of input. These lines give the first, second, third, and fourth digits of the phone number, respectively. Each digit is an integer between 0 and 9.

Output

If the phone number belongs to a telemarketer, output `ignore`; otherwise, output `answer`.

Boolean Operators

What has to be true about a phone number that belongs to a telemarketer? Its first digit has to be 8 *or* 9. *And,* its fourth digit has to be 8 *or* 9. *And,* the second and third digits have to be the same. We can encode this "or" and "and" logic using Python's *Boolean operators.*

or Operator

The or operator takes two Boolean expressions as its operands. It returns `True` if at least one operand is `True`, and `False` otherwise:

```
>>> True or True
True
>>> True or False
True
>>> False or True
True
>>> False or False
False
```

The only way to get `False` out of the or operator is if both of its operands are False.

We can use or to tell us whether a digit is an 8 or a 9:

```
>>> digit = 8
>>> digit == 8 or digit == 9
True
>>> digit = 3
>>> digit == 8 or digit == 9
False
```

Remember from "Integer and Floating-Point Numbers" in Chapter 1 that Python uses operator precedence to determine the order that operators are applied. The precedence of or is lower than the precedence of relational operators, which means that we don't often need parentheses around operands. For example, in digit == 8 or digit == 9, the two operands to or are digit == 8 and digit == 9. It's the same as if we'd written it as (digit == 8) or (digit == 9).

In English, it makes sense if someone says "if the digit is 8 or 9." But writing that won't work in Python:

```
>>> digit = 3
>>> if digit == 8 or 9:
```

```
...     print('yes!')
...
yes!
```

Notice that I've (incorrectly!) written the second operand as 9 instead of digit == 9. Python responds by outputting yes!, which is certainly not what we'd want given that digit refers to 3. The reason is that Python considers nonzero numbers to be True. Since 9 is considered True, this makes the whole or expression True. Carefully double-check your Boolean expressions to avoid these kinds of mistakes when translating from natural language to Python.

and Operator

The and operator returns True if both of its operands are True, and returns False otherwise:

```
>>> True and True
True
>>> True and False
False
>>> False and True
False
>>> False and False
False
```

The only way to get True out of the And operator is if both of its operands are True.

The precedence of and is higher than or. Here's an example of why this matters:

```
>>> True or True and False
True
```

Python interprets that expression like this, with the and happening first:

```
>>> True or (True and False)
True
```

The result is True because the first operand of or is True.

We can force the or to happen first by including parentheses:

```
>>> (True or True) and False
False
```

The result is False because the second operand of and is False.

not Operator

Another important Boolean operator is not. Unlike or and and, not takes only one operand (not two). If its operand is True, not returns False, and vice versa:

```
>>> not True
False
>>> not False
True
```

The precedence of not is higher than or and and.

CONCEPT CHECK

Here's an expression and versions of that expression with parentheses. Which of them evaluates to True?

A. not True and False

B. (not True) and False

C. not (True and False)

D. None of the above

Answer: C. The expression (True and False) evaluates to False; the not therefore makes the full expression True.

CONCEPT CHECK

Consider the expression not a or b.

Which of the following makes the expression False?

A. a False, b False

B. a False, b True

C. a True, b False

D. a True, b True

E. More than one of the above

Answer: C. If a is True, then not a is False. Since b is False, too, both operands to or are False, so the whole expression evaluates to False.

Solving the Problem

With Boolean operators at the ready, we can tackle the Telemarketers problem. Our solution is in Listing 2-2.

```
num1 = int(input())
num2 = int(input())
num3 = int(input())
num4 = int(input())

❶ if ((num1 == 8 or num1 == 9) and
       (num4 == 8 or num4 == 9) and
       (num2 == num3)):
    print('ignore')
else:
    print('answer')
```

Listing 2-2: Solving Telemarketers

As in Winning Team, we start by reading the input and converting it to integers.

The high-level structure of our if statement ❶ is three expressions connected by and operators; each of them must be True for the entire expression to be True. We require that the first number be 8 or 9, that the fourth number be 8 or 9, and that the second and third numbers be equal. If all three of these conditions hold, then we know that the phone number belongs to a telemarketer, and we output ignore. Otherwise, the phone number does not belong to a telemarketer, and we output answer.

I've split the Boolean expression over three lines. This requires wrapping the entire expression in an additional pair of parentheses, as I have done. (Without those parentheses, you'll get a syntax error, because there's no indication to Python that the expression is continuing on the next line.)

Python style guides suggest that a line be no longer than 79 characters. A line with the full Boolean expression would squeak in there at 76 characters. But I think the three-line version is clearer, highlighting each condition that must be True on its own line.

We have a good solution here. To explore a little further, let's discuss some alternate approaches.

Our code uses a Boolean expression to detect when a phone number belongs to a telemarketer. We could have also chosen to write code that detects when a phone number does *not* belong to a telemarketer. If the phone number doesn't belong to a telemarketer, we should output answer; otherwise, we should output ignore.

If the first digit isn't 8 and isn't 9, then the phone number doesn't belong to a telemarketer. Or, if the fourth digit isn't 8 and isn't 9, then the phone number doesn't belong to a telemarketer. Or, if the second and third digits aren't equal, then the phone number doesn't belong to a telemarketer. If even one of these expressions is True, then the phone number doesn't belong to a telemarketer.

See Listing 2-3 for a version of the code that captures this logic.

```
num1 = int(input())
num2 = int(input())
num3 = int(input())
num4 = int(input())

if ((num1 != 8 and num1 != 9) or
        (num4 != 8 and num4 != 9) or
        (num2 != num3)):
    print('answer')
else:
    print('ignore')
```

Listing 2-3: Solving Telemarketers, alternate approach

It's not easy getting all of those !=, or, and and operators correct! Notice, for example, that we've had to change all == operators to !=, all or operators to and, and all and operators to or.

An alternate approach is to use the not operator to negate the "is a telemarketer" expression in one shot. See Listing 2-4 for that code.

```
num1 = int(input())
num2 = int(input())
num3 = int(input())
num4 = int(input())

if not ((num1 == 8 or num1 == 9) and
        (num4 == 8 or num4 == 9) and
        (num2 == num3)):
    print('answer')
else:
    print('ignore')
```

Listing 2-4: Solving Telemarketers, not operator

Which of these solutions do you find most intuitive? There's often more than one way to structure the logic of an if statement, and we should use the one that's easiest to get right. To me, Listing 2-2 is the most natural, but you may feel otherwise!

Choose your favorite version and submit it to the judge. You should see that all test cases pass.

Comments

We should always strive to make our programs as clear as possible. This helps to avoid introducing errors when programming and makes it easier to fix our code when errors do slip in. Meaningful variable names, spaces around operators, blank lines to segment the program into its logical pieces, simple `if` statement logic: all of these practices can improve the quality of the code we write. Another good habit is adding *comments* to our code.

A comment is introduced by the # character and continues until the end of the line. Python ignores comments, so they have no impact on what our program does. We add comments to remind ourselves, or others, about design decisions that we've made. Assume that the person reading the code knows Python, so avoid comments that simply restate what the code is doing. Here's code with an unnecessary comment:

```
>>> x = 5
>>> x = x + 1  # Increase x by 1
```

That comment adds nothing beyond what we already know about assignment statements.

See Listing 2-5 for a version of Listing 2-2 with comments.

❶ # ccc18j1, Telemarketers

```
num1 = int(input())
num2 = int(input())
num3 = int(input())
num4 = int(input())
```

❷ # Telemarketer number: first digit 8 or 9, fourth digit 8 or 9,
```
# second digit and third digit are same
if ((num1 == 8 or num1 == 9) and
        (num4 == 8 or num4 == 9) and
        (num2 == num3)):
    print('ignore')
else:
    print('answer')
```

Listing 2-5: Solving Telemarketers, comments added

I've added three comment lines: the one at the top ❶ reminds us of the problem code and name, and the two before the `if` statement ❷ remind us of the rules for detecting a telemarketer phone number.

Don't go overboard with comments. Whenever possible, write code that doesn't require comments in the first place. But for tricky code or to document why you chose to do something in a particular way, a well-placed comment now can save time and frustration later.

Input and Output Redirection

When you submit Python code to the judge, it runs many test cases to determine whether your code is correct. Is someone there, dutifully waiting for new code and then frantically hammering test cases at it from the keyboard?

No way! It's all automated. There's no one typing test cases at the keyboard. How does the judge test our code, then, if we satisfy a call to input by typing something from the keyboard?

The truth is that input isn't necessarily reading input from the keyboard. It's reading from a source of input called *standard input*, which, by default, is the keyboard.

It's possible to change standard input so that it refers to a file rather than the keyboard. The technique is called *input redirection*, and it's what the judge uses to provide input.

We can also try input redirection ourselves. For programs whose input is small—just a line of text or a couple of integers—input redirection may not save us much. But for programs whose test cases can be tens or hundreds of lines long, input redirection makes it much easier to test our work. Rather than typing the same test case over and over, we can store it in a file and then run our program on it as many times as we want.

Let's try input redirection on Telemarketers. Navigate to your *programming* folder and create a new file called *telemarketers_input.txt*. In that file, type the following:

```
8
1
1
9
```

The problem specifies that we should provide one integer per line, so we've written them one per line here.

Save the file. Now enter **python telemarketers.py < telemarketers_input.txt** to run your program using input redirection. Your program should output ignore, just as it would if you'd typed the test case from the keyboard.

The < symbol instructs your operating system to use a file rather than the keyboard to provide input. After the < symbol comes the name of the file that contains the input.

To try your program on different test cases, just modify the *telemarketers _input.txt* file and run your program again.

We can also change where our output goes, though we won't need to for this book. The print function outputs to *standard output*, which, by default, is the screen. We can change standard output so that it instead refers to a file. We do so using *output redirection*, which is written as a > symbol followed by a filename.

Enter **python telemarketers.py > telemarketers_output.txt** to run your program using output redirection. Provide four integers of input, and you should be back to your operating system prompt. But you shouldn't see any output from your Telemarketers program! That's because we've redirected the output to file telemarketers_output.txt. If you open telemarketers_output .txt in your text editor, you should see the output there.

Be careful with output redirection. If you use a filename that already exists, your old file will be overwritten! Always double-check that you're using the filename you intended.

Summary

In this chapter, we learned how to use `if` statements to direct what our programs do. The key ingredient of an `if` statement is a Boolean expression, which is an expression with a `True` or `False` value. To build up Boolean expressions, we use relational operators such as `==` and `>=`, and we use Boolean operators such as `and` and `or`.

Deciding what to do based on what is `True` and `False` makes our programs more flexible, able to adapt to the situation at hand. But our programs are still limited to handling small amounts of input and output—whatever we can do with individual calls to `input` and `print`. In the next chapter, we'll start learning about loops, which let us repeat code so that we can process as much input and output as we like.

Want to work with 100 values? How about 1,000? And with just a small amount of Python code? It is a little early for me to be provoking you, I know, because you still have the following exercises to do. But when you're ready, read on!

Chapter Exercises

Here are some exercises for you to try.

1. DMOJ problem ccc06j1, Canadian Calorie Counting
2. DMOJ problem ccc15j1, Special Day
3. DMOJ problem ccc15j2, Happy or Sad
4. DMOJ problem dmopc16c1p0, C.C. and Cheese-kun
5. DMOJ problem ccc07j1, Who is in the Middle

Notes

Winning Team is originally from the 2019 Canadian Computing Competition, Junior Level. Telemarketers is originally from the 2018 Canadian Computing Competition, Junior Level.

3

REPEATING CODE: DEFINITE LOOPS

Computers shine when we have them repeat a process over and over. They tirelessly do exactly what we ask, whether it involves doing something 10, 100, or a billion times. In this chapter, we'll learn about loops, statements that instruct the computer to repeat the execution of part of our program.

We'll use loops to solve three problems: tracking the location of a ball under a cup, counting the number of occupied parking spaces, and determining how much data is available on a cell phone plan.

Problem #5: Three Cups

In this problem, we'll track the location of a ball under a cup as the cups move. But the cups can move many times, so we won't be able to write code for each move separately. Instead, we'll learn about and use the for loop, which allows us to more easily run code for each move.

This is DMOJ problem coci06c5p1.

The Challenge

Borko has a row of three opaque cups: one at the left (location 1), one at the middle (location 2), and one at the right (location 3). There is a ball under the cup at the left. It's our job to keep track of the location of the ball as Borko swaps the locations of the cups.

Borko can make three types of swap:

A Swap the left and middle cups

B Swap the middle and right cups

C Swap the left and right cups

For example, if Borko's first swap is type A, then he swaps the left and middle cups; because the ball starts at the left, this swap moves it to the middle. If instead his first swap is type B, then he swaps the middle and right cups; the left cup stays where it is, so the ball doesn't change locations.

Input

The input is one line of at most 50 characters. Each character specifies a type of swap that Borko makes: A, B, or C.

Output

Output the final location of the ball:

- 1 if the ball is at the left
- 2 if the ball is at the middle
- 3 if the ball is at the right

Why Loops?

Consider this test case:

ACBA

There are four swaps here. To determine the final location of the ball, we need to carry out each one.

The first swap is type A, which swaps the cups at the left and middle. Since the ball starts at the left, this results in the ball moving to the middle. The second swap is type C, which swaps the cups at the left and right. Since the ball is currently at the middle, this has no effect on the location of the ball. The third swap is type B, which swaps the cups at the middle and right. This moves the ball from the middle to the right. The fourth swap is type A, which swaps the cups at the left and middle. This has no effect on the ball. The correct output is therefore 3, because the ball ends up at the right.

Notice that for each swap, we have to make a decision to determine whether the ball moves and, if it does, to move the ball appropriately. Making decisions is something we know how to do from Chapter 2. For example, if the swap type is A and the ball is at the left, then the ball moves to the middle. That looks like this:

```
if swap_type == 'A' and ball_location == 1:
    ball_location = 2
```

We could add an elif for each other case where the ball moves: swap type A and ball is at the middle, swap type B and ball is at the middle, swap type B and ball is at the right, and so on. This big if statement would be enough to handle one swap. But that's not enough to solve the Three Cups problem, because we could have a test case of up to 50 swaps. We'd need to repeat the if statement logic for each swap. And we certainly wouldn't want to copy and paste the same code 50 times. Imagine if you had made a typo and had to fix it 50 times. Or if you suddenly became interested in test cases with up to a million swaps. No, what we have learned so far is not going to cut it. We need a way to walk through the swaps, performing the same logic for each one. We need a loop.

for Loops

Python's for statement produces *for loops*. for loops allow us to process each element of a sequence. The only sequence type we've seen so far is the string. We'll learn others as we go; for loops work on all of them.

Here's our first example of a for loop:

```
>>> secret_word = 'olive'
>>> for char in secret_word:
...     print('Letter: ' + char)
...
Letter: o
Letter: l
Letter: i
Letter: v
Letter: e
```

Following the keyword for, we write the name of a *loop variable*. A loop variable is one that refers to different values as a loop progresses. In a for loop on a string, the loop variable refers to each of the string's characters.

I've chosen the variable name char (for "character") to remind us that the variable refers to a character from the string. Sometimes, it's clearer if we use a contextual variable name. For example, in Three Cups, we could instead use the name swap_type to remind us that it refers to a type of swap.

After the variable name, we have the keyword in and then the string that we want to loop over. In our example, we're looping over the string referred to by secret_word, which is 'olive'.

Like the if, elif, and else lines of an if statement, the for line ends with a colon (:). And, also like an if statement, a for statement has an indented block of one or more statements.

An execution of the indented statements is referred to as an *iteration* of the loop. Here's a walk-through of what our loop does on each iteration:

- On the first iteration, Python sets char to refer to 'o', the first character of 'olive'. It then runs the loop block, which consists only of the call to print. As char refers to 'o', the output produced is Letter: o.

- On the second iteration, Python sets char to refer to 'l', the second character of 'olive'. It then calls print, outputting Letter: l.

- This process repeats three more times, once for each remaining character in 'olive'.

- The loop then terminates. We have no code after the loop, so our program has finished running. If there was additional code after the loop, then execution would continue with that code.

You can put multiple statements in the block of a for loop. Here's an example:

```
>>> secret_word = 'olive'
>>> for char in secret_word:
...     print('Letter: ' + char)
...     print('*')
...
Letter: o
*
Letter: l
*
Letter: i
*
Letter: v
*
Letter: e
*
```

Now we have two statements executing on each iteration of the loop: one that outputs the current letter of the string, and one that outputs a * character.

A for loop loops through the elements of a sequence, so the sequence's length tells us how many iterations there will be. The len function takes a string and returns its length:

```
>>> len('olive')
5
```

Our for loop on 'olive' will therefore consist of five iterations:

```
>>> secret_word = 'olive'
❶ >>> print(len(secret_word), 'iterations, coming right up!')
>>> for char in secret_word:
```

```
...     print('Letter: ' + char)
...
5 iterations, coming right up!
Letter: o
Letter: l
Letter: i
Letter: v
Letter: e
```

I called print with multiple arguments ❶, rather than using concatenation, to avoid having to convert the length to a string.

. A for loop is what's called a *definite loop*, referring to the idea that the number of iterations is predetermined. There are also *indefinite loops*, whose iterations depend on the vagaries of what happens when your program runs. We'll study those in the next chapter.

CONCEPT CHECK

What is the output of the following code?

```
s = 'garage'
total = 0

for char in s:
    total = total + s.count(char)

print(total)
```

A. 6

B. 10

C. 12

D. 36

Answer: B. For each character in 'garage', we add its count to total. There are two g's, two a's, one r, two a's (again!), two g's (again!), and 1 e.

Nesting

The for loop block is one or more statements. Those statements can include one-line statements such as function calls and assignment statements. But they can also include multiline statements such as if statements and loops.

Let's start with an example of an if statement inside a for loop. Suppose we wanted to output only the uppercase characters from a string. Strings have an `isupper` method that we can use to determine whether a character is uppercase:

```
>>> 'q'.isupper()
False
>>> 'Q'.isupper()
True
```

We can use `isupper` in an `if` statement to control what happens on each iteration of a for loop:

```
>>> title = 'The Escape'
>>> for char in title:
...     if char.isupper():
...         print(char)
...
T
E
```

Be careful with the indentation here. We need one level of indentation for the `for` loop, and an extra level of indentation for the nested `if` statement.

On the first iteration, `char` refers to `'T'`. Since `'T'` is uppercase, the `isupper` test returns `True`, and the `if` statement block runs. That results in the output of `T`. On the second iteration, `char` refers to `'h'`. This time, the `isupper` test returns `False`, so the `if` statement block doesn't run. Overall, the `for` loop loops through each character of the string, but the nested `if` statement fires only twice: on the `'T'` at the beginning of the string and on the `'E'` at the beginning of `'Escape'`.

What about a `for` loop nested in a `for` loop? We can do that! Here's an example:

```
>>> letters = 'ABC'
>>> digits = '123'
>>> for letter in letters:
...     for digit in digits:
...         print(letter + digit)
...
A1
A2
A3
B1
B2
B3
C1
C2
C3
```

The code produces all two-character strings whose first character is from letters and whose second character is from digits.

On the first iteration of the outer (letters) loop, letter refers to 'A'. This iteration involves completely running the inner (digits) loop. The whole time the inner loop runs, letter refers to 'A'. On the first iteration of the inner loop, digit refers to 1, which explains the A1 output. On the second iteration of the inner loop, digit refers to 2, and A2 is output. On the third and final iteration of the inner loop, digit refers to 3, and A3 is output.

We're not done! We've gone through only one iteration of the outer loop. On the second iteration of the outer loop, letter refers to 'B'. Now the three iterations of the inner loop run again, this time with letter referring to 'B'. This accounts for the B1, B2, and B3 outputs. Finally, on the third iteration of the outer loop, letter refers to 'C', and the inner loop produces C1, C2, and C3.

CONCEPT CHECK

What is the output of the following code?

```
title = 'The Escape'
total = 0

for char1 in title:
    for char2 in title:
        total = total + 1

print(total)
```

A. 10

B. 20

C. 100

D. This code produces a syntax error because two nested loops cannot both use title

---

Answer: C. total starts off as 0 and is increased by 1 on each iteration of the inner loop. The length of 'The Escape' is 10. The outer loop therefore has 10 iterations. For each of those iterations, the inner loop has 10 iterations. The inner loop therefore has 10*10 = 100 iterations in all.

Solving the Problem

Back to Three Cups. The structure we need is a for loop to go through each swap, and a nested if statement to keep track of where the ball is:

```
for swap_type in swaps:
    # Big if statement to keep track of the ball
```

There are three types of swaps (A, B, and C) and three possible locations for the ball, so it's tempting to conclude that we have to write an if statement with 3 * 3 = 9 Boolean expressions (one after the if and one after each of eight elifs). In fact, we need only six Boolean expressions. Three of the nine don't move the ball at all: swap type A when the ball is at the right, swap type B when the ball is at the left, and swap type C when the ball is at the middle.

Listing 3-1 has a solution to Three Cups.

```
swaps = input()

ball_location = 1

❶ for swap_type in swaps:
    ❷ if swap_type == 'A' and ball_location == 1:
        ❸ ball_location = 2
    elif swap_type == 'A' and ball_location == 2:
        ball_location = 1
    elif swap_type == 'B' and ball_location == 2:
        ball_location = 3
    elif swap_type == 'B' and ball_location == 3:
        ball_location = 2
    elif swap_type == 'C' and ball_location == 1:
        ball_location = 3
    elif swap_type == 'C' and ball_location == 3:
        ball_location = 1

print(ball_location)
```

Listing 3-1: Solving Three Cups

I've used input to assign the string of swaps to the swaps variable. The for loop ❶ loops through these swaps. Each swap is processed by the nested if statement ❷. The if and elif branches each encode what happens with a given type of swap and a given ball location and then move the ball accordingly. For example, if the swap type is A and the ball is at location 1 ❷, then the ball ends up at location 2 ❸.

This is a code example where it matters whether we use multiple elifs (one big if statement) or multiple ifs (multiple if statements). If we change the elifs to ifs, then our code is no longer correct. Listing 3-2 shows the incorrect code.

```
# This code is incorrect

swaps = input()

ball_location = 1

for swap_type in swaps:
 ❶ if swap_type == 'A' and ball_location == 1:
        ball_location = 2
 ❷ if swap_type == 'A' and ball_location == 2:
        ball_location = 1
    if swap_type == 'B' and ball_location == 2:
        ball_location = 3
    if swap_type == 'B' and ball_location == 3:
        ball_location = 2
    if swap_type == 'C' and ball_location == 1:
        ball_location = 3
    if swap_type == 'C' and ball_location == 3:
        ball_location = 1

print(ball_location)
```

Listing 3-2: Solving Three Cups incorrectly

If we say that the code is incorrect, we're claiming that it fails at least one test case. Can you find a test case where this code produces the wrong answer?

Here's one such test case:

```
A
```

It may make sense to us that the ball can move at most once per swap. But Python robotically runs the code you have written, whether it matches what we expect or not. In this case, we have only one swap, so the ball should move at most once. On the first and only iteration of the for loop, Python checks the expression ❶. It's True, so Python sets ball_location to 2. Then, Python checks the expression ❷. Because we just changed ball_location to 2, this expression is True! Python therefore sets ball_location to 1. The output of the program is 1 when it should be 2.

This is an example of a *logic error*: an error that causes a program to follow the wrong logic and produce the wrong answer. A common term for logic error is a *bug*. When programmers work through their code to fix bugs, it's called *debugging*.

It often takes only a simple test case to demonstrate when a program is incorrect. When you're trying to narrow down what's going wrong with your code, don't start with long test cases. Such test case results are hard to verify by hand and often set in motion complex execution paths from which we may learn very little. A small test case, by contrast, doesn't cause our program to do much; if what it does is wrong, then we don't have far to look for the culprit. Devising small, targeted test cases is not always easy. It's a skill that you can hone through practice.

Submit our correct code to the judge, and then let's move on.

Before continuing, you might like to try solving exercises 1 and 2 from "Chapter Exercises" on page 67.

Problem #6: Occupied Spaces

We know how to loop through the characters of a string. But sometimes we need to know where we are in the string, not just the character that's stored there. This problem is one such example.

This is DMOJ problem ccc18j2.

The Challenge

You supervise a parking lot with n parking spaces. Yesterday, you recorded whether each parking space was occupied by a car or was empty. Today, you again recorded whether each parking space was occupied by a car or was empty. Indicate the number of parking spaces that were occupied on both days.

Input

The input consists of three lines.

- The first line contains integer n, the number of parking spaces. n is between 1 and 100.

- The second line contains a string of n characters for yesterday's information, one character for each parking space. A C indicates an occupied parking space (C for car), and a . indicates an empty parking space. For example, CC. means that the first two parking spaces were occupied and the third was empty.

- The third line contains a string of n characters for today's information, in the same format as the second line.

Output

Output the number of parking spaces that were occupied on both days.

A New Kind of Loop

We could have up to 100 parking spaces, so you may not be surprised that a loop will show up here somewhere. The kind of for loop we learned when solving Three Cups can certainly loop through a string of parking-space information:

```
>>> yesterday = 'CC.'
>>> for parking_space in yesterday:
...     print('The space is ' + parking_space)
...
The space is C
The space is C
The space is .
```

That tells us whether each space was occupied yesterday. But we also need to know whether each space was also occupied today.

Consider this test case:

```
3
CC.
.C.
```

The first parking space was occupied yesterday. Was that parking space occupied on both days? To answer that, we need to look at the corresponding character in today's string. It's a . (empty), so this parking space was not occupied on both days.

What about the second parking space? That one was also occupied yesterday. And, looking at the second character of today's string, it was also occupied today. So this *is* a parking space that was occupied on both days. (This is the only such parking space; the correct output for this test case is 1.)

Looping through the characters of one string doesn't help us find the corresponding characters in the other string. But if we could keep track of where we were in the string—we're at the first parking space, we're at the second parking space, and so on—we could look up the corresponding character from each string. The for loops we've learned so far are not the way to do this. The way to do this is using indexing and a new type of for loop.

Indexing

Each character in a string has an *index*, which indicates its location. The first character is at index 0, the second character is at index 1, and so on. In natural language, we often start counting at 1. In English, no one says "the character at position 0 of *hello* is *h*." But most programming languages, Python included, start at 0.

To use indexing, we follow a string by an index in square brackets. Here are some examples of indexing:

```
>>> word = 'splore'
>>> word[0]
's'
```

```
>>> word[3]
'o'
>>> word[5]
'e'
```

If we like, we can use variables in an index:

```
>>> where = 2
>>> word[where]
'l'
>>> word[where + 2]
'r'
```

The highest index that we can use on a nonempty string is its length minus 1. (There is no valid index for an empty string.) For example, 'splore' is length 6, so index 5 is its highest index. Any bigger and we get an error:

```
>>> word[len(word)]
Traceback (most recent call last):
  File "<stdin>", line 1, in <module>
IndexError: string index out of range
>>> word[len(word) - 1]
'e'
```

How can we access the second character from the right of a string? This will do it:

```
>>> word[len(word) - 2]
'r'
```

But there's an easier way. Python supports negative indices as another option for accessing characters. Index -1 is the rightmost character, index -2 is the second character from the right, and so on:

```
>>> word[-2]
'r'
>>> word[-1]
'e'
>>> word[-5]
'p'
>>> word[-6]
's'
>>> word[-7]
Traceback (most recent call last):
  File "<stdin>", line 1, in <module>
IndexError: string index out of range
```

The plan is to use indexing to access corresponding positions of yesterday's and today's parking information. We can use index 0 of each string to access information about the first parking space, index 1 to access information about the second parking space, and so on. But before we can carry out that plan, we need to learn a new kind of for loop.

Range for loops

Python's range function generates ranges of integers, and we can use those ranges to control for loops. Rather than looping through the characters of a string, a range for loop loops through integers. If we provide one argument to range, we get a range from 0 to 1 less than that argument:

```
>>> for num in range(5):
...     print(num)
...
0
1
2
3
4
```

Notice that 5 is not output.

If we provide two arguments to range, we get a sequence from the first argument up to but not including the second argument:

```
>>> for num in range(3, 7):
...     print(num)
```

```
...
3
4
5
6
```

We can count up by a different *step size* by including a third argument. The default step size is 1, which counts up by one. Let's try a couple of other step sizes:

```
>>> for num in range(0, 10, 2):
...     print(num)
...
0
2
4
6
8
>>> for num in range(0, 10, 3):
...     print(num)
...
0
3
6
9
```

We can count backward, too, but *not* like this:

```
>>> for num in range(6, 2):
...     print(num)
...
```

That doesn't work, because by default range counts up. A step size of -1 lets us go backward, one at a time:

```
>>> for num in range(6, 2, -1):
...     print(num)
...
6
5
4
3
```

To count down from 6 to 0, including 0, we need a value of -1 for the second argument:

```
>>> for num in range(6, -1, -1):
...     print(num)
...
6
```

```
5
4
3
2
1
0
```

It's sometimes helpful to quickly look at the numbers in a range without coding a loop. Unfortunately, the range function doesn't directly show us those numbers:

```
>>> range(3, 7)
range(3, 7)
```

We can pass that result to the list function to get what we want:

```
>>> list(range(3, 7))
[3, 4, 5, 6]
```

When called with a range, the list function produces a list of the range's integers. We'll learn all about lists later; for now, keep list in mind as an aid to diagnosing errors with ranges.

CONCEPT CHECK

How many iterations are performed by the following loop?

```
for i in range(10, 20):
    # Some code here
```

A. 9

B. 10

C. 11

D. 20

Answer: B. The range goes through the numbers 10, 11, 12, 13, 14, 15, 16, 17, 18, and 19. There are 10 numbers and hence 10 iterations.

Range for Loops Through Indices

Suppose we have strings giving yesterday's and today's parking-space information:

```
>>> yesterday = 'CC.'
>>> today = '.C.'
```

Given an index, we can look at yesterday's and today's information for that index:

```
>>> yesterday[0]
'C'
>>> today[0]
'.'
```

We can use a range for loop through the indices to process each pair of corresponding characters. We know that yesterday and today are the same length. But that length could be anything from 1 to 100, so we can't write something like range(3). We want to iterate with indices 0, 1, 2, and so on, all the way up to the length of the string minus 1. We can do that by using the length of one of the strings as the argument to range:

```
>>> for index in range(len(yesterday)):
...     print(yesterday[index], today[index])
...
...
C .
C C
. .
```

I've called the loop variable index. Other popular names include i (the first letter of index) and ind. I'll use i from here on out.

Don't call this loop variable status or information. Those names imply that it takes on 'C' and '.' values, when really it takes on integers.

Solving the Problem

With our range for loops, we're ready to solve Occupied Spaces. Our strategy is to loop through each index from the beginning of the strings to the end. We can check what's at each index in both yesterday's information and today's information. Using a nested if statement, we'll determine whether the parking space was occupied on both days.

Listing 3-3 has our solution.

```
n = int(input())
yesterday = input()
today = input()

❶ occupied = 0

❷ for i in range(len(yesterday)):
    ❸ if yesterday[i] == 'C' and today[i] == 'C':
        ❹ occupied = occupied + 1

print(occupied)
```

Listing 3-3: Solving Occupied Spaces

The program starts by reading the three lines of input: n refers to the number of parking spaces; and yesterday and today refer to yesterday's and today's parking-space information, respectively.

Notice that we don't refer to the number of parking spaces (n) again. We could make use of it to tell us the length of the strings, but I've chosen to ignore it because it's often not provided in real-life scenarios.

We use the occupied variable to count the number of parking spaces that were occupied both yesterday and today. We start that variable off at 0 ❶.

Now we reach the range for loop, which loops through the valid indices of yesterday and today ❷. For each such index, we check whether the parking space was occupied yesterday and occupied today ❸. If it was, then we include this parking space in our total by increasing occupied by 1 ❹.

When the range for loop terminates, we'll have gone through all parking spaces. The total number of parking spaces that were occupied yesterday and today can be accessed through the occupied variable. All that's left is to output that total.

That'll do it for this problem. Time to submit your code to the judge.

Problem #7: Data Plan

We've learned that for loops are useful for processing data after we've read it from the input. They're also often useful for reading the data itself. In this problem, we'll tackle data that's spread over many lines and use a for loop to help us read it all.

This is DMOJ problem coci16c1p1.

The Challenge

Pero has a data plan with his cell phone provider that offers him x megabytes of data per month. In addition, any data he doesn't use in a given month carries over to the next month. For example, if x is 10 and Pero uses only 4MB in a given month, the remaining 6MB carry over to the next month (in which he'd now have 10 + 6 = 16MB available).

We're given the number of megabytes of data that Pero uses in each of the first n months. Our task is to determine the number of megabytes available for the following month.

Input

The input consists of the following lines:

- A line containing integer x, the number of megabytes given to Pero per month. x is between 1 and 100.

- A line containing integer n, the number of months that Pero has had the data plan. n is between 1 and 100.

- *n* lines, one for each month, giving the integer number of megabytes that Pero uses in that month. Each number is at least 0 and will never outstrip the number of available megabytes. (For example, if *x* is 10 and Pero currently has 30MB available, the next number will be at most 30.)

Output

Output the number of megabytes available for the next month.

Looping to Read Input

In all of our problems so far, we've known exactly how many lines to read from the input. For example, in Three Cups, we read one line; in Occupied Spaces, we read three lines. Here in Data Plan, we don't know in advance how many lines to read, because it depends on the number that we read from the second line.

We can read the first line of input:

```
monthly_mb = int(input())
```

(I've used variable name `monthly_mb` rather than x to imbue it with some meaning.)

And we can read the second line of input:

```
n = int(input())
```

But we can't read any more without a loop. A range `for` loop is perfect here, because we can use it to loop exactly n times:

```
for i in range(n):
    # Process month
```

Solving the Problem

My strategy for solving the problem is to keep track of the number of megabytes that are carried over from previous months. I call this the *excess*.

Consider this test case:

```
10
3
4
12
1
```

In each month, Pero is given 10MB of data, and we have to process the data that he used in the provided three months. In the first month, Pero is given 10MB and uses 4MB, so the excess that carries forward is 6MB. In the second month, Pero is given 10MB more, so now he has 16MB total. He uses

12MB this month, so the excess that carries forward is 16 – 12 = 4MB. In the third month, Pero is given 10MB more, so now he has 14MB total. He uses 1MB this month, so the excess that carries forward is 14 – 1 = 13MB.

We need to know the number of megabytes that Pero has available for the next (that is, fourth) month. He has 13MB that carry over from the first three months, and he's given his usual 10MB for this month, so he has a total of 13 + 10 = 23MB to use.

When I went to write the code based on this explanation, I neglected to add this final 10, so my output was 13 instead of 23. I was focusing exclusively on the excess and forgot that what we need is not the excess going into the next month, but the total number of megabytes available. That total is the excess plus whatever Pero is given per month.

See Listing 3-4 for the (corrected!) code.

```
monthly_mb = int(input())
n = int(input())

excess = 0

❶ for i in range(n):
      used = int(input())
    ❷ excess = excess + monthly_mb - used

❸ print(excess + monthly_mb)
```

Listing 3-4: Solving Data Plan

The excess variable begins at 0. On each iteration of the range for loop, we assign a value to excess that considers the number of megabytes given per month and the number of megabytes used in that month.

The range for loop loops n times, once for each month that Pero has had the data plan ❶. The values that i takes on—0, 1, and so on—aren't of interest to us, because we have no reason to care about which month we're processing. For that reason, we don't use the value of i anywhere in the program. You can replace i with _ (an underscore) to be explicit about the variable's "don't care" status, but I'll leave it as i for consistency with other examples.

In the range for loop, we read the number of megabytes used in this month. Then, we update the number of excess megabytes ❷: it's what it was before, plus the number of megabytes that Pero gets per month, minus the number of megabytes that Pero uses this month.

Having computed the excess number of megabytes after n months, we report the number of megabytes available for the next month ❸.

There are always multiple ways to solve a problem. Programming is creative, and I enjoy observing the range of solution strategies that people come up with. Even if you've succeeded in solving a problem, you might like to Google the problem to learn from how others have solved it. In addition, some online judges, like DMOJ, allow you to view other people's submissions once you've solved the problem. For submissions that pass all of the test cases: did those programmers do things differently from you? For submissions that fail some test cases: what's wrong with the code? Reading other people's code is a great way to improve your own programming skill!

Can you think of another way to solve Data Plan?

Here's a hint: you can start by calculating the total number of megabytes that Pero is given and then subtracting the number of megabytes that he uses. I encourage you to take some time to work out how to do this before continuing!

The total number of megabytes given to Pero, including those given in the next month, is $x * (n + 1)$, where x is the number of megabytes given per month. To determine the number of megabytes available for the next month, we can start with that total and subtract what Pero uses each month. That strategy is coded in Listing 3-5.

```
monthly_mb = int(input())
n = int(input())

total_mb = monthly_mb * (n + 1)

for i in range(n):
    used = int(input())
    total_mb = total_mb - used

print(total_mb)
```

Listing 3-5: Solving Data Plan, alternate approach

Choose whichever solution is your favorite, and submit to the judge.

What's intuitive to one person may not be intuitive to another. You might read an explanation or code and not be able to make sense of it. This doesn't mean that you're not smart enough. It just means you need a different presentation, one that aligns more closely to your current thinking. You might also flag difficult explanations and examples for later review. They may prove to be surprisingly useful once you've gained further practice.

Summary

In this chapter, we learned about for loops. Standard for loops loop through the characters of a sequence; range for loops loop through integers in a range. Each problem that we solved required us to process many pieces of input, and we wouldn't have been able to manage that without a loop.

The for loop is the loop of choice whenever you need to repeat code a specified number of times. Python has one other type of loop, and we'll learn how to use it in the next chapter. Why do we need anything besides for loops? What can't for loops do? Good questions! I'll tell you this for now: practicing with for loops is a wonderful way to prepare for what's to come.

Chapter Exercises

Here are some exercises for you to try.

1. DMOJ problem `wc17c3j3`, Uncrackable
2. DMOJ problem `coci18c3p1`, Magnus
3. DMOJ problem `ccc11s1`, English or French
4. DMOJ problem `ccc11s2`, Multiple Choice
5. DMOJ problem `coci12c5p1`, Ljestvica
6. DMOJ problem `coci13c3p1`, Rijeci
7. DMOJ problem `coci18c4p1`, Elder

Notes

Three Cups is originally from the 2006/2007 Croatian Open Competition in Informatics, Contest 5. Occupied Spaces is originally from the 2018 Canadian Computing Competition, Junior Level. Data Plan is originally from the 2016/2017 Croatian Open Competition in Informatics, Contest 1.

4

REPEATING CODE: INDEFINITE LOOPS

The for loops and range for loops that you learned in Chapter 3 are convenient for looping through a string or range of indices. But what do we do when we have no string or when the indices do not follow a fixed pattern? We use a while loop, the topic of this chapter. while loops are more general than for loops and can handle situations that a for loop cannot.

We'll solve three problems where for loops fall short: determining the number of times slot machines can be played, organizing a song playlist until the user wants to stop, and decoding an encoded message.

Problem #8: Slot Machines

How many times can slot machines be played before we run out of money? This is a subtle question that depends not only on our starting money but also on the pattern of winnings as we play. We'll see that we need a while loop, not a for loop, for this situation.

This is DMOJ problem ccc00s1.

The Challenge

Martha goes to a casino and brings n quarters. The casino has three slot machines, and she plays them in order until she has no quarters left. That is, she plays the first slot machine, then the second, then the third, then back to the first, then the second, and so on. Each play costs one quarter.

The slot machines operate according to the following rules:

- The first slot machine pays 30 quarters every 35th time it is played.

- The second slot machine pays 60 quarters every 100th time it is played.

- The third slot machine pays 9 quarters every 10th time it is played.

- No other plays pay anything.

Determine the number of times Martha plays before she has no quarters left.

Input

The input consists of four lines.

- The first line contains an integer n, the number of quarters that Martha brings to the casino. n is between 1 and 1,000.

- The second line contains an integer indicating the number of times that the first slot machine has been played since it last paid. These plays occurred prior to Martha arriving, and Martha's plays continue from there. For example, suppose that the first slot machine has been played 34 times since it last paid. Then, Martha will win 30 quarters the first time she plays it.

- The third line contains an integer indicating the number of times that the second slot machine has been played since it last paid.

- The fourth line contains an integer indicating the number of times that the third slot machine has been played since it last paid.

Output

Output the following sentence, where x is the number of times Martha plays before she has no quarters left:

Martha plays x times before going broke.

Exploring a Test Case

Let's run through an example, just to make sure that everything in this problem is clear. Here's the test case we'll use:

7

28

To carefully trace Martha's plays, we'll need to keep track of six pieces of information. It's convenient to use a table to do this, since a row can tell us the state after each play. Here are our columns:

Plays   the number of slot machines that Martha has played

Quarters   the number of quarters that Martha has

Next play   the slot machine that Martha would play next

First plays   the number of times that the first machine has been played since it last paid

Second plays   the number of times that the second machine has been played since it last paid

Third plays   the number of times that the third machine has been played since it last paid

To start, Martha has played zero slot machines, she has seven quarters, and she'll next play the first slot machine. The first slot machine has been played 28 times since it last paid, the second has been played 0 times since it last paid, and the third has been played 8 times since it last paid. Our state looks like this:

Plays	Quarters	Next play	First plays	Second plays	Third plays
0	7	first	28	0	8

Martha starts by playing the first slot machine. That costs one quarter. Because this is the 29th time this machine has been played since it last paid, not the 35th, the slot machine pays Martha nothing. Martha will play the second slot machine next. This is our new state:

Plays	Quarters	Next play	First plays	Second plays	Third plays
1	6	second	29	0	8

Playing the second slot machine costs one quarter. Because this is the first time this machine has been played since it last paid, not the 100th, the slot machine pays Martha nothing. Martha will play the third slot machine next. This is our new state:

Plays	Quarters	Next play	First plays	Second plays	Third plays
2	5	third	29	1	8

Playing the third slot machine costs one quarter. Because this is the 9th time this machine has been played since it last paid, not the 10th, the slot machine pays Martha nothing. Next, Martha will cycle back to the first slot machine. This is our new state:

Plays	Quarters	Next play	First plays	Second plays	Third plays
3	4	first	29	1	9

Now Martha plays the first slot machine:

Plays	Quarters	Next play	First plays	Second plays	Third plays
4	3	second	30	1	9

Then Martha plays the second slot machine:

Plays	Quarters	Next play	First plays	Second plays	Third plays
5	2	third	30	2	9

Martha is almost out of quarters! But there's good news coming, because she's next going to play the third slot machine. It has been played nine times since it last paid. The next play is therefore its 10th, which pays Martha nine quarters. She had two quarters, pays one to play this machine, and then gets paid nine, so she'll have 2 − 1 + 9 = 10 quarters after this play:

Plays	Quarters	Next play	First plays	Second plays	Third plays
6	10	first	30	2	0

Notice that the third slot machine has now been played zero times since it last paid.

That's six plays so far. I encourage you to keep tracing. You should see that Martha never gets paid again and that after 10 more plays (for a total of 16), Martha is broke.

A Limitation of for loops

In Chapter 3, we studied for loops. Standard for loops loop through a sequence, such as a string. We certainly have no string in the Slot Machines problem.

Range for loops loop through a range of integers and can be used to loop a specified number of times. But how many times should we loop for Slot Machines? Ten? Fifty? Who knows. It depends on the number of plays that Martha can make before she's out of quarters.

We have no string and don't know how many iterations are required. If all we had were for loops, we'd be stuck.

Enter the *while loop*, the most general looping structure that Python offers. We can write while loops that have nothing to do with strings or sequences of integers. In return for this added flexibility, we'll need to be a little more careful and take a little more responsibility with writing our loops. Let's dig in!

while loops

To write a while loop, we use Python's while statement. A while loop is controlled by a Boolean expression. If the Boolean expression is True, then Python executes one iteration of the while loop. If the expression is still True, then Python executes another iteration of the while loop, and so on, until the Boolean expression is False. If the Boolean expression is False at the outset, then the loop does not run at all.

while loops are *indefinite loops*: the number of iterations may not be known in advance.

Using while loops

Let's start with the following example of a while loop:

```
❶ >>> num = 0
❷ >>> while num < 5:
   ...     print(num)
❸ ...     num = num + 1
   ...
   0
   1
   2
   3
   4
```

In a for loop, the loop variable is created for us; we don't have to use an assignment statement to create the variable prior to the loop. But in a while loop, we get nothing for free. If we need a variable to loop through values in a while loop, then we have to create that variable ourselves. We do that here by making num refer to 0 prior to the loop ❶.

The while loop itself is controlled by the Boolean expression num < 5 ❷. If num < 5 is True, then the code in the loop block will run. Right now, num refers to 0, so the Boolean expression is True. We therefore run the loop block, which outputs 0 and then increases num to 1 ❸.

We jump back to the top of the loop and evaluate the num < 5 Boolean expression again. As num refers to 1, the expression is True. We therefore run the loop block again, which outputs 1 and then increases num to 2.

Back to the top of the loop: is num < 5 still True? It is, because num is only 2. That kicks off another iteration of the loop, which outputs 2 and increases num to 3.

This pattern continues, with two more iterations of the loop: one when num refers to 3 and one when num refers to 4. When num refers to 5, the num < 5 Boolean expression is finally False, which terminates the loop.

It's important that we remember to increase num ❸. A for loop automatically steps our loop variable through the appropriate values. But, again, we get nothing for free in a while loop and must update variables ourselves to bring us closer and closer to loop termination. If we forget to increase num, this happens:

```
>>> num = 0
>>> while num < 5:
...     print(num)
...
0
0
0
0
0
0
0
0
... forever
```

If you run this code on your computer, your screen will fill up with zeros, and you'll have to terminate your program. You can do that by pressing CTRL-C or by closing the Python window.

The problem is that num < 5 stays True forever; nothing in the loop can ever make it False. This situation, where a loop never terminates, is called an *infinite loop*. It's surprisingly easy to inadvertently produce infinite while loops. If you see the same values repeating or your program appears to be doing nothing at all, it's likely that you're stuck in an infinite loop. Carefully check the while loop's Boolean expression and that the loop block is making progress toward termination.

We can do whatever we like with the num variable. Here's a while loop counting up by three:

```
>>> num = 0
>>> while num < 10:
...     print(num)
...     num = num + 3
...
0
3
6
9
```

And here's a while loop counting down from 4 to 0:

```
>>> num = 4
❶ >>> while num >= 0:
...     print(num)
...     num = num - 1
...
4
3
2
1
0
```

Notice that I've used >= here rather than > ❶. This way, the while loop runs when num refers to 0, as desired.

CONCEPT CHECK

What is the output of the following code?

```
n = 3
while n > 0:
    if n == 5:
        n = -100
    print(n)
    n = n + 1
```

A.
```
3
4
```

B.
```
3
4
5
```

C.
```
3
4
-100
```

(continued)

D.
```
3
4
5
-100
```

Answer: C. A while loop's Boolean expression is checked only at the start of each iteration. Even if it becomes False at some point during the iteration, the remainder of the iteration completes.

As 3 is greater than 0, an iteration of the loop runs. The if statement block is skipped (because its Boolean expression is False), so this iteration outputs 3 and sets n to 4. As 4 is greater than 0, we have another iteration of the loop, this one outputting 4 and setting n to 5. As 5 is greater than 0, we have yet another iteration of the loop. This time, the if statement block runs, which sets n to -100. Next, -100 is output, and n is set to -99. And here we stop, because n > 0 is False.

CONCEPT CHECK

What is the output of the following code?

```
x = 6
while x > 4:
    x = x - 1
    print(x)
```

A.
```
6
5
```

B.
```
6
5
4
```

C.
```
5
4
```

D.
```
5
4
3
```

E.
```
6
5
4
3
```

Answer: C. Many while loops do something and then update the loop variable, but not this one. This one first decrements the loop variable x and *then* outputs it. As 6 is greater than 4, an iteration of the loop runs, which assigns 5 to x and then outputs 5. Next, 5 is greater than 4, so we have another iteration, this one assigning 4 to x and outputting 4. And that's it: 4 is not greater than 4, so the loop terminates.

Nesting Loops in Loops

We can nest loops inside of while loops, much as we can nest loops inside of for loops. In "Nesting" in Chapter 3, I noted that the inner for loop completes all of its iterations before the next iteration of the outer loop begins. The same holds for while loops. Here's an example:

```
>>> i = 0
>>> while i < 3:
...     j = 8
...     while j < 11:
...         print(i, j)
...         j = j + 1
...     i = i + 1
...
0 8
0 9
0 10
1 8
1 9
1 10
2 8
2 9
2 10
```

Each value of i is involved in three lines of output, one for each iteration of the inner j loop.

Adding Boolean Operators

To solve Slot Machines, we want to loop while Martha has at least one quarter. That looks like this:

```
while quarters >= 1:
```

That simple Boolean expression will suffice for this problem. But just like for if statements, the Boolean expression following the word while can include relational or Boolean operators. Here's an example:

```
>>> x = 4
>>> y = 10
>>> while x <= 10 and y <= 13:
...     print(x, y)
...     x = x + 1
...     y = y + 1
```

```
...
4 10
5 11
6 12
7 13
```

The `while` loop is controlled by the Boolean expression `x <= 10 and y`
`<= 13`. As with any `and` operator, both of its operands must be `True` for the
whole expression to be `True`. When x refers to 8 and y refers to 14, the loop
terminates because the `y <= 13` operand is `False`.

Solving the Problem

To solve Slot Machines, we know that we need a `while` loop, not a `for` loop,
because we can't predict the number of iterations in advance. Each iteration
of the loop will play the current slot machine. When the loop terminates,
Martha will have no quarters left, and we will output the number of times
she played.

Here's what we need to do on each iteration:

- Decrease Martha's quarters by one (since it costs one quarter to play
  a slot machine).

- If Martha is currently on the first slot machine, play that machine.
  This involves increasing the number of times this machine has been
  played. If this is the 35th play, then pay Martha and reset the number of times that this machine has been played to 0.

- If Martha is currently on the second slot machine, play that machine
  (similar to how we played the first machine).

- If Martha is currently on the third slot machine, play that machine
  (similar to how we played the first machine).

- Increase the number of Martha's plays (since we just played a machine).

- Move to the next machine. If Martha just played the first machine,
  we want to move to the second; if she just played the second, we
  want to move to the third; and if she just played the third, we want
  to cycle back to the first.

Our programs are getting longer now, so outlining the plan as I just did
is a useful technique for keeping the complexity under control and guiding
us toward correct code. We can use the outline to make sure we're following
the plan and not forgetting anything.

Our code is in Listing 4-1.

```
quarters = int(input())
first = int(input())
second = int(input())
third = int(input())
```

```
      plays = 0
❶ machine = 0

❷ while quarters >= 1:
    ❸ quarters = quarters - 1

    ❹ if machine == 0:
          first = first + 1
        ❺ if first == 35:
              first = 0
              quarters = quarters + 30
      elif machine == 1:
          second = second + 1
          if second == 100:
              second = 0
              quarters = quarters + 60
      elif machine == 2:
          third = third + 1
          if third == 10:
              third = 0
              quarters = quarters + 9

    ❻ plays = plays + 1
    ❼ machine = machine + 1
    ❽ if machine == 3:
          machine = 0

print('Martha plays', plays, 'times before going broke.')
```

Listing 4-1: Solving Slot Machines

The quarters variable tracks the number of quarters that Martha has. The first, second, and third variables track the number of plays since the last payment for the first, second, and third slot machines, respectively.

The machine variable tracks the slot machine that Martha will play next. The first slot machine is referred to by the number 0, the second by the number 1, and the third by 2. Making machine refer to 0 therefore indicates that the first slot machine will be played next ❶.

We could have referred to the slot machines using 1, 2, and 3 instead of 0, 1, and 2. Or we could have used strings: 'first', 'second', and 'third'. But numbering items starting from zero is customary, so that's what I've done here.

The final variable in this program is plays, which tracks the number of slot machines that Martha has played. We'll output this once Martha is out of quarters.

The bulk of the program consists of a while loop that loops as long as Martha has quarters ❷.

Each iteration of the loop plays one slot machine. As such, the first thing we do is decrease Martha's quarters by one ❸. Next, we play the current slot machine.

Are we on slot machine 0? Slot machine 1? Slot machine 2? We need an if statement to answer that.

We first check whether we're on slot machine 0 ❹. If we are, then we increase the number of plays since this slot machine paid by one. To determine whether Martha gets paid, we then check whether this machine has been played exactly 35 times since it last paid ❺. If it has, then we reset this machine's plays to 0 and increase Martha's quarters by 30.

There are several levels of nesting here, so take some time to convince yourself that the logic of the code is correct. In particular, note that every time we play the first machine, we increase its number of plays by one. But we only pay Martha after every 35 plays—that's why we have the inner if statement ❺!

We handle the second and third slot machines just as we handled the first. The only difference is that each slot machine pays Martha after its own number of plays and pays Martha its own amount of quarters.

Having played a slot machine, we increase Martha's number of plays by one ❻. Now all that's left is to move to the next machine so that we'll be at the right machine if there's a next iteration of the loop.

To move to the next machine, we increase machine by one ❼. If we were on machine 0, this would move us to machine 1. If we were on machine 1, this would move us to machine 2. If we were on machine 2, this would move us to machine 3.

. . . Machine 3? There's no machine 3! If we just played machine 2, then we want to start over at machine 0. To do that, we add a check: if we just moved to machine 3 ❽, then we know that we just played machine 2, so we reset machine to machine 0.

When the loop terminates, we know that Martha has no quarters left. As a last step, we output the required sentence, including Martha's number of plays.

This code has a lot going on: stopping when Martha has no quarters left, keeping track of the current machine, paying Martha when appropriate, and counting Martha's plays. Feel free to submit this code now, but also to consider whether you'd have written parts of it in a different way. What happens if you increase plays by 1 at the top of the loop instead of the bottom? Does it matter whether you decrease quarters by 1 at the top of the loop or the bottom? Would you have used new variables to keep track of the number of times that Martha played each slot machine, rather than modifying first, second, and third? I strongly encourage you to experiment with variations of what we've done here. If you make changes and the code no longer passes the tests, great! Now you have a new learning opportunity to fix the code and learn why your changes led to undesired behavior.

The next two sections offer further refinement of the code. We'll use the % operator to reduce the number of variables that we need and learn about f-strings to streamline how we build strings.

The Mod Operator

In "Integer and Floating-Point Numbers" in Chapter 1, I introduced the mod (%) operator for calculating the remainder of an integer division. For example, 16 divided by 5 has a remainder of 1:

```
>>> 16 % 5
1
```

And 15 divided by 5 has a remainder of 0 (because 5 divides 15 exactly):

```
>>> 15 % 5
0
```

The second operand dictates the range of values that % can possibly return. The possible return values are 0 up to but not including the second operand. For example, if the second operand is 3, then the only values that can be returned by % are 0, 1, and 2. In addition, as we increase the first operand, we cycle through all possible return values. Here's an example:

```
>>> 0 % 3
0
>>> 1 % 3
1
>>> 2 % 3
2
>>> 3 % 3
0
>>> 4 % 3
1
>>> 5 % 3
2
>>> 6 % 3
0
>>> 7 % 3
1
```

Notice the pattern: 0, 1, 2, 0, 1, 2, and so on.

This behavior is useful for counting up to a specified number and then cycling back to 0. It's exactly the behavior that we need when playing the slot machines: we play slot machine 0, then 1, then 2, then 0, then 1, then 2, then 0, then 1, and so on. (This is another reason why I used 0, 1, and 2, rather than other values, to refer to the slot machines.)

Suppose that variable plays refers to the number of times that Martha has played. To determine the next machine to play (0, 1, or 2), we can use the % operator. For example, suppose that Martha has played one slot machine so far, and we want to know which she will play next. She'll play slot machine 1 next, and the % operator tells us that:

```
>>> plays = 1
>>> plays % 3
1
```

If Martha has played six times so far, then she's played slot machines 0, 1, 2, 0, 1, 2. The next slot machine she'll play is machine 0. And, as she's played all three machines twice, with no other plays beyond that, the % operator gives us 0:

```
>>> plays = 6
>>> plays % 3
0
```

As a final example, suppose that Martha has played 11 times so far. She's done three complete cycles: 0, 1, 2, 0, 1, 2, 0, 1, 2. That's nine of the plays. The remaining two plays put Martha on slot machine 2 for her next play:

```
>>> plays = 11
>>> plays % 3
2
```

That is, we can figure out the slot machine to play without explicitly maintaining a machine variable.

We can also use % to simplify the logic of determining whether the next play on the current slot machine pays Martha. Consider the first slot machine. In Listing 4-1, we counted the number of plays since the slot machine paid. If that number is 35, then we pay Martha and reset the count to 0. But there's no need to reset the count if we're using the % operator. We can just check whether the slot machine has been played a multiple of 35 times and pay Martha if so. To test whether a number is a multiple of 35, we can use the % operator. A number is a multiple of 35 if dividing it by 35 yields no remainder:

```
>>> first = 35
>>> first % 35
0
>>> first = 48
>>> first % 35
13
>>> first = 70
>>> first % 35
0
>>> first = 175
>>> first % 35
0
```

We can just check `first % 35 == 0` to determine whether to pay Martha.

I've updated Listing 4-1 to use the % operator. The new code is in Listing 4-2.

```
quarters = int(input())
first = int(input())
second = int(input())
third = int(input())

plays = 0

while quarters >= 1:
❶   machine = plays % 3
    quarters = quarters - 1

    if machine == 0:
        first = first + 1
❷       if first % 35 == 0:
            quarters = quarters + 30
    elif machine == 1:
        second = second + 1
        if second % 100 == 0:
            quarters = quarters + 60
    elif machine == 2:
        third = third + 1
        if third % 10 == 0:
            quarters = quarters + 9

    plays = plays + 1

print('Martha plays', plays, 'times before going broke.')
```

Listing 4-2: Solving Slot Machines using %

I've used % in the two ways described in this section: to determine the current machine based on the number of plays ❶ and to determine whether Martha gets paid on a play (for example, at ❷).

Associating % with returning the remainder of a division belies its flexibility. Whenever you need to count in a cycle (0, 1, 2, 0, 1, 2), consider whether you can use % to simplify your code.

F-Strings

The final thing we do in our solution to Slot Machines is output the required sentence, like this:

```
print('Martha plays', plays, 'times before going broke.')
```

We have to remember to end the first string so that we can output the number of plays and then start a new string for the second half of the sentence. In addition, we're using multiple arguments to print to avoid having to convert plays to a string. If we were storing the resulting string rather than printing it, we'd need the str conversion:

```
>>> plays = 6
>>> result = 'Martha plays ' + str(plays) + ' times before going broke.'
>>> result
'Martha plays 6 times before going broke.'
```

Gluing strings and integers together is fine for a simple sentence like this, but it doesn't scale. Here's how it looks when we try to embed three integers instead of one:

```
>>> num1 = 7
>>> num2 = 82
>>> num3 = 11
>>> 'We have ' + str(num1) + ', ' + str(num2) + ', and ' + str(num3) + '.'
'We have 7, 82, and 11.'
```

We don't want to have to keep track of all of those quotes, pluses, and spaces.

The most flexible way to build a string consisting of strings and numbers is to use an *f-string*. Here's how the previous example looks with an f-string:

```
>>> num1 = 7
>>> num2 = 82
>>> num3 = 11
>>> f'We have {num1}, {num2}, and {num3}.'
'We have 7, 82, and 11.'
```

Notice the f before the opening quote of the string. The f stands for format, because f-strings allow you to format the contents of a string. Inside of an f-string, we can place expressions inside curly brackets. As the string is being built, each expression is replaced by its value and inserted into the string. The result is just a regular old string—there's no new type here:

```
>>> type(f'hello')
<class 'str'>
>>> type(f'{num1} days')
<class 'str'>
```

The expressions in the curly brackets can be more complex than bare variable names:

```
>>> f'The sum is {num1 + num2 + num3}'
'The sum is 100'
```

We can use f-strings in the final line of Slot Machines. Here's how that would look:

```
print(f'Martha plays {plays} times before going broke.')
```

Even in this simplest of string-formatting contexts, I think f-strings add clarity. Keep them in the back of your mind for whenever you catch yourself building a string from smaller pieces.

One warning about f-strings: they were added in Python 3.6, which at the time of writing is still a reasonably recent version of Python. In older versions of Python, f-strings cause syntax errors.

If you use f-strings, be sure to check that the judge you're submitting to is using Python 3.6 or newer to test your code.

Before continuing, you might like to try solving exercise 1 from "Chapter Exercises" on page 99.

Problem #9: Song Playlist

Sometimes we don't know in advance how much input will be provided. We'll see in this problem that a while loop is what we need in such cases.

This is DMOJ problem ccc08j2.

The Challenge

We have five favorite songs named A, B, C, D, and E. We've created a playlist of these songs and are using an app to manage the playlist. The songs start off in the order A, B, C, D, E. The app has four buttons:

- Button 1: Moves the first song of the playlist to the end of the playlist. For example, if the playlist is currently A, B, C, D, E, then it changes to B, C, D, E, A.

- Button 2: Moves the last song of the playlist to the beginning of the playlist. For example, if the playlist is currently A, B, C, D, E, then it changes to E, A, B, C, D.

- Button 3: Swaps the first two songs of the playlist. For example, if the playlist is currently A, B, C, D, E, then it changes to be B, A, C, D, E.

- Button 4: Plays the playlist!

We're provided a user's button presses. When the user presses button 4, output the order of songs in the playlist.

Input

The input consists of pairs of lines, where the first line of a pair gives the number of a button (1, 2, 3, or 4), and the second gives the number of times that the user pressed this button (between 1 and 10). That is, the first line is the number of a button, the second line is the number of times it is pressed, the third line is the number of a button, the fourth line is the number of times it is pressed, and so on. The input ends with these two lines:

```
4
1
```

indicating that the user pressed button 4 once.

Output

Output the order of songs in the playlist after all button presses. The output must be on one line, with a space separating each pair of songs.

String Slicing

The high-level plan of our solution to Song Playlist will be a while loop that keeps going as long as we haven't found the press of button 4. On each iteration, we'll read two lines of input and process them. That leads to this structure:

```
❶ button = 0

while button != 4:
    # Read button
    # Read number of presses
    # Process button presses
```

Prior to the while loop, we create the variable button and make it refer to the number 0 ❶. Without this, the button variable would not exist, and we'd get a NameError in the while loop's Boolean expression. Any number besides 4 would work here to trigger the first iteration of the loop.

Within this while loop, we'll use a for loop to process the button presses. For each press, we'll use an if statement to check which button was pressed. We'll need four indented blocks of statements in the if statement, one for each of the four buttons.

Let's talk about how to handle each of the buttons. Button 1 moves the first song of the playlist to the end of the playlist. Because we have a small, known number of songs, we can get away with using string indexing to concatenate each character. Remember that the first character of a string is at index 0, not 1. We can put that character at the end of the string like this:

```
>>> songs = 'ABCDE'
>>> songs = songs[1] + songs[2] + songs[3] + songs[4] + songs[0]
>>> songs
'BCDEA'
```

This is rather unwieldy and is specific to having exactly five songs. We can use string slicing to write more general and less error-prone code.

Slicing is a Python feature that lets us refer to a substring of a string. (In fact, it works on any sequence, as we'll see later in the book.) It takes two indices: the index where we want to start, and the index one to the right of where we want to end. If we use indices 4 and 8, for example, then we get the characters at indices 4, 5, 6, and 7. Slicing uses square brackets, with a colon between the two indices:

```
>>> s = 'abcdefghijk'
>>> s[4:8]
'efgh'
```

The slicing doesn't change what s refers to. We can make s refer to the slice by using an assignment statement:

```
>>> s
'abcdefghijk'
>>> s = s[4:8]
>>> s
'efgh'
```

It's easy to make an off-by-one error here and think that s[4:8] includes the character at index 8. But it doesn't, just like range(4, 8) doesn't include the 8. So while this behavior may be a little counterintuitive, it's applied consistently in both range and slicing.

We must always include the colon when performing string slicing, but the start and end indices are optional. If we leave off the start index, Python starts slicing at index 0:

```
>>> s = 'abcdefghijk'
>>> s[:4]
'abcd'
```

If we leave off the end index, Python slices until the end of the string:

```
>>> s[4:]
'efghijk'
```

And leaving out both indices? That gives us a slice consisting of the entire string:

```
>>> s[:]
'abcdefghijk'
```

We can even use negative indices in a slice. Here's an example:

```
>>> s[-4:]
'hijk'
```

The start index refers to the fourth character from the right, which is 'h', and the end index is omitted. We therefore get a slice from the 'h' to the end of the string.

Unlike indexing, slicing never produces an index error. If we use indices that are outside of the string, Python slices to the appropriate end of the string:

```
>>> s[8:20]
'ijk'
>>> s[-50:2]
'ab'
```

We'll use string slicing to implement the behaviors of buttons 1, 2, and 3. Here's what the code looks like for button 1:

```
>>> songs = 'ABCDE'
>>> songs = songs[1:] + songs[0]
>>> songs
'BCDEA'
```

The slice gives us the entire string except for the character at index 0. (There's nothing specific to a string of length 5 here; this code would work on a nonempty string of any length.) Appending that missing character results in the first song moving to the end of the playlist. The slicing for the other buttons is similar; you'll see that code next.

CONCEPT CHECK

What is the output of the following code?

```
game = 'Lost Vikings'

print(game[2:-6])
```

A. st V
B. ost V
C. iking
D. st Vi
E. Viking

Answer: A. The character at index 2 is the 's' in 'Lost'. The character at index -6 is the first 'i' in 'Vikings'. Since we go from index 2 up to but not including index -6, we get the slice 'st V'.

Which password gets us out of the following loop?

```
valid = False

while not valid:
    s = input()
    valid = len(s) == 5 and s[:2] == 'xy'
```

A. xyz

B. xyabc

C. abcxy

D. More than one of the above passwords get us out of the loop

E. None; the loop never executes and no passwords are obtained

Answer: B. The while loop terminates when valid is True (because then not valid is False). The only one of the given passwords whose length is 5 and whose first two characters are 'xy' is xyabc. This is therefore the only given password that sets valid to True and ends the loop.

Solving the Problem

Now that we have some practice using while loops to loop as long as there are more buttons to handle, and using slicing for string manipulation, we're ready to solve Song Playlist. See Listing 4-3 for the code.

```
songs = 'ABCDE'

button = 0

❶ while button != 4:
    button = int(input())
    presses = int(input())
    ❷ for i in range(presses):
        if button == 1:
            ❸ songs = songs[1:] + songs[0]
        elif button == 2:
            ❹ songs = songs[-1] + songs[:-1]
        elif button == 3:
            ❺ songs = songs[1] + songs[0] + songs[2:]

❻ output = ''
```

```
    for song in songs:
        output = output + song + ' '

❼ print(output[:-1])
```

Listing 4-3: Solving Song Playlist

The while loop continues as long as button 4 hasn't been pressed ❶. On each iteration of the while loop, we read the button number and then read the number of times that this button was pressed.

Now, nested in the outer while loop, we need to loop once per button press. Keep all of the loop types in mind as you decide which to use. Here, a range for loop is the best choice ❷, since it's the easiest way to loop exactly the number of times we specify.

The behavior inside the range for loop depends on which button is pressed. We therefore use an if statement to check the button number and modify the playlist accordingly. If button 1 is pressed, we use slicing to move the first song to the end of the playlist ❸. If button 2 is pressed, we use slicing to move the last song to the beginning of the playlist ❹. To do that, we start with the character at the right end of the string and then use slicing to append all other characters. For button 3, we need to modify the playlist so that the first two songs swap positions. We build a new string with the character at index 1, then the character at index 0, and then all of the characters starting at index 2 ❺.

Once we escape the while loop, we need to output the songs, with a space between each pair of songs. We can't just output songs, because that doesn't have spaces. Instead, we build an output string that has the appropriate spaces. To do that, we start with the empty string ❻ and then use a for loop to concatenate each song and a space. One small annoyance is that this adds a space to the end of the string, after the last song, and we don't want that. We therefore use slicing to remove that final space character ❼.

You're now ready to submit to the judge.

Before continuing, you might like to try solving exercise 3 from "Chapter Exercises" on page 99.

Problem #10: Secret Sentence

Even if we have a string and even if we know how much input will be provided, a while loop may still be the required type of loop. This problem demonstrates why this can be the case.

This is DMOJ problem coci08c3p2.

The Challenge

Luka is writing a secret sentence in class. He doesn't want the teacher to be able to read it, so instead of writing down the original sentence, he writes down an encoded version. After each vowel in the sentence (*a*, *e*, *i*, *o*, or *u*), he adds the letter *p* and that vowel again. For example, rather than write down the sentence *i like you*, he would write *ipi lipikepe yopoupu*.

The teacher acquires Luka's encoded sentence. Recover Luka's original sentence for the teacher.

Input

The input is one line of text, Luka's encoded sentence. It consists of lowercase letters and spaces. There is exactly one space between each pair of words. The maximum length of the line is 100 characters.

Output

Output Luka's original sentence.

Another Limitation of for loops

In Chapter 3, we learned how for loops can be used to process strings. A for loop plods through the string, from beginning to end, one character at a time. In many cases, that's precisely what we want. In Three Cups, for example, we needed to look at each swap from left to right, so we used a for loop over the string of swaps.

In other cases, that's too restrictive, and a range for loop may be more appropriate. A range for loop gives us access to indices rather than characters. It also allows us to skip through a sequence with whatever step size we choose. For example, we can use a range for loop to visit every third character of a string:

```
>>> s = 'zephyr'
>>> for i in range(0, len(s), 3):
...     print(s[i])
...
z
h
```

We can also use a range for loop to process a string from right to left instead of left to right:

```
>>> for i in range(len(s) - 1, -1, -1):
...     print(s[i])
...
r
y
h
p
e
z
```

All of this assumes that we want to step by a fixed amount on each iteration.

What if sometimes we want to move one character to the right and other times we want to move three characters to the right? That's not at all far-fetched. In fact, if we could do that, then we'd be well on our way to solving Secret Sentence.

To see why, consider this test case:

```
ipi lipikepe yopoupu
```

Imagine that we're reconstructing Luka's original sentence by copying characters to it. The first character in the encoded sentence is the vowel i. This is the first character of Luka's original sentence, too. Based on how Luka encodes sentences, we know that the next two characters will be p and i. We don't want to include those in Luka's original sentence, so we need to skip over them. That is, after processing index 0, we want to jump to index 3.

Index 3 is a space character. Since it isn't a vowel, we copy this character as is to Luka's original sentence and then move to index 4. Index 4 is l, another nonvowel, so we copy that too and move to index 5. Here at index 5 we have a vowel; after copying it, we want to jump to index 8.

What's the step size here? Sometimes we jump by three, but not always. And sometimes we jump by one, but not always. It's a mix of threes and ones. for loops are not designed for this kind of processing.

With a while loop, we can zip around a string however we please, unencumbered by predefined step sizes.

while Loops Through Indices

Writing a while loop that loops through string indices isn't any different from writing any other kind of while loop. We just need to incorporate the string's length. Here's how we can loop through each character of a string from left to right:

```
>>> s = 'zephyr'
>>> i = 0
❶ >>> while i < len(s):
...     print('We have ' + s[i])
...     i = i + 1
...
We have z
We have e
We have p
We have h
We have y
We have r
```

The variable i allows us to access each character of the string. It begins at 0 and increases by one each time through the loop.

I used < in the loop's Boolean expression ❶ to continue as long as we haven't reached the length of the string. Had I used <= instead of <, we'd have received an IndexError:

```
>>> i = 0
>>> while i <= len(s):
...     print('We have ' + s[i])
...     i = i + 1
...
We have z
We have e
We have p
We have h
We have y
We have r
Traceback (most recent call last):
  File "<stdin>", line 2, in <module>
IndexError: string index out of range
```

The length of the string is 6. We get this error because the loop tries to access s[6], which is not a valid index in the string.

Want to loop through the string jumping by three characters at a time instead of one? No problem; just increase i by 3 instead of 1:

```
>>> i = 0
>>> while i < len(s):
...     print('We have ' + s[i])
...     i = i + 3
...
We have z
We have h
```

We can also go from right to left instead of left to right. We have to start at len(s) - 1 instead of 0, and we have to decrease i on each iteration rather than increase it. We also have to change the loop's Boolean expression to detect when we're at the beginning of the string rather than the end. Here's how we go from right to left, looping through each character:

```
>>> i = len(s) - 1
>>> while i >= 0:
...     print('We have ' + s[i])
...     i = i - 1
...
We have r
We have y
We have h
We have p
We have e
We have z
```

A final use case for a while loop on a string: stopping at the first index that meets some criterion.

The strategy is to use the Boolean and operator to continue while there are more characters to check and we haven't yet met our criterion. For example, here is how we can find the index of the first 'y' in a string:

```
>>> i = 0
>>> while i < len(s) and s[i] != 'y':
...     i = i + 1
...
>>> print(i)
4
```

If there's no 'y' anywhere in the string, the loop stops when i equals the string length:

```
>>> s = 'breeze'
>>> i = 0
>>> while i < len(s) and s[i] != 'y':
...     i = i + 1
...
>>> print(i)
6
```

When i refers to 6, the first operand of and is False, so the loop terminates. You might wonder why the second operand of and doesn't cause an error here, since index 6 is not a valid index in the string. The reason is that the Boolean operators use *short-circuiting evaluation*, which means that they stop evaluating their operands if the result of the operator is already known. For and, if the first operand is False, then we know that, no matter what the second operand is, and will return False; Python therefore doesn't evaluate the second operand. Similarly, for or, if the first operand is True, then or is guaranteed to return True, so Python doesn't evaluate the second operand.

Solving the Problem

Now we know how to use a while loop to loop through a string.

For Secret Sentence, we need to do something different depending on whether we're looking at a vowel or a nonvowel. If we're looking at a vowel, then we need to copy the character and jump ahead by three characters (to skip over the p and the second occurrence of this vowel). If we're looking at a nonvowel, then we need to copy the character and move to the next character. So, we always copy the current character but then move by three or one based on whether the current character is a vowel. We can use an if statement inside the while loop to make this decision for each character that we see.

A solution for Secret Sentence is in Listing 4-4.

```
  sentence = input()

❶ result = ''
  i = 0

❷ while i < len(sentence):
      result = result + sentence[i]
  ❸ if sentence[i] in 'aeiou':
          i = i + 3
      else:
          i = i + 1

  print(result)
```

Listing 4-4: Solving Secret Sentence

The result variable ❶ is used to build the original sentence, one character at a time.

The while loop's Boolean expression is the standard one for looping until we reach the end of a string ❷. In that loop, we first concatenate the current character to the end of the result. Then we check whether the current character is a vowel ❸. Recall from "Relational Operators" in Chapter 2 that the in operator can be used to check whether the first string occurs in the second. If the current character is found in the string of vowels, we jump ahead by three characters; if not, we move to the next character.

Once the loop terminates, we have gone through the entire encoded sentence and copied the correct characters into result. The last thing to do is therefore to output this variable.

You're ready to submit our code to the judge. Grepeapat wopork!

break and continue

In this section, I'll show you two other loop keywords that Python supports: break and continue. It's my experience that introducing these keywords leads learners to overuse them to the detriment of the clarity of their loops, so I've decided to avoid them elsewhere in the book. Nonetheless, they are occasionally useful, and you're likely to see them in other Python code, so let's have a brief discussion.

break

The break keyword immediately terminates a loop, no questions asked.

Back when we solved Song Playlist, we used a while loop that looped while the button was not 4. We could also solve that problem using break; see Listing 4-5 for the code.

```
songs = 'ABCDE'

❶ while True:
        button = int(input())
    ❷ if button == 4:
        ❸ break
        presses = int(input())
        for i in range(presses):
            if button == 1:
                songs = songs[1:] + songs[0]
            elif button == 2:
                songs = songs[-1] + songs[:-1]
            elif button == 3:
                songs = songs[1] + songs[0] + songs[2:]

output = ''
for song in songs:
    output = output + song + ' '

print(output[:-1])
```

Listing 4-5: Solving Song Playlist using break

The loop's Boolean expression ❶ looks suspicious: True is always True, so at first glance it seems that this loop never terminates. (That's the downside to break. We can't just look at the Boolean expression to understand what must happen for the loop to terminate.) But it can terminate, because of our use of break. If button 4 is pressed ❷, then we hit a break ❸, which terminates the loop.

Let's see one more example of using break. In "while Loops Through Indices" in this chapter, we wrote code to find the index of the first 'y' in a string. Here's how that looks using break:

```
>>> s = 'zephyr'
>>> i = 0
>>> while i < len(s):
...     if s[i] == 'y':
...         break
...     i = i + 1
...
>>> print(i)
4
```

Again, notice that the loop's Boolean expression is misleading: it suggests that the loop always runs until the end of the string, but further scrutiny reveals that a break is lurking and can influence termination.

A break terminates only its own loop, not any outer loops. Here's an example:

```
>>> i = 0
>>> while i < 3:
...     j = 10
...     while j <= 50:
...         print(j)
...         if j == 30:
❶ ...             break
...         j = j + 10
...     i = i + 1
...
10
20
30
10
20
30
10
20
30
```

Notice how the break ❶ cuts the j loop short. But it doesn't affect the i loop: there are three iterations of that loop, exactly as there would be without the break ❶.

continue

The continue keyword ends the current iteration of the loop without running any more of its code. Unlike break, it does not end the loop altogether. If the loop condition is True, then further iterations of the loop occur.

Here's an example that uses continue to print each vowel and its index in a string:

```
>>> s = 'zephyr'
>>> i = 0
>>> while i < len(s):
❶ ...     if not s[i] in 'aeiou':
...         i = i + 1
❷ ...         continue
❸ ...     print(s[i], i)
...     i = i + 1
...
e 1
```

If the current character is not a vowel ❶, then we don't want to print it. So, we increase i by 1 to take us past this character and then use continue ❷ to end the current iteration. If we get below the if statement ❸, then it must mean that we're looking at a vowel (otherwise `continue` would have prevented us from getting here). We therefore output that character and increase i by 1 to take us past this character.

The `continue` keyword is enticing because it seems to give us a way to get us out of an iteration that we don't want to be in. "This isn't a vowel. I'm out of here!" But an `if` statement can also be used to obtain the same behavior, and the logic is often clearer:

```
>>> s = 'zephyr'
>>> i = 0
>>> while i < len(s):
...     if s[i] in 'aeiou':
...         print(s[i], i)
...     i = i + 1
...
e 1
```

Rather than skip the iteration when the current character is not a vowel, the `if` statement processes it when it *is* a vowel.

Summary

The unifying feature of the problems in this chapter is that we don't know in advance how many iterations of a loop will be required.

Slot Machines   The number of iterations depends on the initial number of quarters and the payouts of the slot machines.

Song Playlist   The number of iterations depends on how many buttons were pressed.

Secret Sentence   The number of iterations, and what to do on each iteration, depends on where vowels are located in a string.

When the number of iterations is unknown, we turn to the `while` loop, which runs as long as needed. Using a `while` loop is more error-prone than code that uses a `for` loop. It's also more flexible, as we are freed from the `for` loop constraint of systematically looping through a sequence.

In the next chapter, we'll learn about lists, which allow us to store large amounts of numeric or string data. And how do you suppose we'll process all of that data? Yes: loops! Practice the following exercises to hone your loop skills. You'll be using them a lot when we solve problems using lists.

Chapter Exercises

You now have three types of loops at your disposal: `for` loops, range `for` loops, and `while` loops. Part of the challenge of solving problems using loops is knowing which loop to use! For each of the following exercises, experiment with using different types of loops to arrive at the solution that you like best.

1. DMOJ problem `ccc20j2`, Epidemiology

2. DMOJ problem `coci08c1p2`, Ptice

3. DMOJ problem `ccc02j2`, AmeriCanadian

4. DMOJ problem `eco013r1p1`, Take a Number

5. DMOJ problem `eco015r1p1`, When You Eat Your Smarties

6. DMOJ problem `ccc19j3`, Cold Compress

Notes

Slot Machines is originally from the 2000 Canadian Computing Competition, Junior/Senior Level. Song Playlist is originally from the 2008 Canadian Computing Competition, Junior Level. Secret Sentence is originally from the 2008/2009 Croatian Open Competition in Informatics, Contest 3.

5

ORGANIZING VALUES USING LISTS

We've seen that we can use strings to work with a sequence of characters. In this chapter, we'll learn about lists, which help us work with sequences of other types of values, such as integers and floats. We'll also learn that we can nest lists inside of lists, which lets us work with grids of data.

We'll solve three problems using lists: finding the smallest neighborhood of a collection of villages, determining whether sufficient money has been raised for a school trip, and calculating the number of bonuses offered by a bakery.

Problem #11: Village Neighborhood

In this problem, we're going to find the size of the smallest neighborhood of a collection of villages. We'll find it helpful to store all of the neighborhood sizes. We might have as many as 100 villages, though, and using a separate variable for each village would be a nightmare. We'll see that lists allow us to aggregate what would otherwise be separate variables into one collection. We'll also learn about Python's powerful list operations for modifying, searching, and sorting a list.

This is DMOJ problem ccc18s1.

The Challenge

There are *n* villages located at distinct points on a straight road. Each village is represented by an integer that indicates its position on the road.

A village's left neighbor is the village with the next smallest position; a village's right neighbor is the village with the next biggest position. The *neighborhood* of a village consists of half the space between that village and its left neighbor, plus half the space between that village and its right neighbor. For example, if there's a village at position 10, with its left neighbor at position 6 and its right neighbor at position 15, then this village's neighborhood starts from position 8 (halfway between 6 and 10) and ends at position 12.5 (halfway between 10 and 15).

The leftmost and rightmost villages have only one neighbor, so the definition of a neighborhood doesn't make sense for them. We'll ignore the neighborhoods of those two villages in this problem.

The *size* of a neighborhood is calculated as the neighborhood's rightmost position minus the neighborhood's leftmost position. For example, the neighborhood that goes from 8 to 12.5 has size 12.5 − 8 = 4.5.

Determine the size of the smallest neighborhood.

Input

The input consists of the following lines:

- A line containing integer *n*, the number of villages. *n* is between 3 and 100.

- *n* lines, each of which gives the position of a village. Each position is an integer between −1,000,000,000 and 1,000,000,000. The positions need not come in order from left to right; the neighbor of a village could be anywhere in these lines.

Output

Output the size of the smallest neighborhood. Include exactly one digit after the decimal point.

Why Lists?

As part of reading the input, we'll need to read *n* integers (the integers that represent the positions of the villages). We dealt with this once already when solving Data Plan in Chapter 3. There, we used a range for loop to loop exactly *n* times. We'll do that here, too.

There's one crucial difference between Data Plan and Village Neighborhood. In Data Plan, we read an integer, used it, and never referred to it again. We didn't need to keep it around. But in Village Neighborhood, it's not enough to see each integer just once. A village's neighborhood depends on its left and right neighbors. Without access to those neighbors, we can't calculate the size of the village's neighborhood. We need to store all of the village positions for later use.

For an example of why we need to store all of the village positions, consider this test case:

6

20

50

4

19

15

1

There are six villages here. To find the size of a village's neighborhood, we need that village's left and right neighbors.

The first village in the input is at position 20. What's the size of that village's neighborhood? To answer that, we need access to all of the village positions so that we can find its left and right neighbors. Scanning through the positions, you can identify that the left neighbor is at position 19 and the right neighbor is at position 50. The size of this village's neighborhood is therefore $(20 - 19)/2 + (50 - 20)/2 = 15.5$.

The second village in the input is at position 50. What's the size of that village's neighborhood? Again, we need to look through the positions to figure it out. This village happens to be the rightmost one, so we ignore this village's neighborhood.

The third village in the input is at position 4. The left neighbor is at position 1, and the right neighbor is at position 15, so the size of this village's neighborhood is $(4 - 1)/2 + (15 - 4)/2 = 7$.

The fourth village in the input is at position 19. The left neighbor is at position 15, and the right neighbor is at position 20, so the size of this village's neighborhood is $(19 - 15)/2 + (20 - 19)/2 = 2.5$.

The only remaining village that we need to consider is at position 15. If you calculate its neighborhood size, you should get an answer of 7.5.

Comparing all of the neighborhood sizes that we calculated, we see that the minimum—and the correct answer for this test case—is 2.5.

We need a way to store all of the village positions so that we can find the neighbors of each village. A string won't help, because strings store characters, not integers. Python lists to the rescue!

Lists

A *list* is a Python type that stores a sequence of values. (You'll sometimes see list values referred to as *elements*.) We use opening and closing square brackets to delimit the list.

We can store only characters in strings, but we can store any type of value in lists. This list of integers holds the village positions from the prior section.

```
>>> [20, 50, 4, 19, 15, 1]
[20, 50, 4, 19, 15, 1]
```

Here's a list of strings:

```
>>> ['one', 'two', 'hello']
['one', 'two', 'hello']
```

We can even create a list whose values are of different types:

```
>>> ['hello', 50, 365.25]
['hello', 50, 365.25]
```

Much of what you learned about strings applies to lists as well. For example, lists support the + operator for concatenation and the * operator for replication:

```
>>> [1, 2, 3] + [4, 5, 6]
[1, 2, 3, 4, 5, 6]
>>> [1, 2, 3] * 4
[1, 2, 3, 1, 2, 3, 1, 2, 3, 1, 2, 3]
```

We even have the in operator, which tells us whether a value is in a list or not:

```
>>> 'one' in ['one', 'two', 'hello']
True
>>> 'n' in ['one', 'two', 'three']
False
```

And we have the len function to give us the length of a list:

```
>>> len(['one', 'two', 'hello'])
3
```

A list is a sequence, and we can use a for loop to loop through its values:

```
>>> for value in [20, 50, 4, 19, 15, 1]:
...     print(value)
...
20
50
4
19
15
1
```

We can make variables refer to lists, just as we make them refer to strings, integers, and floats. Let's make two variables refer to lists and then concatenate them to produce a new list.

```
>>> lst1 = [1, 2, 3]
>>> lst2 = [4, 5, 6]
>>> lst1 + lst2
[1, 2, 3, 4, 5, 6]
```

While we displayed the concatenated list, we did not store it, as we can see by looking at the lists again:

```
>>> lst1
[1, 2, 3]
>>> lst2
[4, 5, 6]
```

To make a variable refer to the concatenated list, we use assignment:

```
>>> lst3 = lst1 + lst2
>>> lst3
[1, 2, 3, 4, 5, 6]
```

Names like lst, lst1, and lst2 can be used when there's no need to be more specific about what a list contains.

But don't use list itself as a variable name. It's already a name that we can use to convert a sequence to a list:

```
>>> list('abcde')
['a', 'b', 'c', 'd', 'e']
```

If you make a variable named list, you'll lose this valuable behavior, and you'll confuse readers who will expect list not to be tampered with.

Finally, lists support indexing and slicing. Indexing returns a single value, and slicing returns a list of values:

```
>>> lst = [50, 30, 81, 40]
>>> lst[1]
30
>>> lst[-2]
81
>>> lst[1:3]
[30, 81]
```

If we have a list of strings, we can access one of its string's characters by indexing twice, first to select a string and then to select a character:

```
>>> lst = ['one', 'two', 'hello']
>>> lst[2]
'hello'
>>> lst[2][1]
'e'
```

List Mutability

Strings are *immutable*, which means they cannot be modified. When it looks like we're changing a string (for example, using string concatenation), we're really creating a new string, not modifying one that already exists.

Lists, on the other hand, are *mutable*, which means they *can* be modified.

We can observe this difference by using indexing. If we try to change a character of a string, we get an error:

```
>>> s = 'hello'
>>> s[0] = 'j'
Traceback (most recent call last):
  File "<stdin>", line 1, in <module>
TypeError: 'str' object does not support item assignment
```

The error message says that strings don't support item assignment, which just means that we can't change their characters.

But because lists are mutable, we can change their values:

```
>>> lst = ['h', 'e', 'l', 'l', 'o']
>>> lst
['h', 'e', 'l', 'l', 'o']
```

```
>>> lst[0] = 'j'
>>> lst
['j', 'e', 'l', 'l', 'o']
>>> lst[2] = 'x'
>>> lst
['j', 'e', 'x', 'l', 'o']
```

Without a precise understanding of the assignment statement, mutability can lead to seemingly bewildering behavior. Here's an example:

```
>>> x = [1, 2, 3, 4, 5]
❶ >>> y = x
>>> x[0] = 99
>>> x
[99, 2, 3, 4, 5]
```

No surprises yet. But you might be surprised by this:

```
>>> y
[99, 2, 3, 4, 5]
```

How did the 99 get into y like that?

When we assign x to y ❶, y is set to refer to the same list as x. The assignment statement doesn't copy the list. There's only one list, and it happens to have two names (or *aliases*) that refer to it. So if we make a change to that list, we see that change whether we refer to the list by x or y.

Mutability is useful because it directly models what we might want to do with the values in a list. If we want to change a value, we just change it. Without mutability, changing one value isn't possible. We'd have to create a new list that was the same as the old list except for the value that we wanted to change. That would work, but it is a roundabout and less transparent way of changing a value.

If you really do want a copy of a list, not just another name for it, you can use slicing. Leave out both the start and end indices, which results in a copy of the entire list:

```
>>> x = [1, 2, 3, 4, 5]
>>> y = x[:]
>>> x[0] = 99
>>> x
[99, 2, 3, 4, 5]
>>> y
[1, 2, 3, 4, 5]
```

Observe this time that the y list didn't change when the x list changed. They're separate lists.

Learning About Methods

Like strings, lists have many useful methods. I'll show you some of them in the next section, but first I'd like to show you how you can learn about methods on your own.

You can use Python's `dir` function to get a list of methods for a particular type. Just call `dir` with a value as the argument, and you'll get the methods for the type of that value.

Here's what we get when we call `dir` using a string value as the argument:

```
>>> dir('')
['__add__', '__class__', '__contains__', '__delattr__',
<more stuff with underscores>
'capitalize', 'casefold', 'center', 'count', 'encode',
'endswith', 'expandtabs', 'find', 'format',
'format_map', 'index', 'isalnum', 'isalpha', 'isascii',
'isdecimal', 'isdigit', 'isidentifier', 'islower',
'isnumeric', 'isprintable', 'isspace', 'istitle',
'isupper', 'join', 'ljust', 'lower', 'lstrip',
'maketrans', 'partition', 'replace', 'rfind', 'rindex',
'rjust', 'rpartition', 'rsplit', 'rstrip', 'split',
'splitlines', 'startswith', 'strip', 'swapcase', 'title',
'translate', 'upper', 'zfill']
```

Notice that we called `dir` with an empty string. We could have called `dir` with any string value; the empty string is just fastest to type.

Ignore the names at the top with underscores; those names are for Python's internal use and not generally of interest to programmers. The rest of the names are string methods that you can call. In that list, you'll find string methods that you already know, such as `isupper` and `count`, and many others that we haven't come across yet.

To learn how to use a method, you can use the name of that method in a call to `help`. Here's the help we get on the string `count` method:

```
>>> help(''.count)
Help on built-in function count:

count(...) method of builtins.str instance
❶ S.count(sub[, start[, end]]) -> int

    Return the number of non-overlapping occurrences of
    substring sub in string S[start:end].  Optional
    arguments start and end are interpreted as in
    slice notation.
```

The help tells us how to call the method ❶.

Square brackets identify optional arguments. You would use `start` and `end` if you wanted to count the occurrences of `sub` within only a slice of the string.

It's worth browsing the list of methods to check whether one is available to help with your current programming task. Even if you've used a method before, looking at the help can show you features that you didn't know existed!

To see which list methods are available, call `dir([])`. To learn about them, call `help([].xxx)`, where *xxx* is the name of a list method.

CONCEPT CHECK

Here is the help for the string `center` method:

```
>>> help(''.center)
Help on built-in function center:

center(width, fillchar=' ', /) method of builtins.str instance
    Return a centered string of length width.

    Padding is done using the specified fill character
    (default is a space).
```

(continued)

What is the string produced by the following code?

```
'cave'.center(8, 'x')
```

A. `'xxcavexx'`

B. `'  cave  '`

C. `'xxxxcavexxxx'`

D. `'    cave    '`

Answer: A. We're calling `center` with a `width` of 8 and a `fillchar` of `'x'`. (Had we provided only one argument, a space would have been used for `fillchar`.) The resulting string will therefore be of length 8. The string `'cave'` has four characters, so we need four more characters to get us to length 8. Python therefore adds two spaces at the beginning and two spaces at the end to center the string.

List Methods

Time to make progress on Village Neighborhood. I can think of two operations on a list that would help us solve it.

First, adding to a list. We'll start off with no village positions and read them one at a time from the input. We therefore need a way to add each of these positions to a growing list: first the list will have nothing, and then it will have one village position in it, then two, and so on.

Second, sorting a list. Once we've read in the village positions, we need to find the smallest neighborhood. This involves looking at each village position and the distance to its left and right neighbors. The village positions could come in any order, so in general it's not easy to find the neighbors of a given village. Think back to the work we did in "Why Lists?" in this chapter. For each village, we had to scan the entire list to find its neighbors. It'd be so much easier if we had the villages ordered by position. Then we'd know exactly where the neighbors were: they'd be just to the left and just to the right of a village.

For example, here are our sample villages in the order that we read them:

```
20 50 4 19 15 1
```

That's a mess! On a real street, they'd come in order of position, like this:

```
1 4 15 19 20 50
```

Want the neighbors of the village at position 4? Just look immediately to the left and immediately to the right: 1 and 15. The neighbors of the village at 15? Boom, they're right there—4 and 19. No more searching all over the place. We'll sort the list of village positions to simplify our code.

We can add to a list using the append method and sort a list using the sort method. We'll learn these two methods, and a few others that you'll likely find useful as you continue working with lists, and then we'll come back to solve Village Neighborhood.

Adding to a List

The append method *appends* to a list, which means that it adds a value to the end of the values already there. Here's append adding three village positions to an initially empty list:

```
>>> positions = []
>>> positions.append(20)
>>> positions
[20]
>>> positions.append(50)
>>> positions
[20, 50]
>>> positions.append(4)
>>> positions
[20, 50, 4]
```

Notice that we're using append without using an assignment statement. The append method doesn't return a list; it modifies an existing list.

It's a common error to use an assignment statement with a method that changes a list. Making this error results in the list being lost, like this:

```
>>> positions
[20, 50, 4]
>>> positions = positions.append(19)
>>> positions
```

Nothing is there! Technically, positions now refers to a None value; you can see that using print:

```
>>> print(positions)
None
```

The None value is used to convey that no information is available. That's absolutely not expected here—we wanted our four village positions!—but we've lost the list through an errant assignment statement.

If your list is disappearing or you're getting error messages related to the None value, make sure you're not using an assignment statement with a method that simply modifies a list.

The extend method is related to append. You use extend whenever you'd like to concatenate a list (not a single value) to the end of an existing list. Here's an example:

```
>>> lst1 = [1, 2, 3]
>>> lst2 = [4, 5, 6]
>>> lst1.extend(lst2)
>>> lst1
[1, 2, 3, 4, 5, 6]
>>> lst2
[4, 5, 6]
```

If you want to insert into a list at a position other than its end, you can use the insert method. It takes an index and a value and inserts the value at the index:

```
>>> lst = [10, 20, 30, 40]
>>> lst.insert(1, 99)
>>> lst
[10, 99, 20, 30, 40]
```

Sorting a List

The sort method *sorts* a list, putting its values in order. If we call it with no arguments, it sorts from smallest to largest:

```
>>> positions = [20, 50, 4, 19, 15, 1]
>>> positions.sort()
>>> positions
[1, 4, 15, 19, 20, 50]
```

If we call it with a reverse argument of value True, it sorts from largest to smallest:

```
>>> positions.sort(reverse=True)
>>> positions
[50, 20, 19, 15, 4, 1]
```

The syntax that I've used, reverse=True, is new. Based on how we've called methods and functions to this point in the book, you might expect that True by itself would work. But no: sort requires the whole reverse=True to be there, for reasons I'll explain in Chapter 6.

Removing Values from a List

The pop method removes a value by index. If no argument is provided, pop both removes and returns the rightmost value.

```
>>> lst = [50, 30, 81, 40]
>>> lst.pop()
40
```

We can pass the index of the value to remove as an argument to pop. Here, we remove and return the value at index 0:

```
>>> lst.pop(0)
50
```

Since pop returns something—unlike methods like append and sort—it makes sense to assign its return value to a variable:

```
>>> lst
[30, 81]
>>> value = lst.pop()
>>> value
81
>>> lst
[30]
```

The remove method removes by value, not index. Pass it the value to remove, and it removes the leftmost occurrence of that value from the list. If the value is not present, remove produces an error. In the following, there are two occurrences of 50 in the list, so remove(50) works twice before producing an error:

```
>>> lst = [50, 30, 81, 40, 50]
>>> lst.remove(50)
>>> lst
[30, 81, 40, 50]
>>> lst.remove(50)
>>> lst
[30, 81, 40]
>>> lst.remove(50)
Traceback (most recent call last):
  File "<stdin>", line 1, in <module>
ValueError: list.remove(x): x not in list
```

CONCEPT CHECK

What is the value of lst after the following code runs?

(continued)

```
lst = [2, 4, 6, 8]
lst.remove(4)
lst.pop(2)
```

A. `[2, 4]`

B. `[6, 8]`

C. `[2, 6]`

D. `[2, 8]`

E. This code produces an error

Answer: C. The `remove` call removes the value 4, leaving `[2, 6, 8]`. Now the `pop` call removes the value at index 2, which is value 8. That leaves a final list of `[2, 6]`.

Solving the Problem

Suppose that we've successfully read and sorted the village positions. Here's what our list would look like at that point:

```
>>> positions = [1, 4, 15, 19, 20, 50]
>>> positions
[1, 4, 15, 19, 20, 50]
```

To find the size of the smallest neighborhood, we start by finding the size of the neighborhood for the village at index 1. (Notice that we don't start at index 0: the village at index 0 is the leftmost one, and per the problem description, we can ignore it.) We can find that neighborhood size like this:

```
>>> left = (positions[1] - positions[0]) / 2
>>> right = (positions[2] - positions[1]) / 2
>>> min_size = left + right
>>> min_size
7.0
```

The `left` variable stores the size of the left part of the neighborhood, and `right` stores the size of the right part. We then add them up to obtain the total size of the neighborhood. We get a value of 7.0.

That's the value to beat. How do we know whether any other village has a smaller neighborhood? We can use a loop to process those other villages. If we find a neighborhood that's smaller than our current smallest, we update our current smallest to that smaller size.

The code for our solution is in Listing 5-1.

```
    n = int(input())

❶ positions = []

❷ for i in range(n):
      ❸ positions.append(int(input()))

❹ positions.sort()

❺ left = (positions[1] - positions[0]) / 2
   right = (positions[2] - positions[1]) / 2
   min_size = left + right

❻ for i in range(2, n - 1):
       left = (positions[i] - positions[i - 1]) / 2
       right = (positions[i + 1] - positions[i]) / 2
       size = left + right
     ❼ if size < min_size:
            min_size = size

    print(min_size)
```

Listing 5-1: Solving Village Neighborhood

We begin by reading n, the number of villages, from the input. We also set positions to refer to an empty list ❶.

Each iteration of the first range for loop ❷ is responsible for reading one village position and appending it to the positions list. It does that by using input to read the next village position, int to convert it to an integer, and the list method append to append that integer to the list ❸. That one line ❸ is equivalent to these three separate lines:

```
    position = input()
    position = int(position)
    positions.append(position)
```

Having read the village positions, we next sort them in increasing order ❹. We then find the size of the neighborhood of the village at index 1, storing it using min_size ❺.

Next, in a second loop, we loop through each of the other villages whose neighborhood sizes we need to compute ❻. Those villages start at index 2 and end at index n - 2. (We don't want to consider the village at index n - 1, because that's the rightmost village.) We therefore use range with a first argument of 2 (thus starting at 2) and a second argument of n - 1 (thus ending at n - 2).

Inside the loop, we calculate the size of the current village's neighborhood, exactly as we did for the first village. The size of the smallest neighborhood that we've found so far is referred to by min_size. Is the current village's neighborhood smaller than our smallest so far? To answer that, we use an `if` statement ❼. If this village's neighborhood is smaller than `min_size`, we update `min_size` to the size of this neighborhood. If this village's neighborhood isn't smaller than `min_size`, then we do nothing, because this village doesn't change the size of the smallest neighborhood.

Having gone through all of the villages, `min_size` must be the size of the smallest neighborhood. We therefore output the value of `min_size`.

The "Output" section of this problem description specified "Include exactly one digit after the decimal point." What if the smallest size was something like 6.25 or 8.33333? Shouldn't we do something about that?

No. We're safe with what we've done. The only neighborhood sizes we can get are numbers like `3.0` (with a `0` after the decimal point) and `3.5` (with a `.5` after the decimal point). Here's why. When we calculate the left part of a neighborhood, we subtract two integers and divide that resulting integer by 2. If we have an even integer before dividing by 2, then dividing gives us a `.0` number (no remainder). And if we have an odd integer before dividing by 2, then dividing gives us a `.5` number. The same goes for the right part of the neighborhood: the size will be a `.0` number or a `.5` number. Adding the left and right parts to get the total size is therefore guaranteed to give us another `.0` or `.5` number.

Avoiding Code Duplication: Two More Solutions

It's a little disappointing that we're including the "compute neighborhood size" code both prior to and in the second range `for` loop. In general, repeated code is a sign that we might be able to improve the code's design. We'd like to avoid repeated code because it adds to the amount of code that we must maintain, and it makes it harder to fix problems in the code if it turns out that the repeated code is flawed. Here, the repeated code seems acceptable to me (it's only three lines), but let's talk about two ways to avoid it. These are general approaches that you'll be able to apply to other similar problems.

Using a Huge Size

The only reason we're calculating the size of a village's neighborhood before the loop is so that the loop has something to compare the other neighborhood sizes against. If we entered the loop without a value for `min_size`, we'd get an error when the code tries to compare it to the size of the current village.

If we set `min_size` to `0.0` before the loop, then the loop will never find a smaller size, and we'll incorrectly output `0.0` no matter the test case. Using `0.0` would be a bug!

But a huge value, one at least as big as every possible neighborhood size, *will* work. We just need to make it so huge that the first iteration of the loop is guaranteed to find a size that's no bigger, ensuring that our fake huge size never gets output.

From the "Input" section of this problem description, we know that each position is between −1,000,000,000 and 1,000,000,000. The biggest neighborhood we could ever have, then, occurs when we have a village at position −1,000,000,000, another at position 1,000,000,000, and a village somewhere in between. That in-between village will have a neighborhood size of 1,000,000,000. We can therefore start min_size with a size of 1000000000.0 or greater. This alternate approach is in Listing 5-2.

```
n = int(input())

positions = []

for i in range(n):
    positions.append(int(input()))

positions.sort()

min_size = 1000000000.0

❶ for i in range(1, n - 1):
    left = (positions[i] - positions[i - 1]) / 2
    right = (positions[i + 1] - positions[i]) / 2
    size = left + right
    if size < min_size:
        min_size = size

print(min_size)
```

Listing 5-2: Solving Village Neighborhood with a huge value

Careful! We need to start computing sizes at index 1 now ❶ (not 2); otherwise, we'd forget to include the neighborhood of the village at index 1.

Building a List of Sizes

Another way to avoid the code duplication is to store each neighborhood size in a list of sizes. Python has a built-in min function that takes a sequence and returns its minimum:

```
>>> min('qwerty')
'e'
>>> min([15.5, 7.0, 2.5, 7.5])
2.5
```

(Python also has a max function that returns the maximum of a sequence.)

See Listing 5-3 for a solution that uses `min` on a list of neighborhood sizes.

```
n = int(input())

positions = []

for i in range(n):
    positions.append(int(input()))

positions.sort()

sizes = []

for i in range(1, n - 1):
    left = (positions[i] - positions[i - 1]) / 2
    right = (positions[i + 1] - positions[i]) / 2
    size = left + right
    sizes.append(size)

min_size = min(sizes)
print(min_size)
```

Listing 5-3: Solving Village Neighborhood using min

Feel free to submit any of these solutions to the judge, whichever you like best!

Before continuing, you might like to try solving exercise 1 from "Chapter Exercises" on page 134.

Problem #12: School Trip

Many problems you'll encounter have input with multiple integers or floats per line. We've avoided these problems until now, but they are everywhere! We'll now learn how we can use lists to process the input for these kinds of problems.

This is DMOJ problem ecoo17r1p1.

The Challenge

Students would like to go on a school trip at the end of the year, but they need money to pay for it. To raise money, they have organized a brunch. To attend the brunch, a student in their first year pays $12, a student in their second year pays $10, a student in their third year pays $7, and a student in their fourth year pays $5.

Of all of the money raised at the brunch, 50 percent of it can be used to pay for the school trip (the other 50 percent is used to pay for the brunch itself).

We are told the cost of the school trip, the proportion of students in each year, and the total number of students. Determine whether the students need to raise more money for the school trip.

Input

The input consists of 10 test cases, with three lines per test case (30 lines in all). Here are the three lines for each test case:

- The first line contains the cost in dollars of the school trip; it's an integer between 50 and 50,000.

- The second line contains four numbers indicating the proportion of brunching students who are in first, second, third, and fourth year, respectively. There is a space between each pair of numbers. Each number is between 0 and 1, and their sum is 1 (for 100 percent).

- The third line contains integer n, the number of students attending the brunch. n is between 4 and 2,000.

Output

For each test case: if the students need to raise more money for the school trip, output YES; otherwise, output NO.

A Catch

Suppose that there are 50 students and that 10 percent of them (a proportion of 0.1) are in their fourth year. Then we can calculate that $50 * 0.1 = 5$ students are in their fourth year.

Now suppose that there are 50 students, but that 15 percent of them (a proportion of 0.15) are in their fourth year. If we multiply, we get $50 * 0.15 = 7.5$ students in their fourth year.

Having 7.5 students doesn't make any sense, and I haven't told you what we should do in such a case. The full problem description specifies that we are to round down—so we'd round down to 7 here. This could result in the sum of the students in first year, second year, third year, and fourth year not equaling the total number of students. For the students who are not accounted for, we are to add them to the year with the most students. It's guaranteed that exactly one year will have the most students (there won't be a tie between multiple years).

We'll first solve the problem ignoring this catch. Then we'll incorporate the catch to give us a full solution.

Splitting Strings and Joining Lists

The second line of each test case consists of four proportions, like this:

```
0.2 0.08 0.4 0.32
```

We need a way to extract those four numbers from a string for further processing. We'll learn about the string `split` method for splitting a string into a list of its pieces. While we're at it, we'll also learn about the string `join` method, which lets us go the other way and collapse a list into a single string.

Splitting a String into a List

Remember that the `input` function returns a string, no matter what the input looks like. If the input should be interpreted as an integer, we need to convert the string to an integer. If the input should be interpreted as a float, we need to convert the string to a float. And if the input should be interpreted as four floats? Well, then we had better split it up into individual floats before converting anything!

The string `split` method splits a string into a list of its pieces. By default, `split` splits around spaces, which is exactly what we need for our four floats:

```
>>> s = '0.2 0.08 0.4 0.32'
>>> s.split()
['0.2', '0.08', '0.4', '0.32']
```

The `split` method returns a list of strings, at which point we can access each one independently. Here, I save the list that `split` returns and then access two of its values:

```
>>> proportions = s.split()
>>> proportions
['0.2', '0.08', '0.4', '0.32']
>>> proportions[1]
'0.08'
>>> proportions[2]
'0.4'
```

Data in the wild is often comma-separated rather than space-separated. Piece of cake: we can call `split` with an argument that tells it what to use as a separator:

```
>>> info = 'Toronto,Ontario,Canada'
>>> info.split(',')
['Toronto', 'Ontario', 'Canada']
```

Joining a List into a String

To go the other way, from a list to a string rather than a string to a list, we can use the string `join` method. The string on which `join` is called is used as the separator between list values. Here are two examples:

```
>>> lst = ['Toronto', 'Ontario', 'Canada']
>>> ','.join(lst)
```

```
'Toronto,Ontario,Canada'
>>> '**'.join(lst)
'Toronto**Ontario**Canada'
```

Technically, join can join the values in any sequence, not just in a list. Here's an example of joining the characters from a string:

```
>>> '*'.join('abcd')
'a*b*c*d'
```

Changing List Values

When we use split on a string of four pieces, we get a list of strings:

```
>>> s = '0.2 0.08 0.4 0.32'
>>> proportions = s.split()
>>> proportions
['0.2', '0.08', '0.4', '0.32']
```

In "Converting Between Strings and Integers" in Chapter 1, we learned that strings that look like numbers can't be used in numerical calculations. So, we need to convert this list of strings to a list of floats.

We can convert a string to a float using float, like this:

```
>>> float('45.6')
45.6
```

That's just one float. How can we convert a whole list of strings to a list of floats? It's awfully tempting to try to make that happen using the following loop:

```
>>> for value in proportions:
...     value = float(value)
```

The logic is that this should go through each value in the list and convert it to a float.

Sadly, it doesn't work. The list still refers to strings:

```
>>> proportions
['0.2', '0.08', '0.4', '0.32']
```

What could be wrong? Is float not working? We can see that float is doing just fine by looking at the type of value after conversion:

```
>>> for value in proportions:
...     value = float(value)
...     type(value)
...
<class 'float'>
```

```
<class 'float'>
<class 'float'>
<class 'float'>
```

Four floats! But the list obdurately remains one of strings.

What's happening here is that we're not changing the values referred to in the list. We're changing what the variable value refers to, but that doesn't change the fact that the list refers to the old string values. To actually change the values that the list references, we need to assign new values at the list's indices. Here's how to do it:

```
>>> proportions
['0.2', '0.08', '0.4', '0.32']
>>> for i in range(len(proportions)):
...     proportions[i] = float(proportions[i])
...
>>> proportions
[0.2, 0.08, 0.4, 0.32]
```

The range for loop loops through each index, and an assignment statement changes what's referred to by that index.

Solving Most of the Problem

We're now in good shape to solve the problem minus the catch.

We'll start with an example to highlight what our code will have to do. Then we'll move onto the code itself.

Exploring a Test Case

The input for this problem consists of 10 test cases, but I'll present only one here. If you type this test case from the keyboard, you'll see the answer. But the program won't terminate there, because it's waiting for the next test case. If you use input redirection with this test case, you'll again see the answer. But then you'll get an EOFError. EOF stands for "end of file"; the error is caused by the program trying to read more input than is available. Once your code is working for one test case, you can try adding a few more to your input to make sure that those work, too. Once you have 10, your program should run to completion.

Here's the test case I'd like to trace with you:

```
504
0.2 0.08 0.4 0.32
125
```

The school trip costs $504, and there are 125 students who attend the brunch.

To determine how much money is raised at the brunch, we calculate the money raised from each year of students. There are $125 * 0.2 = 25$ students in their first year, and each of them pays \$12 for the brunch. So, the first-year students raise 25 * 12 = 300 dollars. We can similarly calculate the money raised by the students in second, third, and fourth years. See Table 5-1 for this work.

Table 5-1: School Trip Example

Year	Students in year	Cost per student	Money raised
First year	25	12	300
Second year	10	10	100
Third year	50	7	350
Fourth year	40	5	200

The money raised by each year of students is calculated by multiplying the number of students in that year by the cost per student in that year; see the rightmost column of the table. For the total money raised by all students, we can add the four numbers in this rightmost column. That gives us 300 + 100 + 350 + 200 = 950 dollars. Only 50 percent of that can be used for the school trip. So we're left with 950 / 2 = 475 dollars, not sufficient to pay for the \$504 trip. The correct output is therefore YES, because more money must be raised.

The Code

This partial solution will correctly handle any input where multiplying a proportion by the number of students gives a whole number of students (such as the test case that we just did). See Listing 5-4 for the code.

❶ `YEAR_COSTS = [12, 10, 7, 5]`

❷ `for dataset in range(10):`
`    trip_cost = int(input())`
❸ `    proportions = input().split()`
`    num_students = int(input())`

❹ `    for i in range(len(proportions)):`
`        proportions[i] = float(proportions[i])`

❺ `    students_per_year = []`

`    for proportion in proportions:`
❻ `        students = int(num_students * proportion)`
`        students_per_year.append(students)`

`    total_raised = 0`

```
❼ for i in range(len(students_per_year)):
      total_raised = total_raised + students_per_year[i] * YEAR_COSTS[i]

❽ if total_raised / 2 < trip_cost:
      print('YES')
  else:
      print('NO')
```

Listing 5-4: Solving most of School Trip

To begin, we use variable YEAR_COSTS to refer to a list of costs for attending the brunch: the cost for students in their first, second, third, and fourth year ❶. Once we've determined the number of students in each year, we'll multiply by these values to determine the money raised. The costs never change, so we'll never change what this variable refers to. For such "constant" variables, Python convention is to write their names in capital letters, as I've done here.

The input contains 10 test cases, so we loop 10 times ❷, once for each test case. The rest of the program is inside this loop, because we want to repeat everything 10 times.

For each test case, we read the three lines of input. The second line is the one that has the four proportions, so we use split to split it into a list of four strings ❸. We use a range for loop to convert each of those strings to a float ❹.

Using those proportions, our next task is to determine the number of students in each year. We begin with an empty list ❺. Then, for each proportion, we multiply the total number of students by that proportion ❻ and append it to the list. Notice at ❻ that I'm using int to guarantee that we're appending only integers. When used on a float, int drops the fractional part by rounding toward 0.

Now we have the two lists that we need to calculate how much money has been raised. In students_per_year, we have a list of the number of students in each year, which looks something like this:

```
[25, 10, 50, 40]
```

And in YEAR_COSTS, we have the cost of brunch for students in each year:

```
[12, 10, 7, 5]
```

Each value at index 0 in these lists tells us something about students in their first year, each value at index 1 tells us something about students in their second year, and so on. Such lists are called *parallel lists*, because they work in parallel to tell us more than each does alone.

We use these two lists to calculate the total money raised, by multiplying each number of students by the corresponding cost per student and adding up all of these results ❼.

Has enough money been raised for the school trip? To find out, we use an if statement ❽. Half of the money raised by the brunch can be used for the school trip. If that amount is less than the cost of the school trip, then we need to raise more money (YES); otherwise, we don't (NO).

The code we've written is very general. The only clue that there are four years of students is at ❶. If we wanted to solve a similar problem for a different number of years, all we'd have to do is change that line (and provide input with the expected number of proportions). This is the power of lists: they help us write flexible code that can accommodate changes to problems we are solving.

How to Handle the Catch

Now let's see why our current program does the wrong thing for some test cases, and the Python features we'll use to fix it.

Exploring a Test Case

Here's a test case that our current code gets wrong:

```
50
0.7 0.1 0.1 0.1
9
```

This time, the school trip costs $50, and there are nine students that attend the brunch. For the number of students in their first year, our current program would calculate $9 * 0.7 = 6.3$ and then round down to 6. The fact that we have to round down is why we have to be careful with this test case. To see what our current program would do for all four years, see Table 5-2.

Table 5-2: An Example Case from School Trip That Our Current Program Gets Wrong

Year	Students in year	Cost per student	Money raised
First year	6	12	72
Second year	0	10	0
Third year	0	7	0
Fourth year	0	5	0

In each year besides the first year, there are 0 students because $9 * 0.1 = 0.9$ rounds down to 0. So it looks like all we raise is $72. Half of $72 is $36, not sufficient to pay for the $50 school trip. Our current program outputs YES. We need to raise more money.

...Or not. We're supposed to have nine students here, not six! We've lost three students to rounding. The problem description specifies that we should add those students to the year with the most students, which in this case is the first year. If we do that, we see that we actually raise $9 * 12 = 108$ dollars. Half of $108 is $54, so in fact we do *not* need to raise any more money for the $50 school trip! The correct output is NO.

More List Operations

To fix our program, we need to do two things: figure out how many students were lost to rounding, and add those students to the year with the most students.

Summing a List

To determine the number of students lost to rounding, we can add up the students in our students_per_year list and then subtract that from the total number of students. Python's sum function takes a list and returns the sum of its values:

```
>>> students_per_year = [6, 0, 0, 0]
>>> sum(students_per_year)
6
>>> students_per_year = [25, 10, 50, 40]
>>> sum(students_per_year)
125
```

Finding the Index of the Maximum

Python's max function takes a sequence and returns its maximum value:

```
>>> students_per_year = [6, 0, 0, 0]
>>> max(students_per_year)
6
>>> students_per_year = [25, 10, 50, 40]
>>> max(students_per_year)
50
```

We want the index of the maximum, not the maximum itself, so that we can increase the number of students at that index. Given the maximum value, we can find its index using the index method. It returns the leftmost index where the provided value is found or generates an error if the value is not in the list at all:

```
>>> students_per_year = [6, 0, 0, 0]
>>> students_per_year.index(6)
0
>>> students_per_year.index(0)
1
>>> students_per_year.index(50)
Traceback (most recent call last):
  File "<stdin>", line 1, in <module>
ValueError: 50 is not in list
```

We'll be searching for a value that we know is in the list, so we won't have to worry about getting an error.

Solving the Problem

We're there! We can now update our partial solution to handle any valid test case. The new program is in Listing 5-5.

```
YEAR_COSTS = [12, 10, 7, 5]


for dataset in range(10):
    trip_cost = int(input())
    proportions = input().split()
    num_students = int(input())

    for i in range(len(proportions)):
        proportions[i] = float(proportions[i])

    students_per_year = []

    for proportion in proportions:
        students = int(num_students * proportion)
        students_per_year.append(students)
❶ counted = sum(students_per_year)
    uncounted = num_students - counted
    most = max(students_per_year)
    where = students_per_year.index(most)
❷ students_per_year[where] = students_per_year[where] + uncounted

    total_raised = 0

    for i in range(len(students_per_year)):
        total_raised = total_raised + students_per_year[i] * YEAR_COSTS[i]

    if total_raised / 2 < trip_cost:
        print('YES')
    else:
        print('NO')
```

Listing 5-5: Solving School Trip

The only new code is the five lines starting at ❶. We use sum to calculate how many students we've counted so far and then subtract this from the total number of students to arrive at the number of uncounted students. We then use max and index to identify the index of the year to which we should add the uncounted students. Finally, we add the uncounted students to this index ❷. (Adding 0 to a number doesn't change that number, so don't worry about coding special behavior for when uncounted is 0. This code is safe in that case.)

That's all for this problem. Go ahead and submit to the judge! And then come back—we're about to explore even more general list structures.

Before continuing, you might like to try solving exercise 5 from "Chapter Exercises" on page 134.

Problem #13: Baker Bonus

In this problem, we'll see how lists help us work with two-dimensional data. This kind of data arises often in real-world programs. For example, data in the form of a spreadsheet consists of rows and columns; processing such data requires techniques like those we're about to learn.

This is DMOJ problem ecoo17r3p1.

The Challenge

Baker Brie has a number of franchisees, each of which sells baked goods to consumers. Having reached the milestone of being in business for 13 years, Baker Brie will celebrate by awarding bonuses based on sales. The bonuses depend on sales per day and sales per franchisee. Here's how the bonuses work:

- For every day on which the total sales across all franchisees is a multiple of 13, that multiple will be given as bonuses. For example, a day where the franchisees sold a combined 26 baked goods will add $26 / 13 = 2$ bonuses to the total.

- For every franchisee whose total sales across all days is a multiple of 13, that multiple will be given as bonuses. For example, a franchisee that sold a total of 39 baked goods will add $39 / 13 = 3$ bonuses to the total.

Determine the total number of bonuses awarded.

Input

The input consists of 10 test cases. Each test case contains the following lines:

- A line containing the integer number of franchisees f and integer number of days d, separated by a space. f is between 4 and 130, and d is between 2 and 4,745.

- d lines, one per day, containing f integers separated by spaces. Each integer specifies a number of sales. The first of these lines gives the sales for each franchise on the first day, the second gives the sales for each franchise on the second day, and so on. Each integer is between 1 and 13,000.

Output

For each test case, output the total number of bonuses awarded.

Representing a Table

The data for this problem can be visualized as a table. We'll start with an example and then look at how to represent a table as a list.

Exploring a Test Case

If we have d days and f franchisees, we can lay out the data as a table with d rows and f columns.

Here's a sample test case:

```
6 4
1 13 2 1 1 8
2 12 10 5 11 4
39 6 13 52 3 3
15 8 6 2 7 14
```

The table corresponding to this test case is in Table 5-3.

Table 5-3: Baker Bonus Table

	0	1	2	3	4	5
0	1	13	2	1	1	8
1	2	12	10	5	11	4
2	39	6	13	52	3	3
3	15	8	6	2	7	14

I've numbered the rows and columns starting at 0 to coincide with how we'll shortly store this data in a list.

How many bonuses are awarded in this test case? Let's first look at the rows of the table, which correspond to days. The sum of the sales for row 0 is $1 + 13 + 2 + 1 + 1 + 8 = 26$. As 26 is a multiple of 13, this row gives us $26 / 13 = 2$ bonuses. The sum of row 1 is 44. That's not a multiple of 13, so no bonuses there. The sum of row 2 is 116—again, no bonuses. The sum of row 3 is 52, which gives us $52 / 13 = 4$ bonuses.

Now let's look at the columns, which correspond to franchisees. The sum of column 0 is $1 + 2 + 39 + 15 = 57$. That's not a multiple of 13, so no bonuses. In fact, the only column that gives us any bonuses is column 1. Its sum is 39, giving us $39 / 13 = 3$ bonuses.

The total number of bonuses awarded is $2 + 4 + 3 = 9$. So, 9 is the correct output for this test case.

Nested Lists

To this point, we've seen lists of integers, floats, and strings. We can also create lists of lists, called *nested lists*. Each value of such a list is itself a list. It's common to use a variable name like grid or table to refer to a nested list. Here's a Python list corresponding to Table 5-3:

```
>>> grid = [[ 1, 13,  2,  1,  1,  8],
...         [ 2, 12, 10,  5, 11,  4],
...         [39,  6, 13, 52,  3,  3],
...         [15,  8,  6,  2,  7, 14]]
```

Each list value corresponds to one row. If we index once, we get a row, which is itself a list:

```
>>> grid[0]
[1, 13, 2, 1, 1, 8]
>>> grid[2]
[39, 6, 13, 52, 3, 3]
```

If we index twice, we get a single value. Here's the value in row 1, column 2:

```
>>> grid[1][2]
10
```

Working with columns is a little trickier than working with rows, because each column is spread over multiple lists. To access a column, we need to aggregate one value from each row. We can do that with a loop, which incrementally builds a new list representing a column. Here, I obtain column 1:

```
>>> column = []
>>> for i in range(len(grid)):
❶ ...     column.append(grid[i][1])
...
>>> column
[13, 12, 6, 8]
```

Notice how the first index (the row) varies, but the second (the column) does not ❶. This picks out each value with the same column index.

What about summing rows and columns? To sum a row, we can use the sum function. Here's the sum of row 0:

```
>>> sum(grid[0])
26
```

We can also use a loop, like this:

```
>>> total = 0
>>> for value in grid[0]:
...     total = total + value
```

```
...
>>> total
26
```

Using sum is the easier option, so we'll use that.

To sum a column, we can build a column list and use sum on that, or we can calculate it directly without making a new list. Here's the latter approach for column 1:

```
>>> total = 0
>>> for i in range(len(grid)):
...     total = total + grid[i][1]
...
>>> total
39
```

CONCEPT CHECK

What is the output of the following code?

```
lst = [[1, 1],
       [2, 3, 4]]
x = 0

for i in range(len(lst)):
    for j in range(len(lst[0])):
        x = x + lst[i][j]

print(x)
```

A. 2

B. 7

C. 11

D. This code produces an error (it uses an invalid index)

Answer: B. The variable i goes through the values 0 and 1 (because the length of lst is 2); the variable j also goes through the values 0 and 1 (because the length of lst[0] is 2). The values in the list that are summed are therefore those where each index is 0 or 1. In particular, this does not include the 4 at lst[1][2].

Solving the Problem

Our code to solve this problem is in Listing 5-6.

```
for dataset in range(10):
❶ lst = input().split()
   franchisees = int(lst[0])
   days = int(lst[1])
```

```
        grid = []

❷   for i in range(days):
        row = input().split()
    ❸   for j in range(franchisees):
            row[j] = int(row[j])
    ❹   grid.append(row)

    bonuses = 0

❺   for row in grid:
    ❻   total = sum(row)
        if total % 13 == 0:
            bonuses = bonuses + total // 13

❼   for col_index in range(franchisees):
        total = 0
    ❽   for row_index in range(days):
            total = total + grid[row_index][col_index]
        if total % 13 == 0:
            bonuses = bonuses + total // 13

    print(bonuses)
```

Listing 5-6: Solving Baker Bonus

As with School Trip, the input contains 10 test cases, so we place all of our code inside a loop that iterates 10 times.

For each test case, we read the first line of input and call split to break it into a list ❶. That list will contain two values—the number of franchisees and the number of days—and we convert them to integers and assign them to appropriately named variables.

The grid variable begins as an empty list. It will ultimately refer to a list of rows, where each row is a list of sales for a given day.

We use a range for loop to loop once for each day ❷. We then read a row from the input and call split to split it into a list of individual sales values. These values are strings right now, so we use a nested loop to convert them all to integers ❸. Then, we add the row to our grid ❹.

We've now read the input and stored the grid. It's time to add up the number of bonuses. We take that in two steps: first for the bonuses from the rows and second for the bonuses from the columns.

To find the bonuses from the rows, we use a for loop on grid ❺. As with any for loop on a list, it gives us its values one at a time. Here, each value is a list, so row refers to a different list on each iteration. The sum function works on any list of numbers, so we use it here to add up the values in the current row ❻. If the sum is divisible by 13, then we add the number of bonuses.

We can't loop through columns of the list like we did rows, so we have to resort to looping through indices. We accomplish that by using a range for loop through the indices of the columns ❼. Using sum is not an option for summing the current column, so we'll need a nested loop. That nested loop goes through the rows ❽, adding up each value in the desired column. We then check whether that total is divisible by 13 and add any bonuses if it is.

We finish by printing the total number of bonuses.

Judge time! If you submit our code, you should see that all test cases pass.

Summary

In this chapter, we learned about lists, which help us work with collections of whatever type we choose. Lists of numbers, lists of strings, lists of lists: Python supports whatever we need. We also learned about list methods and why sorting a list can make it easier to process the values in a list.

In contrast to strings, lists are mutable, which means that we can change their contents. This helps us more easily manipulate lists, but we must be careful to modify the list that we think we're modifying.

We're at the point in our learning where we can write programs with many lines of code. We can direct what our programs do using if statements and loops. We can store and manipulate information using strings and lists. We can write programs to solve challenging problems. Such programs can become difficult to design and read. Fortunately, there's a tool we can use to help us organize our programs to keep their complexity under control, and we'll learn that tool in the next chapter. Working through some of the following exercises may deepen your appreciation of the difficulty in writing larger amounts of code. Then you'll be ready to continue!

Chapter Exercises

Here are some exercises for you to try.

1. DMOJ problem ccc07j3, Deal or No Deal Calculator
2. DMOJ problem coci17c1p1, Cezar
3. DMOJ problem coci18c2p1, Preokret
4. DMOJ problem ccc00s2, Babbling Brooks (Check out Python's round function.)
5. DMOJ problem ecoo18r1p1, Willow's Wild Ride
6. DMOJ problem ecoo19r1p1, Free Shirts
7. DMOJ problem dmopc14c7p2, Tides
8. DMOJ problem wac3p3, Wesley Plays DDR
9. DMOJ problem ecoo18r1p2, Rue's Rings (If you use f-strings here, you'll need a way to include the { and } symbols themselves. You can include a { in the f-string by using {{ and a } by using }}.)
10. DMOJ problem coci19c5p1, Emacs

11. DMOJ problem `coci20c2p1`, Crtanje (You'll need to support rows from −100 to 100. But how do we support negative-indexed rows when Python lists start at index 0? Here's a trick: use index `x + 100` any time you need access to row `x`. That shifts the row numbers to be between 0 and 200 rather than between −100 and 100. Also, one small annoyance here with strings: \ is a special character, so you'll have to use `'\\'` rather than `'\'` if you want a \ character.)

12. DMOJ problem `dmopc19c5p2`, Charlie's Crazy Conquest (You'll have to be careful with indices and the game rules for this one!)

Notes

Village Neighborhood is originally from the 2018 Canadian Computing Competition, Senior Level. School Trip is originally from the 2017 Educational Computing Organization of Ontario Programming Contest, Round 1. Baker Bonus is originally from the 2017 Educational Computing Organization of Ontario Programming Contest, Round 3.

6

DESIGNING PROGRAMS WITH FUNCTIONS

When writing large programs, it's important to organize our code into smaller logical pieces, each of which contributes to the overall goal. That way, we'll be able to think about each piece on its own, without worrying about what other pieces are doing. Then we'll put the pieces together. These pieces are called *functions*.

In this chapter, we'll use functions to break down and solve two problems: calculating the score in a two-player card game and determining whether boxes of action figures can be nicely organized.

Problem #14: Card Game

In this problem, we'll implement a two-player card game. As part of thinking through the problem, we'll find that the same bit of logic crops up several times. We'll learn how to bundle this code into a Python function to avoid code duplication and enhance code clarity.

This is DMOJ problem ccc99s1.

The Challenge

Two players, A and B, are playing a card game. (You don't need to know about playing cards or card games to understand this problem.)

The game starts with a deck of 52 cards. Player A takes a card from the deck, then player B takes a card from the deck, then player A, then player B, until there are no cards left in the deck.

There are 13 types of cards in the deck. These types are as follows: two, three, four, five, six, seven, eight, nine, ten, jack, queen, king, ace. There are four cards of each of these types in the deck. For example, there are four twos, four threes, and so on, all the way up to four aces. (That's why there are 52 cards in the deck: 13 types times 4 cards per type.)

A *high card* is a card that is a jack, queen, king, or ace.

When a player takes a high card, they may score some points. Here are the rules by which points are scored:

- If a player takes a jack, after which there is at least one card remaining in the deck, and the next card in the deck is not a high card, then the player scores 1 point.

- If a player takes a queen, after which there are at least two cards remaining in the deck, and neither of the next two cards in the deck is a high card, then the player scores 2 points.

- If a player takes a king, after which there are at least three cards remaining in the deck, and none of the next three cards in the deck is a high card, then the player scores 3 points.

- If a player takes an ace, after which there are at least four cards remaining in the deck, and none of the next four cards in the deck is a high card, then the player scores 4 points.

We're asked to output information each time a player scores, as well as the total score for each player at the end of the game.

Input

The input consists of 52 lines. Each line contains the type of a card in the deck. The lines are in the order that cards will be taken from the deck; that is, the first line is the first card taken from the deck, the second line is the second card taken, and so on.

Output

Whenever a player scores, output the following line:

Player *p* scores *q* point(s).

where *p* is A for player A or B for player B, and *q* is the number of points that they just scored.

When the game ends, output the following two lines:

```
Player A: m point(s).
Player B: n point(s).
```

where *m* is the total score for player A and *n* is the total score for player B.

Exploring a Test Case

If you think through how to solve this problem, you might be left wondering whether we can just solve it, right now, without learning anything new. Indeed, we can! We're in great shape. We can use a list to represent the deck of cards. We know how to use the list append method to add a card to the deck. We can access values in the list to look for high cards. We've even got f-strings to help us output the player and points information.

Rather than dive in, though, let's go through a small example. Doing so is going to highlight that we're missing one crucial feature of Python that will make it easier to organize our solution and solve this problem.

We'll be here all year if we go through a 52-card example, so let's use a smaller one with just 10 cards. This isn't a complete test case, so the program we write won't work on it, but it's enough for us to understand the mechanics of the game and what our solution will have to do. Here's the test case:

```
queen
three
seven
king
nine
jack
eight
king
jack
four
```

Player A takes the first card, which is a queen. A queen is a high card, and player A might score 2 points here. First, we confirm that there are at least two cards remaining in the deck after this queen. Next, we have to check these next two cards, hoping there is no high card among them. The next two cards are not high cards—they are a three and a seven—so player A gets 2 points.

Player B now takes the second card, which is a three. Three isn't a high card, so no points for player B.

Player A now takes the seven. No points.

Player B now takes the king, so there's a chance for 3 points for player B. There are at least three cards remaining in the deck after this king. We have to check these next three cards, hoping there is no high card among them. Sadly, there is a high card, a jack, among those three. No points for player B.

Player A now takes the nine. No points.

Player B now takes the first jack. There is at least one card remaining in the deck after this jack. We have to check this next card, hoping it isn't a high card. Good news: it's not a high card—it's an eight—so player B gets 1 point.

There's only one more point scored, and it's by player A when they take the second-last card (the jack) from the deck.

Therefore, this is the output for this test case:

```
Player A scores 2 point(s).
Player B scores 1 point(s).
Player A scores 1 point(s).
Player A: 3 point(s).
Player B: 1 point(s).
```

Notice that each time a player takes a high card, we need to check two things: that there are at least a certain number of cards remaining in the deck and that there is no high card among these cards. The first we should be able to manage by using a variable that tells us how many cards have been taken. The second is more difficult. We'd need some code to check a given number of cards for a high card. Worse, if we're not careful, we'd end up duplicating very similar code four times: once to check the card after a jack, once to check the two cards after a queen, once to check the three cards after a king, and once to check the four cards after an ace. If we later found a flaw in our logic, we would have to fix it in up to four different places.

Is there a Python feature that lets us package that "no high cards here" logic, just once, and invoke it four times? There is. It's called a *function*, and it's just a named block of code that carries out a small task. Functions are essential to the organization and clarity of our code. All programmers use them. Without them, writing large software systems like games and word processors would be untenable. Let's learn how to use functions.

Defining and Calling Functions

We've already learned how to call functions that come with Python. For example, we've used the input function to read input. Here's a call of input with no arguments:

```
>>> s = input()
hello
>>> s
'hello'
```

We've also used Python's print function to output text. Here's a call of print with one argument:

```
>>> print('well, well')
well, well
```

The built-in Python functions are general-purpose, designed to be used in a wide variety of settings. When we want a function to solve a problem-specific task, we'll have to define it ourselves.

Functions Without Arguments

To *define*, or create, a function, we use Python's `def` keyword. Here's the definition of a function that outputs three lines:

```
>>> def intro():
...     print('********')
...     print('*WELCOME*')
...     print('********')
...
```

The structure of a function definition mirrors that of an `if` statement or loop. The name after `def` is the name of the function that we're defining; here, we're defining a function named `intro`. Following the name of the function, we have a pair of empty parentheses, `()`. We'll see later that we can include information in these parentheses to pass arguments to functions. This `intro` function doesn't take any arguments, which is why the parentheses are empty. Following the parentheses is a colon; as with `if` statements or loops, leaving out the colon is a syntax error. On the following lines, we provide an indented block of statements that will run each time the function is called.

When you defined the `intro` function, you may have expected to see this as output:

```
********
*WELCOME*
********
```

But no: so far we've only defined the function, not called it. Defining a function has no observable effect; it simply stores the function in the computer's memory so we can call it later. We call our own functions just like we call any of Python's built-in functions. Since this `intro` function doesn't take any arguments, we use an empty set of parentheses in the call:

```
>>> intro()
********
*WELCOME*
********
```

You can call this function as many times as you like. It's there as often as we need it.

Functions with Arguments

Our `intro` function isn't very flexible, as it does the same thing each time it's called. We can change the function so that we can pass arguments to it, and the arguments we pass can influence what the function does. Here's a new version of the intro function that allows us to pass a single argument:

```
>>> def intro2(message):
...     line_length = len(message) + 2
...     print('*' * line_length)
...     print(f'*{message}*')
...     print('*' * line_length)
...
```

To call this function, we provide a string argument:

```
>>> intro2('HELLO')
*******
*HELLO*
*******
>>> intro2('WIN')
*****
*WIN*
*****
```

We can't call this intro2 function without an argument—if we try, we get an error:

```
>>> intro2()
Traceback (most recent call last):
  File "<stdin>", line 1, in <module>
TypeError: intro2() missing 1 required positional argument: 'message'
```

The error reminds us that we have not provided an argument for message. The name message is known as a function *parameter*. When we call intro2, Python first makes message refer to whatever our argument refers to; that is, message becomes an alias for our argument.

We can create functions with more than one parameter. Here's a function that takes two parameters, a message to print and the number of times to print it:

```
>>> def intro3(message, num_times):
...     for i in range(num_times):
...         print(message)
...
```

To call this one, we provide two arguments. Python works from left to right, assigning the first argument to the first parameter and the second argument to the second parameter. In the following call, 'high' is assigned to the message parameter and 5 is assigned to the num_times parameter:

```
>>> intro3('high', 5)
high
high
```

Be sure to provide the correct number of arguments. For `intro3`, we need two arguments. Anything else is an error:

```
>>> intro3()
Traceback (most recent call last):
  File "<stdin>", line 1, in <module>
TypeError: intro3() missing 2 required positional arguments: 'message'
and 'num_times'
>>> intro3('high')
Traceback (most recent call last):
  File "<stdin>", line 1, in <module>
TypeError: intro3() missing 1 required positional argument: 'num_times'
```

We also have to be sure to provide values of the proper types. Wrong types won't stop us from calling the function, but they will cause an error within the function:

```
>>> intro3('high', 'low')
Traceback (most recent call last):
  File "<stdin>", line 1, in <module>
  File "<stdin>", line 2, in intro3
TypeError: 'str' object cannot be interpreted as an integer
```

This `TypeError` arises because `intro3` uses a range for loop on variable `num_times`. If the argument we provide for `num_times` is not an integer, the range for loop fails.

Keyword Arguments

It's possible to override the left-to-right correspondence between arguments and parameters when calling a function. To do that, we use the names of parameters in whatever order we like. An argument that uses the name of a parameter is called a *keyword argument*. Here's how it works:

```
>>> def intro3(message, num_times):
...     for i in range(num_times):
...         print(message)
...
>>> intro3(message='high', num_times=3)
high
high
high
>>> intro3(num_times=3, message='high')
```

```
high
high
high
```

Each function call here uses two keyword arguments. A keyword argument is written as the name of a parameter, an equal sign, and its corresponding argument.

You can even start with regular arguments and finish with keyword arguments:

```
>>> intro3('high', num_times=3)
high
high
high
```

But once you use a keyword argument, you can't go back to regular ones:

```
>>> intro3(message='high', 3)
  File "<stdin>", line 1
SyntaxError: positional argument follows keyword argument
```

In "Sorting a List" in Chapter 5 we used a reverse keyword argument when calling the sort method. The Python designers decided that reverse would be a keyword-only parameter, which means that it's impossible to fill in its value without using a keyword argument. Python lets us do that with our functions, too, but we won't need that level of control in this book.

Local Variables

Names of parameters work like regular variables, but are *local* to the function in which they're defined. That is, a function parameter doesn't exist outside of its function:

```
>>> def intro2(message):
...     line_length = len(message) + 2
...     print('*' * line_length)
...     print(f'*{message}*')
...     print('*' * line_length)
...
>>> intro2('hello')
*******
*hello*
*******
>>> message
Traceback (most recent call last):
  File "<stdin>", line 1, in <module>
NameError: name 'message' is not defined
```

What about that `line_length` variable—is it local, too? It is:

```
>>> line_length
Traceback (most recent call last):
  File "<stdin>", line 1, in <module>
NameError: name 'line_length' is not defined
```

What happens if you have a variable and you call a function that uses a parameter or local variable of the same name? Is your value lost? Let's see:

```
>>> line_length = 999
>>> intro2('hello')
*******
*hello*
*******
>>> line_length
999
```

Phew—it's still 999, just as we left it. Local variables are created when a function is called and destroyed when the function terminates, all without affecting other variables with shared names.

A function can access a variable that was created outside of that function. It's ill-advised to rely on that, though, because then that function isn't self-contained, instead hoping that variables it expects to be there are actually there. In this book, we'll write functions so that they only use local variables. All information that a function needs will be provided to the function through its parameters.

Mutable Parameters

Since a parameter is an alias for its corresponding argument, it can be used to change a mutable value. Here's a function that removes all occurrences of value from a list lst:

```
>>> def remove_all(lst, value):
...     while value in lst:
...         lst.remove(value)
...
>>> lst = [5, 10, 20, 5, 45, 5, 9]
>>> remove_all(lst, 5)
>>> lst
[10, 20, 45, 9]
```

Notice that we passed a list to `remove_all` by using a variable. This function won't accomplish anything useful if you call it with a list value directly (rather than with a variable referring to a list):

```
>>> remove_all([5, 10, 20, 5, 45, 5, 9], 5)
```

The function removed all the 5s from the list, but because we didn't use a variable, we have no way to refer to that list ever again.

```
s = 'a'
lst = [1]
mystery(s, lst)

print(s, lst)
```

Return Values

Let's come back to our Card Game problem. Our goal is to define a function that tells us whether there are no high cards in a list of cards. We'll name that function no_high. We haven't written no_high yet, but we can still specify what we hope to accomplish. Here's what we're after:

```
>>> no_high(['two', 'six'])
True
>>> no_high(['eight'])
True
>>> no_high(['two', 'jack', 'four'])
False
>>> no_high(['queen', 'king', 'three', 'queen'])
False
```

We want the first two calls to return True, because there are no high cards in those lists of cards. And we want the third and fourth calls to return False, because there's at least one high card in those lists of cards.

How can we define a function that returns these True and False values? That's the final piece of the function puzzle.

To return a value from a function, we use Python's return keyword. As soon as a return is reached, execution of the function terminates, and the specified value is returned to the caller.

Here's how we can write the no_high function:

```
>>> def no_high(lst):
...     if 'jack' in lst:
...         return False
...     if 'queen' in lst:
...         return False
...     if 'king' in lst:
...         return False
...     if 'ace' in lst:
...         return False
...     return True
...
```

We first check whether there are any `'jack'` cards in the list. If there are, then we know that the list contains one or more high cards, so we immediately return `False`.

If we're still here, then we know that there are no jacks. But there could be other high cards, so we need to check for them. The rest of the if statements check for queens, kings, and aces, respectively, returning `False` if any of them is in the list.

If we don't hit any of those four return statements, then there are no high cards in the list. In that case, we return `True`.

A return by itself, with no value given, returns the value `None`. That's useful if you're writing a function that doesn't return anything useful and you need to terminate the function before reaching the bottom of its code.

If a return is encountered inside a loop, the function still terminates immediately, regardless of how deeply nested it is. Here's an example showing a return getting us out of a nested loop:

```
>>> def func():
...     for i in range(10):
...         for j in range(10):
...             print(i, j)
...             if j == 4:
...                 return
...
>>> func()
0 0
0 1
0 2
0 3
0 4
```

A return is like a super-break! Some people don't like using return from within a loop for the same reason that they don't like break: it can obscure the purpose and logic of a loop. I'll use return within a loop when convenient. Unlike break, which can show up anywhere, a return is restricted to showing up within a function, separated from other code. If we keep our functions small, then using a return within a loop can help us write clear code without interfering with the code around it.

CONCEPT CHECK

Is the following version of no_high correct? That is, does it return `True` if there is at least one high card in the list, and `False` otherwise?

```
def no_high(lst):
    for card in lst:
```

```
        if card in ['jack', 'queen', 'king', 'ace']:
            return False
        else:
            return True
```

A. Yes

B. No; for example, it returns the wrong value for ['two', 'three']

C. No; for example, it returns the wrong value for ['jack']

D. No; for example, it returns the wrong value for ['jack', 'two']

E. No; for example, it returns the wrong value for ['two', 'jack']

Answer: E. The if-else statement causes the loop to always terminate on its first iteration. If the first card is a high card, the function terminates and returns False; if the first card is not a high card, the function terminates and returns True. It doesn't look at any of the other cards! And that's why it fails on ['two', 'jack']: the first card is not a high card, so the function returns True. Returning True tells us that there are no high cards in the list. But that's wrong: there's a jack in there! The function did the wrong thing. It should have returned False.

Function Documentation

It's clear to us right now what our no_high function does and how we should call it. But what about in a few months, when the purpose of our old code doesn't come readily to mind? And what about once we've amassed a large collection of our own functions, making it difficult to remember what each one does?

For each function we write, we'll add documentation that specifies the meaning of each parameter and what the function returns. Such documentation is called a *docstring*, for "documentation string." The docstring should be written starting at the first line of the function's block. Here's the no_high function, this time with documentation:

```
>>> def no_high(lst):
...     """
...     lst is a list of strings representing cards.
...
...     Return True if there are no high cards in lst, False otherwise.
...     """
...     if 'jack' in lst:
...         return False
...     if 'queen' in lst:
...         return False
...     if 'king' in lst:
```

```
...         return False
...      if 'ace' in lst:
...         return False
...      return True
...
```

The docstring begins and ends with three double quotes (`"""`). Like a single quote (`'`) or double quote (`"`), three double quotes can be used to start and end any string. A string created with three quotes is called a *triple-quoted string*. (Three single quotes work as well, but Python convention is to use three double quotes.) They have the bonus of letting us add multiple lines of text to the string by just pressing ENTER after each line; strings created with `'` or `"` can't span lines like that. We use triple-quoted strings for docstrings so that we can include as many lines as we like.

The docstring here tells us what lst is: it's a list of strings representing cards. It also tells us that the function returns a `True` or `False` value and what each return value means. This is sufficient information to enable someone to call the function without having to look at its code. As long as someone knows what a function does, they can just use it. We've been using Python functions all along without ever having looked at their code. How does `print` work? How does `input` work? We don't know! But it doesn't matter: we know what the functions do, so we can just focus on calling them.

For functions with multiple parameters, the docstring should name each one and give its expected type. Here's remove_all, from "Mutable Parameters" in this chapter, with a suitable docstring:

```
>>> def remove_all(lst, value):
...      """
...      lst is a list.
...      value is a value.
...
...      Remove all occurrences of value from lst.
...      """
...      while value in lst:
...          lst.remove(value)
...
```

Notice that this docstring doesn't talk about returning anything. That's because this function doesn't return anything useful! It removes from lst, which is what the docstring says it does.

Solving the Problem

We've just learned the fundamentals of defining and calling functions. For the rest of the book, whenever we're faced with a large problem to solve, we'll be able to break down its solution into smaller tasks, each of which will be solved by a function.

Let's use our no_high function in a solution to Card Game. The code is in Listing 6-1.

❶ ```
NUM_CARDS = 52
```

❷ ```
def no_high(lst):
    """
    lst is a list of strings representing cards.

    Return True if there are no high cards in lst, False otherwise.
    """
    if 'jack' in lst:
        return False
    if 'queen' in lst:
        return False
    if 'king' in lst:
        return False
    if 'ace' in lst:
        return False
    return True
```

❸ ```
deck = []
```

❹ ```
for i in range(NUM_CARDS):
    deck.append(input())

score_a = 0
score_b = 0
player = 'A'
```

❺ ```
for i in range(NUM_CARDS):
    card = deck[i]
    points = 0
```
❻ ```
    remaining = NUM_CARDS - i - 1
```
❼ ```
    if card == 'jack' and remaining >= 1 and no_high(deck[i+1:i+2]):
        points = 1
    elif card == 'queen' and remaining >= 2 and no_high(deck[i+1:i+3]):
        points = 2
    elif card == 'king' and remaining >= 3 and no_high(deck[i+1:i+4]):
        points = 3
    elif card == 'ace' and remaining >= 4 and no_high(deck[i+1:i+5]):
        points = 4
```

❽ ```
    if points > 0:
        print(f'Player {player} scores {points} point(s).')
```

```
❾ if player == 'A':
        score_a = score_a + points
        player = 'B'
    else:
        score_b = score_b + points
        player = 'A'

print(f'Player A: {score_a} point(s).')
print(f'Player B: {score_b} point(s).')
```

Listing 6-1: Solving Card Game

I've introduced the constant NUM_CARDS to refer to 52 ❶. We'll use it a couple of times in the code, and it's easier to remember what NUM_CARDS means than what 52 means.

Next we define the no_high function, including docstring, that we've discussed in depth ❷. We'll always put our functions near the top of our programs. This way, the functions are available to be called by any code that follows them.

The main part of the program starts with creating a list that will hold the cards in the deck ❸. We then read the cards from the input ❹, appending each to the deck. You'll notice that cards are never literally removed or taken from the deck (the deck remains as is throughout program execution). We could have done it that way. Instead, I've chosen to track where we are in the deck so that we know which card would be removed next.

There are three other crucial variables that we maintain: score_a, the current total score for player A; score_b, the current total score for player B; and player, the name of the current player.

Our next task is to look at each card in the deck to give points to the players. A regular for loop would let us look at the current card. But that's not enough: if the current card is a high card, then we have to be able to look at later cards as well. To facilitate that, we use a range for loop ❺.

On each iteration of this loop, we determine the number of points awarded to the current player based on the card that they take from the deck. Each rule for getting points depends on the deck having some number of remaining cards. The remaining variable ❻ tells us the number of remaining cards. When i is 0, the number of remaining cards is 51, because we've just taken the first card. When i is 1, the number of remaining cards is 50, because we've just taken the second card. In general, the expression for the number of remaining cards is the total number of cards, minus i, minus 1.

And now we have four tests, one for each way to score points ❼. Each one checks the current card and the number of cards remaining. If both of those conditions are True, then a call is made to our no_high function with a slice of the deck containing the appropriate number of cards. For example, if the current card is a 'jack' and there is at least 1 card remaining, then we pass a list of length 1 to no_high ❼. If no_high returns True, then there are no high cards in the slice of the list, so the current player gets points. The `points` variable determines the number of points that will be awarded; it starts at 0 on each iteration of the loop and is set to 1, 2, 3, or 4 as appropriate.

If the player scored points ❽, then we output a message indicating the player who scored points and the number of points they scored.

All that's left for the current iteration is to add the points to the current player's score and make it the other player's turn. We accomplish both of these tasks with an `if-else` statement ❾. (If `points` is 0 on this iteration, then a harmless 0 is added to a player's score. There's no reason to explicitly test for and avoid that.)

The final two `print` calls output the total points for each player.

There we go: a solution to the problem that uses a function to organize our code and make it easier to read. Feel free to submit our code to the judge, and you should see that all test cases pass.

Problem #15: Action Figures

To solve Card Game, we first went through an example, and that example highlighted where a function might be useful. Now, we'll solve another problem using functions, but we'll discover the needed functions using a more systematic approach.

This is Timus problem 2144. This is the only problem in the book from the Timus judge. To find the problem, go to *https://acm.timus.ru/*, click **Problem set**, click **Volume 12**, and find problem 2144 (it's called Cleaning the Room on the judge).

The Challenge

Lena has *n* unopened boxes of action figures. The boxes cannot be opened (otherwise the action figures lose their value), so the order of action figures in a box cannot be changed. Further, a box cannot be rotated (otherwise the action figures will be facing the wrong way).

Each action figure is specified by its height. For example, one of the boxes might have three action figures, from left to right, of heights 4, 5, and 7. When I talk about a box of action figures, I'll always list the heights from left to right.

Lena wants to *organize the boxes*, which means to arrange the boxes so that heights of action figures increase or stay the same from left to right.

Whether she can organize the boxes or not depends on the heights of action figures in the boxes. For example, if a first box has action figures of heights 4, 5, and 7, and a second box has action figures of heights 1 and 2, then she can organize these boxes by putting the second box first. But if we keep the first box as is and change the second box to have action figures of heights 6 and 8, then there's no way to organize these boxes.

Determine whether it's possible for Lena to organize the boxes.

Input

The input consists of the following lines:

- A line containing integer n, the number of boxes. n is between 1 and 100.

- n lines, one for each box. Each of these lines begins with integer k, indicating the number of action figures in this box. k is between 1 and 100. (Since k is at least 1, we don't have to worry about empty boxes.) Following k, there are k integers giving the heights of the action figures from left to right in this box. Each height is an integer between 1 and 10,000. There is a space between each pair of integers on the line.

Output

If Lena can organize the boxes, output YES; otherwise, output NO.

Representing the Boxes

This problem consists of several smaller problems, each of which we can solve by writing a function. Let's first see how to represent the boxes in Python, and then we'll design the functions that we need.

In Chapter 5, when we solved Baker Bonus, we learned that lists can have other lists as their values. This allows us to nest lists inside of lists. We can use such an arrangement to represent the boxes of action figures. For example, here's a list that represents two boxes:

```
>>> boxes = [[4, 5, 7], [1, 2]]
```

The first box has three action figures, and the second has two. We can access each box individually:

```
>>> boxes[0]
[4, 5, 7]
>>> boxes[1]
[1, 2]
```

We'll read the contents of the boxes from the input and put that information into a nested list, like the one I've shown. Then we'll use that nested list to determine whether the boxes can be organized.

Top-Down Design

We'll solve this problem using a program design approach called *top-down design*. Top-down design breaks a large problem into several smaller problems. That's useful because each of the smaller problems will be easier to solve. We can then assemble those subproblem solutions to solve the original problem.

Doing Top-Down Design

Here's how top-down design works. We start by writing an incomplete Python program that captures the main tasks in a solution. Some of these tasks won't require much code, so we can proceed to solve them directly. Other tasks will require more from us, and we'll turn each of those into a function that we'll call. We might also solve a task by writing a little code *and* calling a function. However, those functions won't exist yet. We'll have to write them!

To write a needed function, we repeat this same process for that function's task. That is, we start by writing down the tasks for that function. If we can write code for a task outright, then we do it; otherwise, we call another function (that we'll write later) to handle that task.

We keep doing this until we have no more functions to write. At that point, we'll have a solution to our problem.

It's called top-down design because we start at the top, or highest, level of the problem and make our way downward, through the guts of the problem, until each task has been completely written in code. We'll now use this to solve Action Figures.

The Top Level

To begin our design, we focus on the main tasks that we'll need to solve.

We'll certainly have to read the input, so that's our first task.

Now, assume that we've read the input. What should we do to determine whether the boxes can be organized? One important thing to do is check each box on its own to make sure that its action figures have their heights in order. For example, suppose that we had the box [18, 20, 4]. This box, with heights out of order, means that we have no chance of organizing all of the boxes. We can't even organize this one!

So, that's our second task: determine whether each box, on its own, has its action figures in order. If any of these boxes has its action figures out of order, then we know that the boxes can't be organized. If all boxes are OK, then we have more to check.

If each box on its own is OK, the next question is whether we can organize all of the boxes. One important observation we can make here is that the only action figures we care about from now on are the ones at the left and right sides of each box. The action figures between these don't matter anymore.

Consider this example where we have three boxes:

```
[[9, 13, 14, 17, 25],
 [32, 33, 34, 36],
 [1, 6]]
```

The first box starts with an action figure of height 9 and ends with an action figure of height 25. Action figures placed to the left of this box must all have height 9 or less; for example, we can place the third box to the left of this box. Action figures placed to the right of this box must all have height 25 or more; for example, we can place the second box to the right of this box. The action figures of heights 13, 14, and 17 change nothing; they may as well not be there.

That's our third task then: ignore all action figures except those on the ends of boxes.

Following that third task, we'll have a list that looks like this:

```
[[9, 25],
 [32, 36],
 [1, 6]]
```

It's a lot easier to tell whether we can organize these boxes if we first sort them, like this:

```
[[1, 6],
 [9, 25],
 [32, 36]]
```

Now it's easy to see what the neighboring boxes of a box must be. (We used a similar approach when solving Village Neighborhood in Chapter 5.) So, our fourth task is to sort the boxes.

Our fifth and final task is to determine whether these sorted boxes are organized. They are organized if the heights of action figures are sorted from left to right. The action figures of heights 1, 6, 9, 25, 32, and 36 are appropriately sorted, so the previous boxes can be organized. But consider this example:

```
[[1, 6],
 [9, 50],
 [32, 36]]
```

These boxes can't be organized because of that huge action figure in the second box. That second box takes up heights 9 to 50; the third box can't go on the right of the second box because its heights are too small.

We've now finished working through the problem and have decided on five main tasks:

1. Read input.

2. Check whether all boxes are OK.

3. Obtain a new list of boxes with only the left and right action figure heights from each box.

4. Sort these new boxes.

5. Determine whether these sorted boxes are organized.

You might wonder why we have a "Read input" task but not a "Write output" task. For this problem, writing output involves just outputting YES or NO as needed; there won't be much to it. In addition, we'll output YES or NO as soon as we know the answer, so output will be interleaved with other tasks. For those reasons, I've decided not to include it as a main task. When working through top-down design on your own, don't worry if you later realize that you've left out a task. You can just add it and continue with your design.

Here's how we can capture our required tasks in code:

❶ ```
Main Program

TODO: Read input

TODO: Check whether all boxes are OK

TODO: Obtain a new list of boxes with only left and right heights

TODO: Sort boxes

TODO: Determine whether boxes are organized
```

I'm calling this the main program ❶. Any functions we write should be included in the program before this comment.

Each task is written as just a comment for now. The TODO markings are there to highlight that these are tasks for us to convert from English to Python. Once we finish a task, we'll remove its TODO. That way, we'll be able to track which tasks we've completed and which we haven't. Let's do this!

## Task 1: Read Input

We need to read the line containing *n* (the number of boxes) and then read the boxes. Reading an integer is something we can do in a single line, so let's read *n* directly. Reading the boxes, on the other hand, is a well-defined task that will take a few lines of code, so let's solve that one with a function; we'll call it read_boxes. Here's where that leaves us in our main program:

```
# Main Program
```

❶ ```
# Read input
n = int(input())
boxes = read_boxes(n)

TODO: Check whether all boxes are OK

TODO: Obtain a new list of boxes with only left and right heights

TODO: Sort boxes

TODO: Determine whether boxes are organized
```

I've removed the TODO from the comment ❶, since from the perspective of the main program, we've solved that task. We do need to write the read_boxes function, of course, so let's do that now.

The read_boxes function takes an integer n as a parameter and reads and returns n boxes. Here's the code:

```
def read_boxes(n):
    """

    n is the number of boxes to read.

    Read the boxes from the input, and return them as a
    list of boxes; each box is a list of action figure heights.
    """
    boxes = []
❶   for i in range(n):
        box = input().split()
    ❷   box.pop(0)
        for i in range(len(box)):
            box[i] = int(box[i])
        boxes.append(box)
    return boxes
```

We're asked to read n boxes, so we loop n times ❶. On each iteration of this loop, we read the current line and split it into its individual action figure heights. The line starts with an integer indicating the number of heights in the line, so we remove that value from the list (it's at index 0) before continuing ❷. Then we convert each height to an integer and add the current box to the list of boxes. Finally, we return the list of boxes.

We didn't defer any part of read_boxes to some as-yet-written function, so we're done with this task! We'll include this function, along with other functions we write, before the # Main Program comment.

Task 2: Check Whether All Boxes Are OK

Does each box, on its own, have the action figures going from shortest to tallest? Good question, and not one we know how to answer in just a line or two of code. Let's rely on a new function, all_boxes_ok, to tell us. If that function returns False, then at least one box has its heights messed up, so we won't be able to organize the boxes. In that case, we should output NO. If all_boxes_ok returns True, then we should carry out our remaining tasks to determine whether the boxes can be organized. Let's add this bit of if-else logic to our program, too. Here's what we've got:

```
# Main Program

# Read input
n = int(input())
boxes = read_boxes(n)

# Check whether all boxes are OK
❶ if not all_boxes_ok(boxes):
```

```
        print('NO')
else:
    # TODO: Obtain a new list of boxes with only left and right heights

    # TODO: Sort boxes

    # TODO: Determine whether boxes are organized
```

Now we need to write the all_boxes_ok function that we're calling ❶. We can check each box to determine whether it's in order. If it isn't, we return False right away. If it is in order, then we check the next box. If we check every box and they're all in order, then we return True.

Aha, so we need to be able to check an individual box! Sounds like another function to me. Let's call that one box_ok.

Here's what we have for all_boxes_ok:

```
def all_boxes_ok(boxes):
    """
    boxes is a list of boxes; each box is a list of action figure heights.

    Return True if each box in boxes has its action figures in
    nondecreasing order of height, False otherwise.
    """
    for box in boxes:
        if not box_ok(box):
            return False
    return True
```

I've used the word nondecreasing in the comment, rather than increasing, because heights of action figures are allowed to be equal. For example, the box [4, 4, 4] is just fine; claiming that this box is "increasing" would be incorrect.

We've pushed part of the all_boxes_ok task into box_ok, so let's write that function next. Here goes:

```
def box_ok(box):
    """
    box is the list of action figure heights in a given box.

    Return True if the heights in box are in nondecreasing order,
    False otherwise.
    """
    for i in range(len(box)):
        if box[i] > box[i + 1]:
            return False
    return True
```

If any height is greater than the height to its right, we return `False` since the heights are not in order. If we get past the `for` loop, then there are no height violations, so we return `True`.

One nice side effect of using top-down design is that we get little chunks of code, wrapped up as functions, that we can test in isolation. For example, enter the code for `box_ok` into the Python shell. Then we can test it:

```
>>> box_ok([4, 5, 6])
```

We're hoping for `True` to be returned here, because the box is in order from small heights to big heights. We certainly weren't hoping for what we actually get:

```
Traceback (most recent call last):
  File "<stdin>", line 1, in <module>
  File "<stdin>", line 9, in box_ok
IndexError: list index out of range
```

Errors are never fun, and they're even less fun when we have to trawl through pages and pages of code to find them. But here, we know that the error is localized to this little function, so our work to find it is reduced considerably. The problem here is that we'll eventually compare the rightmost height to the height to its right—and of course the latter doesn't exist! So we need to stop one iteration earlier, comparing the second-to-last height to the last height. Here's the updated code:

```
def box_ok(box):
    """
    box is the list of action figure heights in a given box.

    Return True if the heights in box are in nondecreasing order,
    False otherwise.
    """
❶ for i in range(len(box) - 1):
        if box[i] > box[i + 1]:
            return False
    return True
```

The only change is in the call to range ❶. If you test this version of the function, you'll see that it works as required. We're done with Task 2!

Task 3: Obtain a New List of Boxes with Only Left and Right Heights

Now we're getting the hang of top-down design. In this task, we need a way to go from boxes with all of their action figures to boxes only with their leftmost and rightmost action figures. I'll refer to the leftmost and rightmost action figures as box *endpoints*.

One approach is to create a new list of boxes with only the endpoints, and that's what I'll do here. You could also think about actually removing heights from the original boxes, though that's a little trickier.

I've called the function for this task boxes_endpoints. Here's the main part of the program, updated with a call to that function:

```
# Main Program

# Read input
n = int(input())
boxes = read_boxes(n)

# Check whether all boxes are OK
if not all_boxes_ok(boxes):
    print('NO')
else:
    # Obtain a new list of boxes with only left and right heights
❶ endpoints = boxes_endpoints(boxes)

    # TODO: Sort boxes

    # TODO: Determine whether boxes are organized
```

When we call boxes_endpoints with a list of boxes ❶, we expect to get back a new list with only the box endpoints. Here's the boxes_endpoints code that satisfies this description:

```
def boxes_endpoints(boxes):
    """
    boxes is a list of boxes; each box is a list of action figure heights.

    Return a list, where each value is a list of two values:
    the heights of the leftmost and rightmost action figures in a box.
    """
❶ endpoints = []
    for box in boxes:
❷        endpoints.append([box[0], box[-1]])
    return endpoints
```

We create a new list ❶ that will hold the endpoints of each box. Then we loop through the boxes. For each box, we use indexing to find the leftmost and rightmost heights in the box and append them to our endpoints list ❷. Finally, we return the endpoints list.

Wait a sec: what happens if there's a box with just one action figure in it? What will our boxes_endpoints function do with it? According to its docstring, it will give us back a list of two values for any valid box. So that had better happen here; otherwise, the function isn't doing what it promises. Let's test it. Enter the boxes_endpoints function into the Python shell, and try it with a list of one box with one action figure:

```
>>> boxes_endpoints([[2]])
[[2, 2]]
```

Success! The leftmost height is 2, and the rightmost height is 2, so we get a list with two occurrences of 2. Our function works correctly in this case because box[0] and box[-1] both refer to the same value when box has only one value. (Don't worry about the possibility of empty boxes. The problem description prohibits them.)

Task 4: Sort Boxes

At this point, we have a list of endpoints—something like this:

```
>>> endpoints = [[9, 25], [32, 36], [1, 6]]
>>> endpoints
[[9, 25], [32, 36], [1, 6]]
```

We want to sort them. Do we need another function for this? Some sort of sort_endpoints function?

Not this time! The list sort method does exactly what we need:

```
>>> endpoints.sort()
>>> endpoints
[[1, 6], [9, 25], [32, 36]]
```

When called on a list of two-value lists, sort sorts using the first value. (If there's a tie, then it further sorts using the second value.)

We can immediately update the main part of our program with a call to sort and knock off one more TODO. Here's the updated code:

```
# Main Program

# Read input
n = int(input())
boxes = read_boxes(n)

# Check whether all boxes are OK
if not all_boxes_ok(boxes):
    print('NO')
else:
    # Obtain a new list of boxes with only left and right heights
    endpoints = boxes_endpoints(boxes)

    # Sort boxes
    endpoints.sort()

    # TODO: Determine whether boxes are organized
```

We're nearly there. Just one TODO to go.

Task 5: Determine Whether Boxes Are Organized

Our final task is to check the endpoints. They might be in order, like this:

```
[[1, 6],
 [9, 25],
 [32, 36]]
```

Or they might not be, like this:

```
[[1, 6],
 [9, 50],
 [32, 36]]
```

In the former case, we should print YES; in the latter, we should print NO. We need a function to tell us whether the endpoints are in order. Updating the main part of the program for the final time, we end up with this:

```
# Main Program

# Read input
n = int(input())
boxes = read_boxes(n)

# Check whether all boxes are OK
if not all_boxes_ok(boxes):
    print('NO')
else:
    # Obtain a new list of boxes with only left and right heights
    endpoints = boxes_endpoints(boxes)

    # Sort boxes
    endpoints.sort()

    # Determine whether boxes are organized
❶ if all_endpoints_ok(endpoints):
        print('YES')
    else:
        print('NO')
```

All that stands between us and a complete solution to the problem is that all_endpoints_ok function that we're calling ❶. It takes a list where each value is a list of endpoints and returns True if the endpoints are in order and False otherwise.

Let's get a feel for how we can implement this function by working through an example. Here's the list of endpoints we'll use:

```
[[1, 6],
 [9, 25],
 [32, 36]]
```

The first box has a right endpoint of height 6. So, the second box better have a left endpoint of height 6 or more. If it doesn't, then we return False indicating that the endpoints are not in order. But we're good here, because the second box has a left endpoint of height 9.

Now we repeat that check using 25, the right endpoint of the second box. The left endpoint of the third box is 32, so we're good again because 32 is at least 25.

In general, if the left endpoint of a box is ever less than the right endpoint of the previous box, we return False. Otherwise, if all of these checks pass, we return True.

Here's the code:

```
def all_endpoints_ok(endpoints):
    """

    endpoints is a list, where each value is a list of two values:
    the heights of the leftmost and rightmost action figures in a box.

❶   Requires: endpoints is sorted by action figure heights.

    Return True if the endpoints came from boxes that can be
    put in order, False otherwise.
    """
❷   maximum = endpoints[0][1]
    for i in range(1, len(endpoints)):
        if endpoints[i][0] < maximum:
            return False
❸       maximum = endpoints[i][1]
    return True
```

I've added some information to the docstring reminding us what the function requires when it's called ❶. Specifically, we must remember to have the endpoints sorted before calling this function. Otherwise, the function could return the wrong value.

Each value of endpoints is a list with two values: index 0 is the leftmost (minimum) height, and index 1 is the rightmost (maximum) height. The code uses the maximum variable to track the maximum height of a box. Prior to the for loop, it refers to the maximum height in the first box ❷. The for loop compares the minimum of the next box to that maximum. If the minimum of the next box is too small, we return False, because these two boxes cannot be organized correctly. The last thing to do in each iteration is update maximum so that it refers to the maximum of the next box ❸.

Putting It All Together

Having written code for all tasks, including the functions that sprang up as part of the design, we're ready to put it all together into a complete solution. It's up to you whether to keep the comments in the main part of the program. I've left them in, but in practice this may be a case of over-documenting the code, since the function names on their own are chosen to convey what the code is doing. See Listing 6-2 for the complete code.

```python
def read_boxes(n):
    """
    n is the number of boxes to read.

    Read the boxes from the input, and return them as a
    list of boxes; each box is a list of action figure heights.
    """
    boxes = []
    for i in range(n):
        box = input().split()
        box.pop(0)
        for i in range(len(box)):
            box[i] = int(box[i])
        boxes.append(box)
    return boxes


def box_ok(box):
    """
    box is the list of action figure heights in a given box.

    Return True if the heights in box are in nondecreasing order,
    False otherwise.
    """
    for i in range(len(box) - 1):
        if box[i] > box[i + 1]:
            return False
    return True


def all_boxes_ok(boxes):
    """
    boxes is a list of boxes; each box is a list of action figure heights.

    Return True if each box in boxes has its action figures in
    nondecreasing order of height, False otherwise.
    """
    for box in boxes:
        if not box_ok(box):
```

```
                    return False
            return True


def boxes_endpoints(boxes):
    """
    boxes is a list of boxes; each box is a list of action figure heights.

    Return a list, where each value is a list of two values:
    the heights of the leftmost and rightmost action figures in a box.
    """
    endpoints = []
    for box in boxes:
        endpoints.append([box[0], box[-1]])
    return endpoints


def all_endpoints_ok(endpoints):
    """
    endpoints is a list, where each value is a list of two values:
    the heights of the leftmost and rightmost action figures in a box.

    Requires: endpoints is sorted by action figure heights.

    Return True if the endpoints came from boxes that can be
    put in order, False otherwise.
    """
    maximum = endpoints[0][1]
    for i in range(1, len(endpoints)):
        if endpoints[i][0] < maximum:
            return False
        maximum = endpoints[i][1]
    return True


# Main Program

# Read input
n = int(input())
boxes = read_boxes(n)

# Check whether all boxes are OK
if not all_boxes_ok(boxes):
    print('NO')
else:
    # Obtain a new list of boxes with only left and right heights
    endpoints = boxes_endpoints(boxes)
```

```
# Sort boxes
endpoints.sort()

# Determine whether boxes are organized
if all_endpoints_ok(endpoints):
    print('YES')
else:
    print('NO')
```

Listing 6-2: Solving Action Figures

This is the largest program that we've written to this point in the book. But look how tidy and minimal the main part of the program is: it's mostly calls to functions, with a little bit of if-else logic to glue them together.

We're calling each function only once here. Compare that to the no_high Card Game function that we called four times. Even if a function is called only once, it still contributes to organized, readable code.

Time to submit to the Timus judge. You should see that all test cases pass.

CONCEPT CHECK

In Task 2, we wrote function box_ok for determining whether a single box has its heights in order. It uses a range for loop. Is the following while loop version of box_ok correct?

```
def box_ok(box):
    """
    box is the list of action figure heights in a given box.

    Return True if the heights in box are in nondecreasing order,
    False otherwise.
    """
    ok = True
    i = 0
    while i < len(box) - 1 and ok:
        if box[i] > box[i + 1]:
            ok = False
        i = i + 1
    return ok
```

A. Yes

B. No; it can cause an IndexError

C. No; it doesn't cause any errors, but it can return the wrong value

(continued)

Answer: A. This is equivalent to our earlier version using the range `for` loop. The `ok` variable starts off as `True`, meaning that all heights we have checked are fine (because we haven't checked any yet!). The `while` loop continues as long

as there are more boxes to check and there are no height violations. If an action figure is out of order, `ok` is set to `False`, which terminates the loop. If all action figures are in order, then the value of `ok` never changes from `True` to `False`. Therefore, when we `return ok` at the bottom of the function, we return `True` if all action figures are in order and `False` if not.

Summary

In this chapter, we learned about functions. A function is a self-contained block of code that solves a small part of a larger problem. We learned how to pass information to a function (through arguments) and get information back (through a return value).

To determine which functions to write in the first place, we can use top-down design. Top-down design helps us break a solution to a large problem into a number of smaller tasks; for each task, we solve it directly if we can or write a function for it if we can't. If a given task is too unwieldy, we can perform further top-down design on it.

In the next chapter, we'll learn how to work with files of our choosing, rather than using standard input and standard output. As we continue to push the boundaries of what we know, we'll find many uses for functions in that chapter and the rest of the book. Practice with some of the following exercises to increase your confidence using functions.

Chapter Exercises

Here are some exercises for you to try. For each, use top-down design to identify one or more functions that help you organize your code. Include a docstring in each function!

1. DMOJ problem ccc13s1, From 1987 to 2013
2. DMOJ problem ccc18j3, Are we there yet?
3. DMOJ problem ecoo12r1p2, Decoding DNA
4. DMOJ problem crci07p1, Platforme
5. DMOJ problem coci13c2p2, Misa
6. Revisit some of the exercises from Chapter 5 and improve your solutions by using functions. I particularly suggest revisiting DMOJ problem coci18c2p1 (Preokret) and DMOJ problem ccc00s2 (Babbling Brooks).

Notes

Card Game is originally from the 1999 Canadian Computing Competition. Action Figures is originally from the 2019 Ural School Programming Contest.

Many modern programming languages, Python included, support two distinct programming paradigms. One is based on functions; that's what we studied in this chapter. The other is based on *objects* and leads to a paradigm known as *object-oriented programming (OOP)*. OOP involves defining new types and writing methods for those types. We use Python types (such as integers and strings) throughout the book, but we won't otherwise discuss OOP. For an introduction to OOP, and case studies of OOP in practice, I recommend *Python Crash Course*, 2nd edition by Eric Matthes (No Starch Press, 2019).

7

READING AND WRITING FILES

To this point, we've read all input using the input function and written all output using the print function. These functions read from standard input (defaulting to the keyboard) and write to standard output (defaulting to the screen), respectively. While we can change these defaults using input and output redirection, sometimes a program needs more control over its files. For example, your word processor allows you to open whichever document file you like and save a file with whatever name you like, without you messing around with standard input and standard output.

In this chapter, we'll learn how to write programs that manipulate text files. We'll solve two problems using files: correctly formatting an essay and seeding a farm to feed cows.

There's one important difference between this problem and all the problems we've solved to this point: this one requires us to read from and write to specific files! Look out for this as you read the problem description.

This is USACO 2020 January Bronze Contest problem Word Processor. This is the first problem in the book from the USACO (USA Computing Olympiad) judge. To find the problem, go to *http://usaco.org/*, click **Contests**, click **2020 January Contest Results**, and then click **View problem** under Word Processor.

The Challenge

Bessie the cow is writing an essay. Each word in the essay contains only lowercase or uppercase characters. Her teacher has specified the maximum number of characters, not counting spaces, that can occur per line. To satisfy this requirement, Bessie writes down the words of the essay using the following rules:

- If the next word fits on the current line, add it to the current line. Include a space between each pair of words on the line.

- Otherwise, put this word on a new line; this line becomes the new current line.

Output the essay with the correct words on each line.

Input

Read input from the file named *word.in*.
The input consists of two lines.

- The first line contains two integers separated by a space. The first integer is n, the number of words in the essay; it's between 1 and 100. The second integer is k, the maximum number of characters (not counting spaces) that can occur per line; it's between 1 and 80.

- The second line contains n words, with a space between each pair of words. Each word has at most k characters.

Output

Write output to the file named *word.out*.
Output the properly formatted essay.

Working with Files

The Essay Formatting problem requires that we read from file *word.in* and write to file *word.out*. Before we can do those things, though, we need to learn how to open files in our programs.

Opening a File

Using your text editor, create a new file called *word.in*. Put that file in the same directory that you've been using for your *.py* Python programs.

This is the first time that we're creating a file that doesn't end with *.py*. Instead, it ends with *.in*. Be sure to name the file *word.in*, not *word.py*. The *in* is short for input; you'll see it used often for files that contain input for a program.

In that file, let's place valid input for the Essay Formatting problem. Enter the following into the file:

```
12 13
perhaps better poetry will be written in the language of digital computers
```

Save the file.

To open the file in Python, we use the open function. We pass two arguments: the first is the filename, and the second is the mode in which to open the file. The mode determines how we can interact with the file.

Here's how we can open *word.in*:

```
>>> open('word.in', 'r')
```
❶ `<_io.TextIOWrapper name='word.in' mode='r' encoding='cp1252'>`

In this function call, we've provided a mode of 'r'. The r stands for "read" and opens the file so that we can read from it. The mode happens to be an optional parameter whose default is 'r', so we can leave it out if we like. But I'll explicitly include the 'r' throughout the book for consistency.

When we use open, Python gives us some information about how the file was opened ❶. For example, it confirms the filename and mode. The bit about encoding indicates how the file was decoded from its state on disk into a form that we can read. Files can be encoded using a variety of encodings, but we don't need to worry about encodings in this book.

If we try to open a file for reading that doesn't exist, we get an error:

```
>>> open('blah.in', 'r')
Traceback (most recent call last):
  File "<stdin>", line 1, in <module>
FileNotFoundError: [Errno 2] No such file or directory: 'blah.in'
```

If you're getting this error when opening *word.in*, double-check that the file is named correctly and in the directory from which you started Python.

In addition to mode 'r' for reading, there's mode 'w' for writing. If we use 'w', then we're opening a file so that we can put text in it.

Be careful with mode 'w'. If you use 'w' with a file that already exists, the contents of that file will be deleted. I just accidentally did that with my *word.in* file. No big deal, because it was easy to re-create. But no one would be happy if we accidentally overwrote an important file.

If you use 'w' with a filename that doesn't exist, it creates an empty file.

Let's use mode `'w'` to create an empty file called *blah.in*:

```
>>> open('blah.in', 'w')
<_io.TextIOWrapper name='blah.in' mode='w' encoding='cp1252'>
```

Now that *blah.in* exists, we can open it for reading without getting an error:

```
>>> open('blah.in', 'r')
<_io.TextIOWrapper name='blah.in' mode='r' encoding='cp1252'>
```

What's that _io.TextIOWrapper that we keep seeing? That's the type of the value that open returns:

```
>>> type(open('word.in', 'r'))
<class '_io.TextIOWrapper'>
```

Think of this type as a file type. Its values represent open files, and you'll see shortly that it has methods that we can call.

As with any function, if we don't assign what open returns to a variable, then its return value is lost. The way we've been calling open so far doesn't give us any way to refer to the file that we've opened!

Here's how we can make a variable refer to an open file:

```
>>> input_file = open('word.in', 'r')
>>> input_file
<_io.TextIOWrapper name='word.in' mode='r' encoding='cp1252'>
```

We'll be able to use input_file to read from `'word.in'`.

When solving Essay Formatting, we'll also need a way to write to file `'word.out'`. Here's a variable that will help us do that:

```
>>> output_file = open('word.out', 'w')
>>> output_file
<_io.TextIOWrapper name='word.out' mode='w' encoding='cp1252'>
```

Reading from a File

To read a line from an open file, we use the file's readline method. That method returns a string containing the contents of the next line of the file. In that way, it's similar to the input function. Unlike input, however, readline reads from a file rather than from standard input.

Let's open *word.in* and read its two lines:

```
>>> input_file = open('word.in', 'r')
>>> input_file.readline()
'12 13\n'
>>> input_file.readline()
'perhaps better poetry will be written in the language of digital computers\n'
```

What's unexpected here is the \n at the end of each string. We certainly didn't see that when using input to read a line. The \ symbol in a string is an *escape character*. It escapes from the standard interpretation of characters and changes their meaning. We don't treat \n as the two separate characters \ and n. Instead, \n is just one character: a newline character. All lines in a file, perhaps except for the last, end with a newline character. If they didn't, then everything would be on a single line! The readline method is literally giving us the entire line, including its terminating newline character.

Here's how we can embed newlines in our own strings:

```
>>> 'one\ntwo\nthree'
'one\ntwo\nthree'
>>> print('one\ntwo\nthree')
one
two
three
```

The Python shell doesn't process the effects of escape characters, but print does.

The \n sequence is useful in strings because it helps us add multiple lines. But we rarely want those newlines in the lines that we read from files. To get rid of them, we can use the string rstrip method. This method is like strip except that it removes whitespace only from the right of a string (not the left). As far as it's concerned, newlines are whitespace just like spaces:

```
>>> 'hello\nthere\n\n'
'hello\nthere\n\n'
>>> 'hello\nthere\n\n'.rstrip()
'hello\nthere'
```

Let's try reading from the file again, this time stripping out the newlines:

```
>>> input_file = open('word.in', 'r')
>>> input_file.readline().rstrip()
'12 13'
>>> input_file.readline().rstrip()
'perhaps better poetry will be written in the language of digital computers'
```

At this point, we've read the two lines, so there's nothing left to read from the file. The readline method signals this by returning an empty string.

```
>>> input_file.readline().rstrip()
''
```

The empty string means that we've reached the end of the file. If we want to read the lines again, we must reopen the file to start at its beginning.

Let's do that, this time saving each line using variables:

```
>>> input_file = open('word.in', 'r')
>>> first = input_file.readline().rstrip()
>>> second = input_file.readline().rstrip()
>>> first
'12 13'
>>> second
'perhaps better poetry will be written in the language of digital computers'
```

If we need to read all of the lines from a file, no matter how many there are, we can use a for loop. Files in Python act as sequences of lines, so we can loop over them just like we loop over strings and lists:

```
>>> input_file = open('word.in', 'r')
>>> for line in input_file:
...     print(line.rstrip())
...
12 13
perhaps better poetry will be written in the language of digital computers
```

Unlike a string or loop, though, we can't loop over the file a second time, because the first one takes us to its end. If we try, we get nothing:

```
>>> for line in input_file:
...     print(line.rstrip())
...
```

CONCEPT CHECK

We want to use a while loop to output each line of the open file input_file. (The file could be any file; I'm not assuming that it's related to Essay Formatting.) Which of the following pieces of code correctly does this?

A.
```
while input_file.readline() != '':
    print(input_file.readline().rstrip())
```

B.
```
line = 'x'
while line != '':
    line = input_file.readline()
    print(line.rstrip())
```

C.

```
line = input_file.readline()
while line != '':
    line = input_file.readline()
    print(line.rstrip())
```

D. All of the above

E. None of the above

Before looking at the answer, I encourage you to create a file with four or five lines in it and try each piece of code on the file. You might also consider adding a character like * to the beginning of each line that's output so that you can see any otherwise blank lines.

Answer: E. Each piece of code has a subtle error.

Code A outputs only every other line of the file. For example, the while loop's Boolean expression causes the first line to be read . . . and lost, because it isn't assigned to a variable. The first iteration of the loop therefore outputs the second line of the file.

Code B comes very close to doing the right thing. It outputs all the lines of the file, but also outputs an extraneous blank line at the end.

Code C fails to print the first line of the file. That's because the first line is read before the loop, but then the loop reads the second line without having printed the first. It also produces an extraneous blank line at the end, just like code B.

Here's correct code to read and print each line:

```
line = input_file.readline()
while line != '':
    print(line.rstrip())
    line = input_file.readline()
```

Writing to a File

To write a line to an open file, we use the file's write method. We pass it a string, and that string is added to the end of the file.

To solve Essay Formatting, we'll write to *word.out*. We're not ready to solve that problem yet, so let's instead write to *blah.out*. Here's how we can write one line to that file:

```
>>> output_file = open('blah.out', 'w')
>>> output_file.write('hello')
5
```

What's that 5 doing there? The write method returns the number of characters written. It's good confirmation that we've written the quantity of text that we expected to write.

If you open *blah.out* in your text editor, you should see the text `hello` in there.

Let's try writing three lines to the file. Here goes:

```
>>> output_file = open('blah.out', 'w')
>>> output_file.write('sq')
2
>>> output_file.write('ui')
2
>>> output_file.write('sh')
2
```

Based on what I've told you so far, you might expect *blah.out* to look like this:

```
sq
ui
sh
```

But if you open *blah.out* in your text editor, you should instead see the following:

```
squish
```

The characters are on a single line like that because `write` doesn't add newlines for us! If we want separate lines, we need to be explicit, like this:

```
>>> output_file = open('blah.out', 'w')
>>> output_file.write('sq\n')
3
>>> output_file.write('ui\n')
3
>>> output_file.write('sh\n')
3
```

Notice in each case that `write` writes three characters, not two. The newline counts as a character. Now if you open *blah.out* in your text editor, you should see the text spread across three lines:

```
sq
ui
sh
```

Unlike `print`, `write` works only if you call it with a string. To write a number to a file, convert it to a string first:

```
>>> num = 7788
>>> output_file = open('blah.out', 'w')
>>> output_file.write(str(num) + '\n')
5
```

Closing Files

It's good practice to close a file once you're done with it. It signals to readers of your code that the file is no longer being used.

Closing files also helps your operating system manage your computer's resources. When you use the write method, what you write may not end up in the file immediately. Rather, Python or your operating system might wait until it has a bunch of write requests and then write them all at once. Closing a file that you wrote to guarantees that what you wrote to the file is safely stored in the file.

To close a file, call its close method. Here's an example of opening a file, reading a line, and closing it:

```
>>> input_file = open('word.in', 'r')
>>> input_file.readline()
'12 13\n'
>>> input_file.close()
```

Once you've closed a file, you can no longer read from or write to the file:

```
>>> input_file.readline()
Traceback (most recent call last):
  File "<stdin>", line 1, in <module>
ValueError: I/O operation on closed file.
```

Solving the Problem

Back to Essay Formatting. Now we know how to read from *word.in* and write to *word.out*. That takes care of the input and output requirements. It's time to tackle the problem itself.

Let's start by exploring a test case to make sure we know how to solve this problem. Then we'll see the code.

Exploring a Test Case

Here's the *word.in* file I've been using:

```
12 13
perhaps better poetry will be written in the language of digital computers
```

There are 12 words, and the maximum number of characters on a line (not counting spaces) is 13. We should add words to the current line as long as they fit; once a word doesn't fit, we'll start a new line with that word.

The word perhaps contains seven characters, so it fits on the first line. The word better contains six characters. We can put that on the first line, too; with perhaps already there, we're at a total of 13 characters (not including the space between the two words).

The word poetry can't go on the first line, so we start a new line with poetry as its first word. The word will fits next to poetry on the second line. Similarly, be fits next to will. We're at 12 nonspace characters so far. Now we have the word written, and with only one character of room on line 2, we're forced to start the next line with written as its first word.

Following this process to the end, the full essay that we need to write to *word.out* is this:

```
perhaps better
poetry will be
written in the
language of
digital
computers
```

The Code

Our solution is in Listing 7-1.

```
❶ input_file = open('word.in', 'r')
❷ output_file = open('word.out', 'w')

❸ lst = input_file.readline().split()
  n = int(lst[0])   # n not needed
  k = int(lst[1])
  words = input_file.readline().split()

❹ line = ''
  chars_on_line = 0

  for word in words:
    ❺ if chars_on_line + len(word) <= k:
          line = line + word + ' '
          chars_on_line = chars_on_line + len(word)
      else:
        ❻ output_file.write(line[:-1] + '\n')
          line = word + ' '
          chars_on_line = len(word)

❼ output_file.write(line[:-1] + '\n')

  input_file.close()
  output_file.close()
```

Listing 7-1: Solving Essay Formatting

To begin, we open the input file ❶ and output file ❷. Notice the modes: we open the input file with mode 'r' (for reading) and open the output file with mode 'w' (for writing). We could have opened the output file a little later, right before we use it, but I've chosen to open both files here to simplify the organization of the program. Similarly, we could close a file as soon as we no longer need it, but in this book, I've chosen to close all files together at the end of the program. For long-running programs that manipulate many files, you likely want to keep files open only when needed.

Next, we read the first line of the input file ❸. This line contains two space-separated integers: n, the number of words, and k, the maximum number of allowed characters (not counting spaces) per line. As always with space-separated values, we use split to separate them. We then read the second line, which contains the essay words. Again we use split, this time to split the string of words into a list of words. That takes care of the input.

Two variables drive the main portion of the program: line and chars_on_line. The line variable refers to the current line; we start out with it referring to the empty string ❹. The chars_on_line variable refers to the number of characters, not counting spaces, on the current line.

You may wonder why I'm maintaining chars_on_line at all. Couldn't we just use len(line) instead? Well, if we did that, we'd be including spaces in our count, and spaces don't count toward the number of characters allowed per line. We could fix that by subtracting the count of spaces, and I encourage you to try that on your own if you find it more intuitive than keeping the chars_on_line variable in there.

Now it's time to loop through all of the words. For each word, we have to determine whether it goes on the current line or next line.

If the number of nonspace characters on the current line plus the number of characters in the current word is at most k, then the current word fits on the current line ❺. In that case, we add the word plus a space to the current line and update the number of nonspace characters on the line.

Otherwise, the current word doesn't fit on the current line. The current line is done! We therefore write the line to the output file ❻ and update the line and chars_on_line variables to reflect that this is the only word on the now-current line.

There are two things to note about the write call ❻. First, the [:-1] slice is in there to prevent us from outputting the space that follows the last word on the line. Second, you may have expected me to use an f-string here, like this:

```
output_file.write(f'{line[:-1]}\n')
```

However, at the time of writing, the USACO judge is running an older version of Python that doesn't support f-strings.

Why are we outputting line after the loop ends ❼? The reason is that each iteration of the for loop is guaranteed to leave line with one or more words that we have not output yet. Consider what happens with each word that we process. If the current word fits on the current line, we don't output anything. If the current word doesn't fit on the current line, then we output the current line, but not the word on the next line. We therefore need to write `line` to the output file *after* the loop ❼; otherwise, the last line in the essay will be lost.

The final thing we do is close both files.

One annoying aspect of writing to a file rather than the screen is that we aren't shown the output when we run the program. To see the output, we have to open the output file in our text editor.

Here's a tip: develop the program using `print` calls rather than `write` calls so that all output goes to the screen. That should make it easier to find errors in your program and avoid having to switch back and forth between your code and the output file. Once you're happy with the code, you can change the `print` calls back to `write` calls. Then be sure to do a little more testing, just to make sure that everything ends up in the file as it should.

We're ready to submit to the USACO judge. Send it our code! All test cases should pass.

Problem #17: Farm Seeding

We can use a loop to read a specified number of lines from a file. We'll do that in this problem, and we'll see that it's similar to using a loop with `input` to read from standard input.

In Chapter 6, when we solved Action Figures, we learned about top-down design using functions. It's an important skill, composing multiple functions to solve a problem. And since there isn't much more to say about files, I've chosen a problem that doubles as a site for top-down design.

This is a challenging problem. We'll first need to understand exactly what we're being asked to do. After that, we'll need to develop a way to solve the problem and think carefully about why our solution is correct.

This is USACO 2019 February Bronze Contest problem The Great Revegetation.

The Challenge

Farmer John has *n* pastures, all of which he would like to seed with grass. The pastures are numbered 1, 2, . . ., *n*.

Farmer John has four different types of grass seed, numbered 1, 2, 3, and 4. He'll choose one of these grass types for each pasture.

Farmer John also has *m* cows. Each cow has two favorite pastures in which it eats grass. Each cow cares only about its two favorite pastures, no others. For a healthy diet, each cow requires that its two pastures have different types of grass. For example, for some given cow, it would be okay if one of its pastures had grass type 1 and the other had grass type 4. But it would not be okay if both of its pastures had grass type 1.

A pasture might be the favorite of more than one cow. But it's guaranteed that a pasture is the favorite of no more than three cows.

Determine the grass type to use in each pasture. Each pasture is required to use a grass type between 1 and 4, and each cow's two favorite pastures must have different grass types.

Input

Read input from the file named *revegetate.in*.

The input consists of the following lines:

- A line containing two integers separated by a space. The first integer is n, the number of pastures; it's between 2 and 100. The second integer is m, the number of cows; it's between 1 and 150.

- m lines, each of which gives the two favorite pasture numbers for a cow. These pasture numbers are integers between 1 and n and are separated by a space.

Output

Write output to the file named *revegetate.out*.

Output a valid way to seed the pastures. The output is a line of n characters, each of which is a '1', '2', '3', or '4'. The first character is the grass type for pasture 1, the second is the grass type for pasture 2, and so on.

We can interpret these n characters as an integer with n digits. For example, if we have the five grass types '11123', then we can interpret this as the integer 11123.

This integer interpretation comes into play when we have a choice of what to output. If there are multiple valid ways to seed the pastures, we must output the one that's smallest when interpreted as an integer. For example, if both '11123' and '22123' are valid, we output the string '11123' because 11123 is less than 22123.

Exploring a Test Case

We're going to use top-down design to arrive at a solution for this problem. Working through a test case will help us sift the tasks.

Here's the test case:

```
8 6
5 4
2 4
3 5
4 1
2 1
5 2
```

The first line of the test case tells us that we have eight pastures. They're numbered from 1 to 8. The first line also tells us that we have six cows. The problem doesn't specify a numbering for the cows, so I'll just number them starting at 0. The two favorite pastures of each cow are in Table 7-1 for easy reference.

Table 7-1: Farm Seeding Example, Cows

Cow	Pasture 1	Pasture 2
0	5	4
1	2	4
2	3	5
3	4	1
4	2	1
5	5	2

In this problem, we're being asked to make n decisions. What grass type should we use for pasture 1? What grass type should we use for pasture 2? Pasture 3? Pasture 4? And so on, all the way up to pasture n. One strategy for these kinds of problems is to make one decision at a time, without making a mistake on any of them. If we manage to finish with decision n and haven't made any mistakes along the way, then our solution must be correct.

Let's go through the pastures from 1 to 8 and see if we can assign a grass type to each of them. We need to prioritize choosing small-numbered grass types so that we end with the smallest grass types when interpreted as a number.

What grass type should we choose for pasture 1? The only cows that care about pasture 1 are cows 3 and 4, so we focus only on those two. If we had already chosen grass types for some of these cows' pastures, then we'd have to be careful with our choice for pasture 1. We wouldn't want to give some cow two pastures with the same grass type, because that would break the rules! We haven't chosen any grass types yet, so nothing can go wrong no matter what we choose for pasture 1. Since we want the smallest grass types, though, we'll choose grass type 1.

I'll collect our grass-type decisions in tables. Here's the decision we just made, grass type 1 for pasture 1:

Pasture	Grass type
1	1

Let's move on. What grass type should we choose for pasture 2? The cows that care about pasture 2 are cows 1, 4, and 5, so we focus on those. One of cow 4's pastures is pasture 1, and we chose grass type 1 for that pasture, so grass type 1 is eliminated as a grass type for pasture 2. If we used grass type 1 for pasture 2, then we'd be giving cow 4 two pastures with the same grass type, and that would break the rules. Cows 1 and 5, however, don't eliminate any other grass types, because we haven't chosen grass types for their pastures yet. We therefore choose grass type 2, the smallest-numbered grass type that's available. Here's where we stand:

Pasture	Grass type
1	1
2	2

What grass type should we choose for pasture 3? The only cow that cares about pasture 3 is cow 2. Cow 2's pastures are pastures 3 and 5. That cow doesn't eliminate any grass types, however, because we haven't assigned a grass type to pasture 5! To get the smallest number, we'll use grass type 1 for pasture 3. Here's our next snapshot:

Pasture	Grass type
1	1
2	2
3	1

I can see three tasks in our top-down design crystallizing here. First, we need to obtain the cows that care about the current pasture. Second, we need to determine which grass types those cows eliminate from consideration. Third, we need to choose the smallest-numbered grass type that wasn't eliminated. Each of those is a prime candidate for a function.

Let's keep going. We have three cows that care about pasture 4: cows 0, 1, and 3. Cow 0 doesn't eliminate any grass types, because we haven't assigned grass types to its pastures yet. Cow 1 eliminates grass type 2 because we assigned grass type 2 to pasture 2 (its other pasture). And cow 3 eliminates grass type 1 because we assigned grass type 1 to pasture 1 (its other pasture). The smallest available grass type, then, is 3, so that's what we use for pasture 4:

Pasture	Grass type
1	1
2	2
3	1
4	3

On to pasture 5. The cows that care about pasture 5 are cows 0, 2, and 5. Cow 0 eliminates grass type 3; cow 2 eliminates grass type 1; and cow 5 eliminates grass type 2. So grass types 1, 2, and 3 are out. Our only choice is grass type 4.

That was close! We almost ran out of grass types there. Lucky for us, there was no other cow that cared about pasture 5 and eliminated grass type 4.

Or, wait. This wasn't luck at all, because of this bit from the problem description: "It's guaranteed that a pasture is the favorite of no more than three cows." This means that at most three grass types can be eliminated for each pasture. We'll never be stuck! And we don't even have to worry about the ramifications of past choices on our next decision. No matter what we did in the past, we'll always have at least one available grass type.

Let's add pasture 5 to our table:

Pasture	Grass type
1	1
2	2
3	1
4	3
5	4

There are three pastures to go. But no cow cares about any of them, so we can just use grass type 1 in each case. That gives us this:

Pasture	Grass type
1	1
2	2
3	1
4	3
5	4
6	1
7	1
8	1

We can read the grass types from top to bottom to obtain the correct output for this example. The output is as follows:

12134111

Top-Down Design

With a good understanding of the tasks that we'll need to complete, we'll turn to a top-down design of this problem.

The Top Level

We discovered three tasks in the previous section as we worked through a test case. Before our program can solve any of those tasks, we need to read the input, so that's a fourth task. We also need to write the output. That will take some thought and a few lines of code, so let's call that our fifth task.

Here are our five main tasks:

1. Read input.
2. Identify cows that care about current pasture.
3. Eliminate grass types for current pasture.
4. Choose smallest-numbered grass type for current pasture.
5. Write output.

As we did when solving Action Figures in Chapter 6, we'll start with a framework of TODO comments and remove each TODO as we solve it.

We begin with mostly comments. Since we'll need to open the files at the start and close them at the end, I've also added that code.

Here's where we begin:

```
# Main Program

input_file = open('revegetate.in', 'r')
output_file = open('revegetate.out', 'w')

# TODO: Read input

# TODO: Identify cows that care about pasture

# TODO: Eliminate grass types for pasture

# TODO: Choose smallest-numbered grass type for pasture

# TODO: Write output

input_file.close()
output_file.close()
```

Task 1: Read Input

Reading the first line of input, with the integers *n* and *m*, is something we know how to do. It's straightforward enough that I don't think we need a function for it, so let's do it directly. Next we need to read the pasture information for the *m* cows, and here a function seems warranted. Let's remove the TODO in the Read input comment, handle the first line of input, and call the read_cows function, which we'll write shortly:

```
# Main Program

input_file = open('revegetate.in', 'r')
output_file = open('revegetate.out', 'w')

# Read input
lst = input_file.readline().split()
num_pastures = int(lst[0])
num_cows = int(lst[1])
❶ favorites = read_cows(input_file, num_cows)

# TODO: Identify cows that care about pasture

# TODO: Eliminate grass types for pasture

# TODO: Choose smallest-numbered grass type for pasture

# TODO: Write output

input_file.close()
output_file.close()
```

The read_cows function that we're calling ❶ will take a file that's already open for reading, and read the two favorite pastures for each cow. It'll return a list of lists, where each inner list contains the two pasture numbers for a given cow. Here's the code:

```
def read_cows(input_file, num_cows):
    """
    input_file is a file open for reading; cow information is next to read.
    num_cows is the number of cows in the file.

    Read the cows' favorite pastures from input_file.
    Return a list of each cow's two favorite pastures;
    each value in the list is a list of two values giving the
    favorite pastures for one cow.
    """
    favorites = []
    for i in range(num_cows):
❶       lst = input_file.readline().split()
```

```
        lst[0] = int(lst[0])
        lst[1] = int(lst[1])
    ❷ favorites.append(lst)
    return favorites
```

This function accumulates the cows' favorite pastures into the favorites list. It does that using a range for loop that loops num_cows times, once for each cow. We need the loop because the number of lines to read depends on the number of cows in the file.

On each iteration of the loop, we read the next line and split it into its two components ❶. We then use int to convert the components from strings to integers. When we append this list to favorites ❷, we're therefore appending a list of two integers.

The last thing we do is return the list of favorite pastures.

Before we continue, let's make sure that we know how to call this function. We'll practice calling it on its own, independent from the larger program that we're building. It's useful to test functions like this so that we can fix any errors that we might find along the way.

Use your text editor to create a file named *revegetate.in* with the following contents (the same as the test case we studied earlier):

```
8 6
5 4
2 4
3 5
4 1
2 1
5 2
```

Now, in the Python shell, enter the code for our read_cows function. Here's what we do to call read_cows:

```
    >>> input_file = open('revegetate.in', 'r')
❶  >>> input_file.readline()
    '8 6\n'
❷  >>> read_cows(input_file, 6)
    [[5, 4], [2, 4], [3, 5], [4, 1], [2, 1], [5, 2]]
```

The read_cows function reads only the information for the cows. Since we're testing this function in isolation, outside of our program, we need to read the first line of the file ourselves before we call it ❶. When we then call read_cows, we get back a list giving the favorite pastures for each cow. Also notice that we're calling read_cows with an open file, *not* a filename ❷.

Be sure to include our read_cows function, along with the functions we'll write for other tasks, before our # Main Program comment. Then we can move on to Task 2.

Task 2: Identify Cows

Our overall strategy for solving this problem is to consider each pasture in turn, deciding which grass type to use. We'll organize this work inside a loop, with each iteration of the loop responsible for seeding one pasture. For each pasture, we need to identify the cows that care about the pasture, eliminate the used grass types, and choose the smallest-numbered available grass type. These three tasks must run for each pasture, so we'll indent them inside the loop.

We'll write a function called cows_with_favorite that tells us the cows who care about the current pasture.

Here's what we've got now for our main program:

```
# Main Program

input_file = open('revegetate.in', 'r')
output_file = open('revegetate.out', 'w')

# Read input
lst = input_file.readline().split()
num_pastures = int(lst[0])
num_cows = int(lst[1])
favorites = read_cows(input_file, num_cows)

for i in range(1, num_pastures + 1):

    # Identify cows that care about pasture
❶   cows = cows_with_favorite(favorites, i)

    # TODO: Eliminate grass types for pasture

    # TODO: Choose smallest-numbered grass type for pasture

# TODO: Write output

input_file.close()
output_file.close()
```

The cows_with_favorite function that we're calling ❶ takes a list of the cows' favorite pastures and a pasture number and returns the cows that care about that pasture. Here's the code:

```
def cows_with_favorite(favorites, pasture):
    """

    favorites is a list of favorite pastures, as returned by read_cows.
    pasture is a pasture number.

    Return list of cows that care about pasture.
    """
```

```
cows = []
for i in range(len(favorites)):
    if favorites[i][0] == pasture or favorites[i][1] == pasture:
        cows.append(i)
return cows
```

The function loops through favorites, looking for cows that care about pasture number pasture. Each cow that cares about the pasture is added to the cows list that is ultimately returned.

Let's do a little test. Enter our cows_with_favorite function into the Python shell. Here's the call that we'll try:

```
>>> cows_with_favorite([[5, 4], [2, 4], [3, 5]], 5)
```

We have three cows here, and we're asking which ones care about pasture 5. The cows at indices 0 and 2 care about pasture 5, and that's exactly what the function tells us:

```
[0, 2]
```

Task 3: Eliminate Grass Types

Now we know the cows that care about the current pasture. Our next step is to figure out which grass types these cows eliminate from consideration for the current pasture. We eliminate the grass types that are used in a pasture associated with one or more of these cows. We'll write a function called types_used that tells us the grass types that have already been used (and are therefore eliminated for the current pasture).

Here is our main program, updated with a call to this function:

```
# Main Program

input_file = open('revegetate.in', 'r')
output_file = open('revegetate.out', 'w')

# Read input
lst = input_file.readline().split()
num_pastures = int(lst[0])
num_cows = int(lst[1])
favorites = read_cows(input_file, num_cows)
```

❶ `pasture_types = [0]`

```
for i in range(1, num_pastures + 1):

    # Identify cows that care about pasture
    cows = cows_with_favorite(favorites, i)
```

```
        # Eliminate grass types for pasture
❷   eliminated = types_used(favorites, cows, pasture_types)

        # TODO: Choose smallest-numbered grass type for pasture

    # TODO: Write output

    input_file.close()
    output_file.close()
```

In addition to calling the types_used function ❷, I've also added a variable called pasture_types ❶. The list referred to by this variable will keep track of the grass type for each pasture.

Recall that the pastures are numbered starting from 1. Python lists, on the other hand, are indexed starting from 0. I don't like this discrepancy; if we simply started adding grass types to pasture_types, then the grass type for pasture 1 would be at index 0, the grass type for pasture 2 would be at index 1, and so on, always off by one. That's why I added a bogus 0 at the beginning of the list ❶; when we later add the grass type for pasture 1, it'll be placed at index 1 to match.

Suppose we've figured out the grass types for the first four pastures. Here's how pasture_types might look at that point:

```
[0, 1, 2, 1, 3]
```

If we want the grass type for pasture 1, we look at index 1; if we want the grass type for pasture 2, we look at index 2; and so on. If we want the grass type for pasture 5? Well, no, we can't have that, because we haven't figured it out yet. If the length of pasture_types is 5, it means that we've figured out the grass types for only the first four pastures. In general, the number of grass types that we've figured out is one less than the list's length.

Now we're ready for the types_used function. It takes three parameters: the list of favorite pastures for each cow, the cows that care about the current pasture, and the grass types chosen for pastures so far. It returns the list of grass types that are already used and therefore eliminated for the current pasture. Here goes:

```
def types_used(favorites, cows, pasture_types):
    """

    favorites is a list of favorite pastures, as returned by read_cows.
    cows is a list of cows.
    pasture_types is a list of grass types.

    Return a list of the grass types already used by cows.
    """
    used = []
    for cow in cows:
        pasture_a = favorites[cow][0]
        pasture_b = favorites[cow][1]
```

```
❶ if pasture_a < len(pasture_types):
        used.append(pasture_types[pasture_a])
❷ if pasture_b < len(pasture_types):
        used.append(pasture_types[pasture_b])
  return used
```

Each cow has two favorite pastures, which I refer to by `pasture_a` and `pasture_b`. For each of these pastures, we check whether a grass type has already been chosen for it at ❶ and ❷. A grass type has already been chosen if that pasture is already an index in `pasture_types`. These grass types are all added to the `used` list, which the function returns after looping through all of the relevant cows.

What if more than one cow uses the same pasture—what does our code do then? Let's come up with a simple test case to answer that question.

Enter our `types_used` function into the Python shell. Here's a call of that function; let's predict what it returns:

```
>>> types_used([[5, 4], [2, 4], [3, 5]], [0, 1], [0, 1, 2, 1, 3])
```

Let's be careful so we don't get lost. The first argument gives the favorite pastures for three cows. The second argument gives the cows that care about a particular pasture; these are cows 0 and 1. And the third argument gives the grass types that we've decided on so far.

Now, what are the grass types already used, and therefore eliminated, by cows 0 and 1? Cow 0 cares about pasture 4, and pasture 4 uses grass type 3, so grass type 3 is eliminated. Cow 1 cares about pasture 2, and pasture 2 uses grass type 2, so grass type 2 is eliminated. Cow 1 also cares about pasture 4—but we already know, from cow 0, that pasture 4's grass type 3 is eliminated.

The return value of our function is this:

```
[3, 2, 3]
```

Two 3s in there, one coming from cow 0 and the other from cow 1.

It may seem tidier to have just one 3 in there, but what we have—with the duplicate—is just fine. If a grass type is in that list, then it's eliminated, no matter whether it's in there once, twice, or three times.

Task 4: Choose Smallest-Numbered Grass Type

Having obtained the grass types that are eliminated, we can move onto our next task: choosing the smallest-numbered available grass type for the current pasture. To solve this one, we'll call a new function, `smallest_available`. It will return the grass type that we should use for the current pasture.

Here's the main program, updated with a call to the `smallest_available` function:

```
# Main Program

input_file = open('revegetate.in', 'r')
```

```
output_file = open('revegetate.out', 'w')

# Read input
lst = input_file.readline().split()
num_pastures = int(lst[0])
num_cows = int(lst[1])
favorites = read_cows(input_file, num_cows)

pasture_types = [0]

for i in range(1, num_pastures + 1):

    # Identify cows that care about pasture
    cows = cows_with_favorite(favorites, i)

    # Eliminate grass types for pasture
    eliminated = types_used(favorites, cows, pasture_types)

    # Choose smallest-numbered grass type for pasture
❶   pasture_type = smallest_available(eliminated)
❷   pasture_types.append(pasture_type)

# TODO: Write output

input_file.close()
output_file.close()
```

Once we obtain the smallest-numbered grass type for the current pasture ❶, we add it to our list of chosen grass types ❷.

Here's the smallest_available function itself:

```
def smallest_available(used):
    """
    used is a list of used grass types.

    Return the smallest-numbered grass type that is not in used.
    """
    grass_type = 1
    while grass_type in used:
        grass_type = grass_type + 1
    return grass_type
```

The function begins with grass type 1. It then loops until it finds a grass type that isn't already used, increasing the grass type by one on each iteration. Once a free grass type is found, the function returns it. And remember, there are at most three grass types that have been used out of the four available, so this function is guaranteed to be successful.

Task 5: Write Output

We've got our answer, right there in pasture_types! Now all we have to do is output it. Here's the main program a final time:

```
# Main Program

input_file = open('revegetate.in', 'r')
output_file = open('revegetate.out', 'w')

# Read input
lst = input_file.readline().split()
num_pastures = int(lst[0])
num_cows = int(lst[1])
favorites = read_cows(input_file, num_cows)

pasture_types = [0]

for i in range(1, num_pastures + 1):

    # Identify cows that care about pasture
    cows = cows_with_favorite(favorites, i)

    # Eliminate grass types for pasture
    eliminated = types_used(favorites, cows, pasture_types)

    # Choose smallest-numbered grass type for pasture
    pasture_type = smallest_available(eliminated)
    pasture_types.append(pasture_type)

  # Write output
❶ pasture_types.pop(0)
❷ write_pastures(output_file, pasture_types)

input_file.close()
output_file.close()
```

Before writing the output, we remove the bogus 0 at the beginning of pasture_types ❶. We don't want to output that 0, as it isn't a real grass type. Then, we call write_pastures to actually write the output ❷.

All we need now is the write_pastures function. It takes a file open for writing, and a list of grass types, and outputs the grass types to the file. Here's the code:

```
def write_pastures(output_file, pasture_types):
    """
    output_file is a file open for writing.
    pasture_types is a list of integer grass types.
```

```
        Output pasture_types to output_file.
        """
        pasture_types_str = []
❶      for pasture_type in pasture_types:
            pasture_types_str.append(str(pasture_type))
❷      output = ''.join(pasture_types_str)
❸      output_file.write(output + '\n')
```

Right now, pasture_types is a list of integers. As we'll see in a second, it's more convenient to work with a list of strings here, so I create a new list with each integer as a string ❶. I don't modify the pasture_types list itself, because that could shock the caller of this function. The caller calls this function expecting only that output gets written to output_file, not that its pasture_types list is modified. The function has no business modifying its list parameter.

To produce the output, we need to call write with a string, not a list. And we need to output the strings from the list with no spaces between them. The string join method works wonderfully here. As we learned in "Joining a List into a String" in Chapter 5, the string that we call join on serves as the separator that's placed between values in the list. Since we don't want any separator between the values, we use an empty string as the separator ❷. The join method works only on a list of strings, not a list of integers, which is why I converted the list of integers to a list of strings at the start of this function ❶.

With the output as a single string, we can write it to the file ❸.

Putting It All Together

The complete program is in Listing 7-2.

```
def read_cows(input_file, num_cows):
    """
    input_file is a file open for reading; cow information is next to read.
    num_cows is the number of cows in the file.

    Read the cows' favorite pastures from input_file.
    Return a list of each cow's two favorite pastures;
    each value in the list is a list of two values giving the
    favorite pastures for one cow.
    """
    favorites = []
    for i in range(num_cows):
        lst = input_file.readline().split()
        lst[0] = int(lst[0])
        lst[1] = int(lst[1])
        favorites.append(lst)
    return favorites
```

```python
def cows_with_favorite(favorites, pasture):
    """
    favorites is a list of favorite pastures, as returned by read_cows.
    pasture is a pasture number.

    Return list of cows that care about pasture.
    """
    cows = []
    for i in range(len(favorites)):
        if favorites[i][0] == pasture or favorites[i][1] == pasture:
            cows.append(i)
    return cows


def types_used(favorites, cows, pasture_types):
    """
    favorites is a list of favorite pastures, as returned by read_cows.
    cows is a list of cows.
    pasture_types is a list of grass types.

    Return a list of the grass types already used by cows.
    """
    used = []
    for cow in cows:
        pasture_a = favorites[cow][0]
        pasture_b = favorites[cow][1]
        if pasture_a < len(pasture_types):
            used.append(pasture_types[pasture_a])
        if pasture_b < len(pasture_types):
            used.append(pasture_types[pasture_b])
    return used


def smallest_available(used):
    """
    used is a list of used grass types.

    Return the smallest-numbered grass type that is not in used.
    """
    grass_type = 1
    while grass_type in used:
        grass_type = grass_type + 1
    return grass_type
```

```
def write_pastures(output_file, pasture_types):
    """

    output_file is a file open for writing.
    pasture_types is a list of integer grass types.

    Output pasture_types to output_file.
    """
    pasture_types_str = []
    for pasture_type in pasture_types:
        pasture_types_str.append(str(pasture_type))
    output = ''.join(pasture_types_str)
    output_file.write(output + '\n')

# Main Program

input_file = open('revegetate.in', 'r')
output_file = open('revegetate.out', 'w')

# Read input
lst = input_file.readline().split()
num_pastures = int(lst[0])
num_cows = int(lst[1])
favorites = read_cows(input_file, num_cows)

pasture_types = [0]

for i in range(1, num_pastures + 1):

    # Identify cows that care about pasture
    cows = cows_with_favorite(favorites, i)

    # Eliminate grass types for pasture
    eliminated = types_used(favorites, cows, pasture_types)

    # Choose smallest-numbered grass type for pasture
    pasture_type = smallest_available(eliminated)
    pasture_types.append(pasture_type)

# Write output
pasture_types.pop(0)
write_pastures(output_file, pasture_types)

input_file.close()
output_file.close()
```

Listing 7-2: Solving Farm Seeding

We did it! An intimidating problem, made more manageable by the application of top-down design. Feel free to submit our work to the USACO judge.

It's easy to be overwhelmed by a problem when you first read it. But remember that you don't need to tackle it in one huge step. Break it down, solve each task that you can solve, and you'll be well on your way to a solution for the overall problem. You've made huge strides in the amount of Python that you know and your ability to design programs and solve problems. Solving these problems is within your grasp!

CONCEPT CHECK

Let's think about a new version of Farm Seeding where there's no restriction on the number of cows that care about a pasture. A pasture might be the favorite of four cows, five cows, or even more. We're still not allowed to give a cow two pastures with the same grass type.

Suppose that we're solving this new version of the problem and have a test case where a pasture is the favorite of more than three cows. Which of the following is true of that test case?

A. It's *guaranteed* that there's *no way* to solve it with only four grass types.

B. There might be a way to solve it. If there is, it's *possible* that our original solution (Listing 7-2) *will* do so.

C. There might be a way to solve it. If there is, it's *guaranteed* that our original solution (Listing 7-2) *will* do so.

D. There might be a way to solve it. If there is, it's *guaranteed* that our original solution (Listing 7-2) *won't* do so.

Answer: B. We can find a test case that is correctly solved by our program, and we can find a test case that can be solved but not by our program. The former eliminates A and D as correct responses; the latter eliminates C as the correct response.

Here's a test case that is correctly solved by our program:

```
2 4
1 2
1 2
1 2
1 2
```

Each pasture is the favorite of four cows. Nevertheless, we can solve this test case using only two grass types. Try our program, and you should see that it correctly solves this test case.

(continued)

Now here's a test case that can be solved, but not by our program:

```
6 10
2 3
2 4
3 4
2 5
3 5
4 5
1 6
3 6
4 6
5 6
```

The mistake that our program makes is to use grass type 1 for pasture 1. In so doing, it's forced to use grass type 5—which isn't allowed!—for pasture 6. Our program fails, but don't conclude that there isn't a way to solve this test case. In particular, use grass type 2 for pasture 1, and you should be able to find a way to solve this test case using only four grass types. It's possible to solve these kinds of test cases with a more sophisticated program, and I encourage you to think about this on your own if you're interested.

Summary

In this chapter, we learned how to open, read from, write to, and close files. Files are useful whenever you need to store information and use it as input later. They're also useful for communicating information to your users. We also learned that we process files similarly to how we process standard input and standard output.

In the next chapter, we'll learn how to store a collection of values in a Python set or dictionary. Storing a collection of values—that sounds like what a list does. We'll see, though, that sets and dictionaries can make it easier for us to solve some kinds of problems.

Chapter Exercises

Here are some exercises for you to try. All of them are from the USACO judge and require reading and writing files. They'll also require you to dust the cobwebs off material from previous chapters.

1. USACO 2018 December Bronze Contest problem Mixing Milk

2. USACO 2017 February Bronze Contest problem Why Did the Cow Cross the Road

3. USACO 2017 US Open Bronze Contest problem The Lost Cow

4. USACO 2019 December Bronze Contest problem Cow Gymnastics

5. USACO 2017 US Open Bronze Contest problem Bovine Genomics

6. USACO 2018 US Open Bronze Contest problem Team Tic Tac Toe

7. USACO 2019 February Bronze Contest problem Sleepy Cow Herding

Notes

Essay Formatting is originally from the USACO 2020 January Bronze Contest. Farm Seeding is originally from the USACO 2019 February Bronze Contest.

There are many types of files besides text files. You might like to work with HTML files, Excel spreadsheets, PDF files, Word documents, or image files. Python can help! See *Automate the Boring Stuff with Python*, 2nd edition by Al Sweigart (No Starch Press, 2019) for much more information.

The "perhaps better poetry" line is from J. C. R. Licklider, as quoted in *Computers and the World of the Future*, edited by Martin Greenberger (MIT Press, 1962):

> But some people write poetry in the language we speak. Perhaps better poetry will be written in the language of digital computers of the future than has ever been written in English.

8

ORGANIZING VALUES USING SETS AND DICTIONARIES

A Python list is useful whenever we need to store a sequence of values, such as the heights of action figures or the words in an essay. Lists make it easy for us to keep values in order and access a value given its index. As we'll see in this chapter, though, there are operations that lists are not optimized for, including identifying whether a specific value is in a collection and making associations between pairs of values.

In this chapter, we'll learn about Python sets and dictionaries, two alternatives to lists for storing collections of values. We'll see that a set can be the tool of choice when we need to search for specific values and don't care about their order and that a dictionary can be the tool of choice whenever we need to work with pairs of values.

We'll solve three problems using these new collections: determining the number of unique email addresses, finding common words in a list of words, and determining the number of special pairs of cities and states.

In this problem, we'll store a collection of email addresses. We won't care about the number of times that each email address shows up, and we won't care about maintaining the order of the email addresses. These lax storage requirements mean that we can forgo a list for a set—a Python type whose speed leaves lists in the dust. We're going to learn all about sets.

This is DMOJ problem ecoo19r2p1.

The Challenge

Did you know that there are many ways to write someone's Gmail email address?

We can take someone's Gmail address and add a plus (+) symbol and a string before the @ symbol, and they'll get any email we send to that new address. That is, as far as Gmail addresses are concerned, all characters from a + symbol to just before the @ symbol are ignored. For example, I tell people that my Gmail address is *daniel.zingaro@gmail.com*, but that's only one way to write it. If you send email to *daniel.zingaro+book@gmail.com* or *daniel.zingaro +hi.there@gmail.com*, I'll get it. (Choose your favorite. Say hi!)

Dots before the @ symbol are also ignored in Gmail addresses. For example, if you send email to *danielzingaro@gmail.com* (no dot at all), *daniel. .zingaro@gmail.com* (two dots in a row), *da.nielz.in.gar.o..@gmail.com* (chaotic dots), *daniel.zin.garo+blah@gmail.com*, and so on, I'll get it.

Last thing: uppercase and lowercase differences throughout the address are ignored. I hope you're not firing a flurry at me by this point, but I'd get anything you send to *Daniel.Zingaro@gmail.com, DAnIELZIngARO+Flurry@ gmAIL.COM*, and so on.

In this problem, we're provided with email addresses, and we're asked to determine the number of them that are unique. The rules for email addresses in this problem are the same as those discussed for Gmail: characters from a + symbol to just before the @ symbol are ignored, dots before the @ symbol are ignored, and case throughout the entire address is ignored.

Input

The input consists of 10 test cases. Each test case contains the following lines:

- A line containing integer *n*, the number of email addresses. *n* is between 1 and 100,000.

- *n* lines, each of which gives an email address. Each email address consists of at least one character before the @ symbol, followed by the @ symbol itself, followed by at least one character after the @ symbol. Characters before the @ symbol consist of letters, numbers, dots, and pluses. Characters after the @ symbol consist of letters, numbers, and dots.

Output

For each test case, output the number of unique email addresses.
The time limit for solving the test cases is 30 seconds.

Using a List

You've worked through seven chapters of this book. In each one, I posed a problem and then taught you new Python features so that you could solve that problem. You might therefore expect me to teach you some new Python before solving Email Addresses.

And you might object to that: don't we already have what we need? After all, we can write a function to take an email address and return a clean version, with no + stuff, no dots before the @ symbol, and all in lowercase. We can also maintain a list of clean email addresses. For each email address that we see, we can clean it up and check whether it's in the list of clean email addresses. If it isn't, then we can add it; if it is, then we do nothing (since it's already being counted). Once we've gone through all of the email addresses, the length of the list will give us the number of unique email addresses.

Yes. We may already have what we need. Let's try solving this thing.

Cleaning an Email Address

Consider the email address *DAnIELZIngARO+Flurry@gmAIL.COM*. We're going to clean this email address so that it becomes *danielzingaro@gmail.com*. No *+Flurry*, no dots before the @ symbol, and all lowercase. We can think of the clean version as the true email address. Any other email address that represents the same true email address will also match *danielzingaro@gmail.com* once it's been cleaned.

Cleaning an email address is a small, self-contained task, so let's write a function for it. This clean function will take a string representing an email address, clean it up, and return the cleaned email address. We'll carry out three cleaning steps: removing characters from a + symbol to just before the @ symbol, removing dots before the @ symbol, and converting to lowercase. The code for this function is in Listing 8-1.

```
def clean(address):
    """

    address is a string email address.

    Return cleaned address.
    """
    # Remove from '+' up to but not including '@'
❶   plus_index = address.find('+')
    if plus_index != -1:
❷       at_index = address.find('@')
        address = address[:plus_index] + address[at_index:]
```

```
# Remove dots before @ symbol
at_index = address.find('@')
before_at = ''
i = 0
while i < at_index:
  ❸ if address[i] != '.':
        before_at = before_at + address[i]
    i = i + 1

❹ cleaned = before_at + address[at_index:]

# Convert to lowercase
❺ cleaned = cleaned.lower()

return cleaned
```

Listing 8-1: Cleaning an email address

The first step is to remove characters from a + symbol to just before the @ symbol. The string find method is useful here. It returns the index of the leftmost occurrence of its argument, or -1 if the argument isn't found:

```
>>> 'abc+def'.find('+')
3
>>> 'abcdef'.find('+')
-1
```

I use find to determine the index of the leftmost + symbol ❶. If there is no + symbol at all, then there's nothing to do for this step. If there is one, however, then we find the index of the @ symbol ❷ and remove characters from the + symbol up to but not including the @ symbol.

The second step is to remove any dots before the @ symbol. To do that, I use a new string, before_at, to accumulate the part of the address before the @ symbol. Each character before the @ symbol that is not a . is added to before_at ❸.

The before_at string doesn't include the @ symbol or any characters following it. We don't want to lose that part of the email address, so I use a new variable, cleaned, to refer to the whole email address ❹.

The third step is to convert the entire email address to lowercase ❺. After that, the email address is clean, so we can return it.

Let's test this a little. Enter the code for our clean function into the Python shell. Here's the function cleaning a few email addresses:

```
>>> clean('daniel.zingaro+book@gmail.com')
'danielzingaro@gmail.com'
>>> clean('da.nielz.in.gar.o..@gmail.com')
'danielzingaro@gmail.com'
>>> clean('DAnIELZIngARO+Flurry@gmAIL.COM')
```

```
'danielzingaro@gmail.com'
>>> clean('a.b.c@d.e.f')
'abc@d.e.f'
```

If the email address is already clean, clean returns it as is:

```
>>> clean('danielzingaro@gmail.com')
'danielzingaro@gmail.com'
```

The Main Program

We can use our clean function to clean any email address. The strategy now is to maintain a list of clean email addresses. We will add a cleaned email address to this list only if it hasn't been added already. In that way, we'll avoid adding duplicates of the same clean email address.

The main part of our program is in Listing 8-2. Be sure to enter our clean function (Listing 8-1) before this code for a complete solution to the problem.

```
# Main Program

for dataset in range(10):
    n = int(input())
❶   addresses = []
    for i in range(n):
        address = input()
        address = clean(address)
❷       if not address in addresses:
            addresses.append(address)

❸   print(len(addresses))
```

Listing 8-2: Main program, using a list

We have 10 test cases to process, so we surround the rest of the program with a range for loop that loops 10 times.

For each test case, we read the number of email addresses and start with an empty list of clean email addresses ❶.

We then use an inner range for loop to loop through each email address. We read each email address and clean it. Then, if we haven't seen this clean email address before ❷, we add it to our list of clean email addresses.

When the inner loop finishes, we'll have built up a list of all clean email addresses. There are no duplicates in that list. The number of unique email addresses, then, is the length of this list, so that's what we output ❸.

Not bad, eh? Almost like we could have solved this problem after we learned functions in Chapter 6. Or, really, after we learned lists in Chapter 5.

Almost, but not quite. Because if you submit to the judge, you should notice that things don't go according to plan.

The first sign of trouble is that the judge takes a while to show us our results. For example, I just waited one minute here for my results to show up. Compare that to the other problems we solved earlier, where we received feedback very quickly.

The second sign of trouble is that when our results do show up, we're not awarded full points for this problem! I'm being given 3.25 points out of 5. You may receive a little more or a little less, but you shouldn't receive the full 5 points.

The reason we're losing points is not because our program is wrong. Our program is fine. No matter the test case, it will output the correct number of unique email addresses.

So if our program is correct, what's the problem?

The problem is that our program is too slow. The judge lets us know this by putting TLE at the start of each test case. TLE stands for time limit exceeded. For this problem, the judge has allocated 30 seconds to each batch of 10 test cases. If our program takes longer than 30 seconds, the judge terminates our program, and the remaining test cases in the batch are not allowed to run.

This may be the first time limit exceeded error you've received, though it's possible you've seen them as you completed exercises from previous chapters.

The first thing to check when you receive this error is whether your program is getting stuck in an infinite loop. If it is, then it'll never finish, no matter the time limit. The judge terminates the program when the allotted time expires.

If there's no infinite loop, then the likely culprit is the *efficiency* of our program itself. When programmers talk about efficiency, they're referring to how long it takes the program to run. A program that runs faster (takes less time) is more efficient than a program that runs slower (takes more time). To solve the test cases within the time limit, we're going to make our program more efficient.

Efficiency of Searching a List

Appending to a Python list is extremely fast. It doesn't matter whether the list has only a few values or many thousands; appending takes the same small amount of time.

Using the in operator, however, is a different story. Our program uses the in operator to determine whether a clean email address is already in our list of clean email addresses. A test case might have as many as 100,000 email addresses. In the worst case, then, our program could use in 100,000 times. It turns out that in is very slow when used on a list with many values, and this ends up hurting our program's efficiency. To determine whether a value is in the list, in searches the list from beginning to end, list value by list value. It does that until it finds the value it's looking for, or it runs out of list values to check. The more values that in has to look through, the slower it is.

Let's get a feel for the way that in slows down as the length of a list increases. We'll use a function that takes a list and a value and uses in to search the list for the value. It searches for the value 50,000 times; if we searched only once, it would be too fast for us to be able to see what's going on.

The function is in Listing 8-3. Enter its code into the Python shell.

```
def search(collection, value):
    """
    search many times for value in collection.
    """
    for i in range(50000):
        found = value in collection
```

Listing 8-3: Searching a collection many times

Let's create a list of the integers from 1 to 5,000 and search for 5000. By searching for the rightmost value in the list, we make in take as much time as possible on that list. Don't worry that we're exploring this using a list of integers rather than a list of email addresses. The efficiency will be similar, and numbers are so much easier to generate than email addresses!

Here goes:

```
>>> search(list(range(1, 5001)), 5000)
```

On my laptop, this takes about three seconds to run. We don't need precise timing here; we're just looking for a general picture of what happens as we increase the length of the list.

Now let's create a list of the integers from 1 to 10,000 and search for 10000:

```
>>> search(list(range(1, 10001)), 10000)
```

On my laptop, that takes about six seconds. As a summary so far, for a list of length 5000, it takes three seconds; double the list length to 10000, and the time doubles, too, to six seconds.

A list of length 20000? Give it a try:

```
>>> search(list(range(1, 20001)), 20000)
```

This takes about 12 seconds on my laptop. The time has doubled again.

Try it on a list of length 50000. You'll be waiting a while. I just ran this on my laptop:

```
>>> search(list(range(1, 50001)), 50000)
```

It took just over 30 seconds. Remember that our search function is searching the list 50,000 times. So, it's taking 30 seconds to search a list of length 50000 a total of 50,000 times.

We could have a test case that requires this much searching. For example, suppose we add 100,000 unique email addresses to our list, one at a time. Halfway through, we'll have a list of 50,000 values; from then on, the remaining 50,000 uses of in will be on a list of at least 50,000 values.

And that's only for one of the 10 test cases! We need to get through all 10 test cases within a total of 30 seconds. If one test case can take about 30 seconds on its own, we have no chance.

Searching a list is just too slow. The Python list is the wrong type to use. We need a type better suited to the job. We need a Python set. You're not going to believe how fast it is to search a set.

Sets

A *set* is a Python type that stores a collection of values, where repeated values are not allowed. We use opening and closing curly brackets to delimit the set.

Unlike a list, a set might not maintain the values in the order you specify. Here's a set of integers:

```
>>> {13, 15, 30, 45, 61}
{45, 13, 15, 61, 30}
```

Notice that Python jumbled the order of the values. You may see the values in a different order on your computer. The important point is that you cannot rely on any particular order of the values. If order matters to you, a set is not the type to use.

If we try to include multiple occurrences of a value, only one occurrence is retained:

```
>>> {1, 1, 3, 2, 3, 1, 3, 3, 3}
{1, 2, 3}
```

Sets are equal if they contain exactly the same values, even if we write them in different orders:

```
>>> {1, 2, 3} == {1, 2, 3}
True
>>> {1, 1, 3, 2, 3, 1, 3, 3, 3} == {1, 2, 3}
True
>>> {1, 2} == {1, 2, 3}
False
```

We can create a set of strings, like this:

```
>>> {'abc@d.e.f', 'danielzingaro@gmail.com'}
{'abc@d.e.f', 'danielzingaro@gmail.com'}
```

We cannot create a set of lists:

```
>>> {[1, 2], [3, 4]}
Traceback (most recent call last):
  File "<stdin>", line 1, in <module>
```

```
TypeError: unhashable type: 'list'
```

Values in a set must be immutable, which explains why we can't put lists inside a set. The restriction has to do with how Python searches a set for a value. When Python adds a value to a set, it uses the value itself to determine where exactly it gets stored. Later, Python can find this value by looking in the place where it should be located. If a value in the set could change, then Python might look in the wrong place, failing to find the value.

While we can't create a set of lists, there's no problem with a list of sets:

```
>>> lst = [{1, 2, 3}, {4, 5, 6}]
>>> lst
[{1, 2, 3}, {4, 5, 6}]
>>> len(lst)
2
>>> lst[0]
{1, 2, 3}
```

You can use the len function to determine the number of values in a set:

```
>>> len({2, 4, 6, 8})
4
```

You can also loop over the values in a set:

```
>>> for value in {2, 4, 6, 8}:
...     print('I found', value)
...
I found 8
I found 2
I found 4
I found 6
```

You can't index or slice a set, though. Values in a set don't have indices.

To create an empty set, you might expect to use an empty pair of curly brackets, {}. In an inconsistency of Python syntax, that doesn't work:

```
>>> type({2, 4, 6, 8})
<class 'set'>
>>> {}
{}
>>> type({})
<class 'dict'>
```

Using {} gives us the wrong type: a dict (dictionary) instead of a set. We'll talk about dictionaries later in this chapter.

To make an empty set, we use set(), like this:

```
>>> set()
set()
```

```
>>> type(set())
<class 'set'>
```

Set Methods

Sets are mutable, so we can add and remove values. We can perform these tasks by using methods.

You can get a list of set methods by using dir(set()). And you can get help on a specific set method by using help, similar to how we use help to learn about string or list methods. For example, to learn about the add method, type help(set().add).

The add method is what we use to add a value to a set. It's the analog of append on lists:

```
>>> s = set()
>>> s
set()
>>> s.add(2)
>>> s
{2}
>>> s.add(4)
>>> s
{2, 4}
>>> s.add(6)
>>> s
{2, 4, 6}
>>> s.add(8)
>>> s
{8, 2, 4, 6}
>>> s.add(8)
>>> s
{8, 2, 4, 6}
```

To remove a value, we use the remove method:

```
>>> s.remove(4)
>>> s
{8, 2, 6}
>>> s.remove(8)
>>> s
{2, 6}
>>> s = {2, 6}
>>> s.remove(8)
Traceback (most recent call last):
  File "<stdin>", line 1, in <module>
KeyError: 8
```

Use `help` to learn about the set `update` and `intersection` methods.

What is output by the call of `print` in the following code?

```
s1 = {1, 3, 5, 7, 9}
s2 = {1, 2, 4, 6, 8, 10}
s3 = {1, 4, 9, 16, 25}
s1.update(s2)
s1.intersection(s3)
print(s1)
```

A. `{1, 2, 3, 4, 5, 6, 7, 8, 9, 10}`

B. `{1, 1, 2, 3, 4, 5, 6, 7, 8, 9, 10}`

C. `{1, 4, 9}`

D. `{1, 4, 9, 16, 25}`

E. `{1}`

Answer: A. The `update` method adds whatever is in set `s2` but is missing from set `s1` to set `s1`. After the call of `update`, `s1` is the set `{1, 2, 3, 4, 5, 6, 7, 8, 9, 10}`.

Now for the call of `intersection`. The intersection of two sets is the set consisting of the values that are in both sets. Here, the intersection of `s1` and `s3` is `{1, 4, 9}`. However, the `intersection` method *does not* modify a set; rather, it produces a new set! For that reason, it has no effect on `s1`.

Efficiency of Searching a Set

Back to solving Email Addresses.

Do we care about the order of our cleaned email addresses? No! All we care about is whether an email address is already in there or not.

Do we need to allow duplicates in our cleaned email addresses? No again! In fact, we want to explicitly avoid storing duplicate email addresses.

Order doesn't matter, and duplicates are not allowed. These are the two ingredients that suggest that a set may be the right type to use.

We were foiled in our attempt to use a list because searching a list is too slow. A set is going to be an improvement for us because we can search a set faster than we can search a list.

We've already used the search function in Listing 8-3 to search a list. But that function doesn't do anything that specifically requires a list! It uses the `in` operator, and `in` works on both lists and sets. So we can use that function, unchanged, to search a set, too.

Enter the search function from Listing 8-3 into the Python shell. Follow along on your computer to get a sense of the difference between searching a long list and a big set:

```
>>> search(list(range(1, 50001)), 50000)
❶ >>> search(set(range(1, 50001)), 50000)
```

At ❶, I've used set to produce a set, not a list, of the integers from the range.

On my laptop, searching the list takes about 30 seconds. Searching the set, by comparison, is bullet fast, almost instantaneous.

Sets are unstoppable. Don't try this on a list, but here we go, searching for something in a set of 500,000 values:

```
>>> search(set(range(1, 500001)), 500000)
```

Boom! Piece of cake.

Python manages a list in such a way as to allow us to use any index at any time. Python has no flexibility to mess around with the order of values: the first value has to be at index 0, the second at index 1, and so on. But for a set, Python can store it in whatever way it wants, because it makes no promises of keeping things in order for us. And it's that increased latitude that allows Python to optimize searches in a set for speed.

For similar reasons, there are other operations that are extremely slow on large lists but extremely fast on large sets. For example, removing a value from a list is very slow, because Python must decrease the index of each value that's to the right of that value. By contrast, removing a value from a set is very fast: there are no indices to update!

Solving the Problem

We already have a function to clean an email address (Listing 8-1), and we'll use it in our set-based solution. As for the main program, Listing 8-2 gets us most of the way there. We just need to use a set instead of a list.

The new main program is in Listing 8-4. Include Listing 8-1 before this code for a complete solution to the problem.

```
# Main Program

for dataset in range(10):
    n = int(input())
❶   addresses = set()
    for i in range(n):
        address = input()
        address = clean(address)
❷       addresses.add(address)

    print(len(addresses))
```

Listing 8-4: Main program, using a set

Notice that we're now using a set ❶ of email addresses rather than a list. After cleaning each email address, we add it to the set using the set add method ❷.

In Listing 8-2, we used the in operator to check whether an email address is already in the list so that we didn't add duplicates. There's no corresponding in check in our set-based solution. Where did it go? It seems that we're adding each email address to the set without even making sure that it's not already there.

We can get away without the in check when using a set because a set never contains duplicates. The add method handles the in check for us, ensuring that a duplicate doesn't get added. You can think of add carrying out its own in check. There's no timing concern there, because searching a set is so fast.

If you submit this solution to the judge, you should pass all of the test cases well within the time limit.

As you've seen here, choosing the appropriate Python type can mean the difference between an unsatisfactory solution and a satisfactory one. Before you start writing code, ask yourself which operations you'll be frequently performing and which Python type is ideally suited to those operations.

Before continuing, you might like to try solving exercises 1 and 2 from "Chapter Exercises" on page 236.

Problem #19: Common Words

In this problem, we'll need to associate words with their number of occurrences. This is beyond what we can do with sets, so we won't use sets here. Instead, we'll learn about and use Python dictionaries.

This is DMOJ problem cco99p2.

The Challenge

We are given m words. The words are not necessarily distinct; for example, the word brook could appear multiple times. We are also given an integer k.

Our task is to find the kth most common words. A word w is a kth most common word if exactly $k - 1$ distinct words occur more often than does w. Depending on the dataset, the kth most common words could be no words, one word, or more than one word.

Let's make sure we're clear on this definition of the kth most common words. If $k = 1$, then we're being asked for the words for which exactly 0 words occur more often; that is, we're being asked for the words that occur most often. If $k = 2$, then we're being asked for the words for which exactly 1 word occurs more often. If $k = 3$, then we're being asked for the words for which exactly two distinct words occur more often, and so on.

Input

The input contains a line giving the number of test cases, followed by the lines of the test cases themselves. Each test case contains the following lines:

- A line containing the integers *m* (the number of words in the test case) and *k* separated by a space. *m* is between 0 and 1,000; *k* is at least 1.

- *m* lines, each of which gives a word. Each word consists of at most 20 characters, and all characters are lowercase.

Output

For each test case, output the following lines:

- A line containing the following:

```
p most common word(s):
```
---

where *p* is 1st if *k* is 1, 2nd if *k* is 2, 3rd if *k* is 3, 4th if *k* is 4, and so on.

- One line for each of the *k*th most common words. If there are no such words, there are no lines of output here.

- A blank line.

The time limit for solving the test cases is one second.

Exploring a Test Case

Let's start by exploring a test case. It'll boost our understanding of the problem and motivate the use of a new Python type.

Suppose that we're interested in the most common words of all. This means that *k* is 1. Here's the test case:

```
1
14 1
storm
cut
magma
cut
brook
gully
gully
storm
cliff
cut
blast
brook
cut
gully
```

The word that shows up most often is cut. There are four occurrences of cut, and no other word has that many occurrences. The correct output is therefore:

```
1st most common word(s):
cut
```

❶

Notice the required blank line at the end ❶.

Now, what do we do if k were 2? We could answer this by scanning through the words again and counting occurrences, but there's a different way to organize the words that would make our task considerably easier. Rather than a list of words, let's look at each word associated with its number of occurrences. See Table 8-1.

Table 8-1: Words and Number of Occurrences

Word	Number of occurrences
cut	4
gully	3
storm	2
brook	2
magma	1
cliff	1
blast	1

I've sorted the words based on their number of occurrences. Looking at the top row, we can reaffirm that cut is the word to output for $k = 1$. Looking at the second row, we see that gully is the word to output for $k = 2$. The word gully is the only word that has exactly one word with more occurrences.

Now for $k = 3$. This time, there are *two* words to output, storm and brook, because they both have the same number of occurrences. Each of these words has exactly two words with more occurrences. This shows that we sometimes need to output more than one word.

It's also possible that we need to output zero words! For example, consider $k = 4$. There are *no* words that have exactly three words with more occurrences. Looking down the table, you might wonder why we don't output magma for $k = 4$. We don't output magma, because magma has exactly four words (not exactly three words) with more occurrences.

When $k = 5$, we have three words to output: magma, cliff, and blast. Before continuing, verify for yourself that there are no words to output for any other value of k—no words for $k = 6$, $k = 7$, $k = 8$, $k = 9$, $k = 100$, and so on.

Table 8-1 simplifies the problem quite a bit for us. We're now going to learn how to organize information like this in Python.

Dictionaries

A *dictionary* is a Python type that stores a mapping from one group of elements, called *keys*, to another group of elements, called *values*.

We use opening and closing curly brackets to delimit the dictionary. Those are the same symbols that we use for a set, but Python can tell the difference between a set and a dictionary because of what we put inside the curly brackets. For a set, we list values; for a dictionary, we list key:value pairs.

Here's a dictionary mapping some strings to numbers:

```
>>> {'cut':4, 'gully':3}
{'cut': 4, 'gully': 3}
```

In this dictionary, the keys are 'cut' and 'gully', and the values are 4 and 3. The key 'cut' is mapped to the value 4, and the key 'gully' is mapped to the value 3.

Based on our encounters with sets, you might wonder whether dictionaries maintain the pairs in the order we enter them. For example, you might wonder whether this could happen:

```
>>> {'cut':4, 'gully':3}
{'gully': 3, 'cut': 4}
```

As of Python 3.7, the answer is no: dictionaries retain the order in which you added pairs. In earlier versions of Python, dictionaries did not maintain this order, so you could add pairs in one order but get them back in another. It's still a good idea to write code that doesn't rely on the Python 3.7 behavior, though, because older versions of Python are likely to be in use for the foreseeable future.

Dictionaries are equal if they contain the same key:value pairs, even if we write them in different orders:

```
>>> {'cut':4, 'gully':3} == {'cut':4, 'gully':3}
True
>>> {'cut':4, 'gully':3} == {'gully': 3, 'cut': 4}
True
>>> {'cut':4, 'gully':3} == {'gully': 3, 'cut': 10}
False
>>> {'cut':4, 'gully':3} == {'cut': 4}
False
```

Dictionary keys must be unique. If you try to include the same key multiple times, only one pair involving that key is retained:

```
>>> {'storm': 1, 'storm': 2}
{'storm': 2}
```

Repeated values, by contrast, are fine:

```
>>> {'storm': 2, 'brook': 2}
{'storm': 2, 'brook': 2}
```

Keys are required to be immutable values, such as numbers and strings. Values can be immutable or mutable. This means that we can't use a list as a key, but we can use a list as a value:

```
>>> {['storm', 'brook']: 2}
Traceback (most recent call last):
  File "<stdin>", line 1, in <module>
TypeError: unhashable type: 'list'
>>> {2: ['storm', 'brook']}
{2: ['storm', 'brook']}
```

The len function gives us the number of key:value pairs in a dictionary:

```
>>> len({'cut':4, 'gully':3})
2
>>> len({2: ['storm', 'brook']})
1
```

To create an empty dictionary, we use {}. That's why we're stuck with that second-rate set() syntax to create a set—dictionaries got the nice syntax:

```
>>> {}
{}
>>> type({})
<class 'dict'>
```

The type is called dict, not dictionary.

You'll see "dictionary" and "dict" used interchangeably in Python resources and code, but I'll stick with "dictionary" in this book.

CONCEPT CHECK

Which of the following is best suited for a dictionary rather than a list or set?

A. The order in which people finish a race

B. The ingredients necessary for a recipe

C. The names of countries and their capital cities

D. 50 random integers

(continued)

CONCEPT CHECK

What is the type of the values (ignoring the keys) in the following dictionary?

```
{'MLB': {'Bluejays': [1992, 1993],
         'Orioles': [1966, 1970, 1983]},
 'NFL': {'Patriots': ['too many']}}
```

A. Integer

B. String

C. List

D. Dictionary

E. More than one of the above

Answer: D. The value for each key in the dictionary is itself a dictionary. For example, the key 'MLB' is mapped to a dictionary; that dictionary has two key:value pairs of its own.

Indexing Dictionaries

We can use square brackets to look up the value that a key maps to. It's similar to how we index a list, but with the keys serving as the valid "indices":

```
>>> d = {'cut':4, 'gully':3}
>>> d
{'cut': 4, 'gully': 3}
>>> d['cut']
4
>>> d['gully']
3
```

It's an error to use a key that doesn't exist:

```
>>> d['storm']
Traceback (most recent call last):
  File "<stdin>", line 1, in <module>
KeyError: 'storm'
```

We can protect against that error by first using in to check whether a key is in the dictionary. When used on a dictionary, the in operator checks only the keys, not the values. Here's how we can check that a key exists before trying to find its value:

```
>>> if 'cut' in d:
...     print(d['cut'])
...
4
>>> if 'storm' in d:
...     print(d['storm'])
...
```

Indexing and using in on a dictionary are extremely fast operations. They don't require searching any kind of list, no matter how many keys are in the dictionary.

It's sometimes more convenient to use the get method rather than indexing to look up the value for a key. The get method never produces an error, even if the key doesn't exist:

```
>>> print(d.get('cut'))
4
>>> print(d.get('storm'))
None
```

If the key exists, get returns its value. Otherwise, it returns None to signify that the key does not exist.

In addition to looking up the value for a key, we can use square brackets to add keys to a dictionary or change the value that a key maps to. Here's some code that shows how to do each of these, starting with an empty dictionary:

```
>>> d = {}
>>> d['gully'] = 1
>>> d
{'gully': 1}
>>> d['cut'] = 1
>>> d
{'gully': 1, 'cut': 1}
>>> d['cut'] = 4
>>> d
{'gully': 1, 'cut': 4}
>>> d['gully'] = d['gully'] + 1
>>> d
{'gully': 2, 'cut': 4}
>>> d['gully'] = d['gully'] + 1
>>> d
{'gully': 3, 'cut': 4}
```

Use `help({}.get)` to learn more about the dictionary `get` method.

What is the output of the following code?

```
d = {3: 4}
d[5] = d.get(4, 8)
d[4] = d.get(3, 9)
print(d)
```

A. {3: 4, 5: 8, 4: 9}

B. {3: 4, 5: 8, 4: 4}

C. {3: 4, 5: 4, 4: 3}

D. Error caused by `get`

Answer: B. The first call of `get` returns 8, because key 4 does not exist in the dictionary. That line therefore adds key 5 with value 8.

The second call of `get` returns 4: key 3 is in the dictionary already, so the second parameter, 9, is ignored. That line therefore adds key 4 with value 4.

Looping Through Dictionaries

If we use a `for` loop on a dictionary, we get the dictionary's keys:

```
>>> d = {'cut': 4, 'gully': 3, 'storm': 2, 'brook': 2}
>>> for word in d:
...     print('a key is', word)
...
a key is cut
a key is gully
a key is storm
a key is brook
```

We might also want to access the value associated with each key, and we can do that by using each key as an index in the dictionary. Here's a loop that accesses both the key and its value:

```
>>> for word in d:
...     print('key', word, 'has value', d[word])
...
key cut has value 4
```

```
key gully has value 3
key storm has value 2
key brook has value 2
```

Dictionaries have methods that let us access the keys, values, or both. The keys method gives us the keys, and the values method gives us the values:

```
>>> d.keys()
dict_keys(['cut', 'gully', 'storm', 'brook'])
>>> d.values()
dict_values([4, 3, 2, 2])
```

These aren't lists, but we can pass them to list to convert them:

```
>>> keys = list(d.keys())
>>> keys
['cut', 'gully', 'storm', 'brook']
>>> values = list(d.values())
>>> values
[4, 3, 2, 2]
```

With the keys available as a list, we can sort the keys and then loop through them in sorted order:

```
>>> keys.sort()
>>> keys
['brook', 'cut', 'gully', 'storm']
>>> for word in keys:
...     print('key', word, 'has value', d[word])
...
key brook has value 2
key cut has value 4
key gully has value 3
key storm has value 2
```

We can also loop through the values:

```
>>> for num in d.values():
...     print('number', num)
...
number 4
number 3
number 2
number 2
```

Looping through keys is often preferred over looping through values. It's easy to go from a key to its value. As we'll see in the next subsection, though, it's not as easy to go from a value back to its key.

One final method that's relevant here is `items`. It gives us access to both the keys and values:

```
>>> pairs = list(d.items())
>>> pairs
[('cut', 4), ('gully', 3), ('storm', 2), ('brook', 2)]
```

This gives us another way to loop through the `key:value` pairs of a dictionary:

```
>>> for pair in pairs:
...     print('key', pair[0], 'has value', pair[1])
...
key cut has value 4
key gully has value 3
key storm has value 2
key brook has value 2
```

Look carefully at the `pairs` value:

```
>>> pairs
[('cut', 4), ('gully', 3), ('storm', 2), ('brook', 2)]
```

There's something fishy here: there are parentheses around each inner value, not square brackets. It turns out that this is *not* a list of lists, but a list of *tuples*:

```
>>> type(pairs[0])
<class 'tuple'>
```

Tuples are similar to lists in that they store a sequence of values. The most important difference between tuples and lists is that tuples are immutable. You can loop over them, index them, and slice them, but you can't modify them. If you try to modify a tuple, you get an error:

```
>>> pairs[0][0] = 'river'
Traceback (most recent call last):
  File "<stdin>", line 1, in <module>
TypeError: 'tuple' object does not support item assignment
```

You can create your own tuples using parentheses. For a tuple with a single value, we need a trailing comma. For a tuple with multiple values, we don't:

```
>>> (4,)
(4,)
>>> (4, 5)
(4, 5)
>>> (4, 5, 6)
(4, 5, 6)
```

Tuples have methods—but only a few, because methods that would change a tuple are not allowed. I encourage you to learn more about tuples if you're interested, but we won't use tuples any further in this book.

Inverting a Dictionary

We're close to being able to solve Common Words using dictionaries. Here's the plan. We maintain a dictionary that maps from words to their number of occurrences. Whenever we process a word, we check whether that word is already in the dictionary. If it isn't, then we add it with a value of 1. If it is, then we increase its value by 1.

Here's an example of adding two words, one that we have seen before and one that we haven't:

```
>>> d = {'storm': 1, 'cut': 1, 'magma': 1}
>>> word = 'cut'  # 'cut' is already in the dictionary
>>> if not word in d:
...     d[word] = 1
... else:
...     d[word] = d[word] + 1
...
>>> d
{'storm': 1, 'cut': 2, 'magma': 1}
>>> word = 'brook'  # 'brook' is not in the dictionary
>>> if not word in d:
...     d[word] = 1
... else:
...     d[word] = d[word] + 1
...
>>> d
{'storm': 1, 'cut': 2, 'magma': 1, 'brook': 1}
```

Dictionaries make it easy to go from a key to a value. For example, given the key 'brook', we can easily look up the value 1:

```
>>> d['brook']
1
```

Referring to Table 8-1, that's like going from a word in the left column to its number of occurrences in the right column. That doesn't directly tell us the words that have a specified number of occurrences, though. What we really need to be able to do is go from the right column to the left, from number of occurrences to words. Then we'll be able to sort the numbers of occurrences from most to least to find the words we need.

That is, we need to go from this kind of dictionary:

```
{'storm': 2, 'cut': 4, 'magma': 1, 'brook': 2,
 'gully': 3, 'cliff': 1, 'blast': 1}
```

to this kind, the *inverted dictionary*:

```
{2: ['storm', 'brook'], 4: ['cut'], 1: ['magma', 'cliff', 'blast'],
 3: ['gully']}
```

The original dictionary maps from strings to numbers. The inverted dictionary maps from numbers to strings. Well, not quite: the inverted dictionary maps from numbers to *lists* of strings. Remember that each key is allowed only once in a dictionary. In the inverted dictionary, we need to map each key to multiple values, so we store all of those values in a list.

To invert a dictionary, each key becomes a value, and each value becomes a key. If a key doesn't exist yet in the inverted dictionary, we create a list for its value. If a key is already in the inverted dictionary, then we add its value to its list.

We can now write a function to return the inverted version of a dictionary. See Listing 8-5 for the code.

```
def invert_dictionary(d):
    """

    d is a dictionary mapping strings to numbers.

    Return the inverted dictionary of d.
    """
    inverted = {}
❶ for key in d:
    ❷ num = d[key]
        if not num in inverted:
          ❸ inverted[num] = [key]
        else:
          ❹ inverted[num].append(key)
    return inverted
```

Listing 8-5: Inverting a dictionary

We're using a for loop over the dictionary d ❶, which gives us each key. We index d to obtain the value mapped to by this key ❷. Then we add this key:value pair to the inverted dictionary. If num is not yet a key in the inverted dictionary, then we add it and make it map to the associated key in d ❸. If num is already a key in the inverted dictionary, then its value is already a list. We can therefore use append to add the key from d as another value ❹.

Enter the code for our invert_dictionary function into the Python shell. Let's give it a try:

```
>>> d = {'a': 1, 'b': 1, 'c': 1}
>>> invert_dictionary(d)
{1: ['a', 'b', 'c']}
>>> d = {'storm': 2, 'cut': 4, 'magma': 1, 'brook': 2,
...      'gully': 3, 'cliff': 1, 'blast': 1}
```

```
>>> invert_dictionary(d)
{2: ['storm', 'brook'], 4: ['cut'], 1: ['magma', 'cliff', 'blast'],
 3: ['gully']}
```

Now we're ready to solve Common Words with an inverted dictionary.

Solving the Problem

If you'd like more practice with top-down design, you might like to solve the problem on your own before continuing. In the interest of space, I won't follow the steps of top-down design here. Rather, I'll present the solution in its entirety, and then we'll discuss each function and how it is used.

The Code

The solution is in Listing 8-6.

```
def invert_dictionary(d):
    """

    d is a dictionary mapping strings to numbers.

    Return the inverted dictionary of d.
    """
    inverted = {}
    for key in d:
        num = d[key]
        if not num in inverted:
            inverted[num] = [key]
        else:
            inverted[num].append(key)
    return inverted


❶ def with_suffix(num):
    """

    num is an integer >= 1.

    Return a string of num with its suffix added; e.g. '5th'.
    """
❷   s = str(num)
❸   if s[-1] == '1' and s[-2:] != '11':
        return s + 'st'
    elif s[-1] == '2' and s[-2:] != '12':
        return s + 'nd'
    elif s[-1] == '3' and s[-2:] != '13':
        return s + 'rd'
    else:
        return s + 'th'
```

```
❹ def most_common_words(num_to_words, k):
    """
    num_to_words is a dictionary mapping number of occurrences to
        lists of words.
    k is an integer >= 1.

    Return a list of the kth most-common words in num_to_words.
    """
    nums = list(num_to_words.keys())
    nums.sort(reverse=True)

    total = 0
    i = 0
    done = False
❺ while i < len(nums) and not done:
        num = nums[i]
    ❻ if total + len(num_to_words[num]) >= k:
            done = True
        else:
            total = total + len(num_to_words[num])
            i = i + 1

    ❼ if total == k - 1 and i < len(nums):
        return num_to_words[nums[i]]
    else:
        return []


❽ n = int(input())

for dataset in range(n):
    lst = input().split()
    m = int(lst[0])
    k = int(lst[1])

    word_to_num = {}

    for i in range(m):
        word = input()
        if not word in word_to_num:
            word_to_num[word] = 1
        else:
            word_to_num[word] = word_to_num[word] + 1

    ❾ num_to_words = invert_dictionary(word_to_num)
```

```
ordinal = with_suffix(k)
words = most_common_words(num_to_words, k)

print(f'{ordinal} most common word(s):')
for word in words:
    print(word)

print()
```

Listing 8-6: Solving Common Words

The first function is `invert_dictionary`. We've already discussed that, in "Inverting a Dictionary" earlier in this chapter. We'll now go through each other piece of the program.

Adding the Suffix

The `with_suffix` function ❶ takes a number and returns a string with the correct suffix added to the number. We need this function because of the pesky requirement to output *k* with a suffix. For example, if *k* = 1, then we'll have to produce this line as part of the output:

```
1st most common word(s):
```

If *k* = 2, we'll have to produce this line as part of the output:

```
2nd most common word(s):
```

and so on. Our `with_suffix` function makes sure that we add the correct suffix to the number. We first convert the number to a string ❷ so that we can easily access its digits. Then we use a series of tests to determine whether the suffix is `st`, `nd`, `rd`, or `th`. For example, if the last digit is a 1 but the last two digits aren't 11 ❸, then the correct suffix is `st`. That gives us `1st`, `21st`, and `31st`, but not `11st` (which would be incorrect).

Finding the kth Most Common Words

The `most_common_words` function ❹ is the function that actually finds the words that we need. It takes an inverted dictionary (which maps numbers of occurrences to lists of words) and an integer k and returns a list of the kth most common words.

To see how it works, let's look at a sample inverted dictionary. I've organized its keys in order from most occurrences to fewest occurrences, as that's the order that `most_common_words` goes through the keys. Here's the dictionary:

```
{4: ['cut'],
 3: ['gully'],
 2: ['storm', 'brook'],
 1: ['magma', 'cliff', 'blast']}
```

Suppose that k is 3. Therefore, exactly two words must be more common than the words that we return. The words we need are not provided by the first dictionary key. That key gives us only one word (cut), so it can't be the third most common word. Similarly, the words we need are not provided by the second dictionary key. That key gives us one more word (gully). We've processed a total of two words now but haven't found the third most common words yet. The words we need, however, *are* provided by the third dictionary key. That key gives us two more words; each of these words (storm and brook) has exactly two words with more occurrences, so these are the words for when k is 3.

What if k were 4? This time, exactly three words must be more common than the words that we return. The candidate words are still those from the third key (storm and brook), but there are only two words that occur more often than each of these words. There are therefore *no* words for when k = 4.

In summary, we need to total up the words we see when going through the keys until we find the key that might contain the words we need. If exactly k - 1 words occur more often, then we have words for k; otherwise, we don't, and there are no words to output.

Now let's walk through the code itself. We begin by obtaining a list of the dictionary's keys and sorting them from biggest to smallest. We then loop through the keys in that reverse-sorted order ❺. The done variable tells us whether we've looked at k or more words yet. As soon as we have ❻, we exit the loop.

When the loop is done, we check whether there are any words for k. If there are exactly k - 1 words that occur more often, and we haven't gone past the end of our keys ❼, then we indeed have words to return. Otherwise, there are no words to return, so we return the empty list.

The Main Program

Now we arrive at the main part of the program ❽. We build dictionary word _to_num, which maps each word to its number of occurrences. We then build the inverted dictionary num_to_words ❾, which maps each number of occurrences to the associated list of words. Notice how the names of these dictionaries convey the direction of mapping: word_to_num goes from words to numbers, and num_to_words goes from numbers to words.

The rest of the code calls our other helper functions and outputs the appropriate words.

With that, you're ready to submit to the judge. Well done: that's the first problem that you've solved with dictionaries. Whenever you need to map between two types of values, think about whether you can organize the information using a dictionary. If you can, it's likely that you'll be well on your way to an efficient solution!

Problem #20: Cities and States

Here's another problem where we'll be able to use a dictionary. As you read the problem description, think about what we could use as the keys and what we could use as the values.

This is USACO 2016 December Silver Contest problem Cities and States.

The Challenge

The United States is divided into geographical regions called *states*, each of which contains one or more cities. Each state has been given a two-character abbreviation. For example, the abbreviation for Pennsylvania is PA, and the abbreviation for South Carolina is SC. We'll write city names and state abbreviations in all uppercase.

Consider the pair of cities SCRANTON PA and PARKER SC. This pair of cities is *special* because the first two characters of each city give the abbreviation for the other city's state. That is, the first two characters of SCRANTON give us SC (PARKER's state), and the first two characters of PARKER give us PA (SCRANTON's state).

A pair of cities is *special* if they meet this property and are not in the same state.

Determine the number of special pairs of cities in the provided input.

Input

Read input from the file named *citystate.in*.
The input consists of the following lines:

- A line containing n, the number of cities. n is between 1 and 200,000.

- n lines, one per city. Each line gives the name of a city in uppercase, a space, and its state's abbreviation in uppercase. The name of each city is between 2 and 10 characters; the abbreviation for each state is exactly two characters. The same city name can exist in multiple states but will not appear more than once in the same state. The name of a city or state in this problem is any string that meets these requirements; it might not be the name of an actual US city or state.

Output

Write output to the file named *citystate.out*.
Output the number of special pairs of cities.
The time limit for solving each test case is four seconds.

Exploring a Test Case

Perhaps you're thinking that you could solve this problem with a list. That's a good thought to have! If you're interested, I suggest giving that a try before continuing. The strategy would be to use two nested loops to consider each pair of cities and check whether each pair is special. It's possible to come up with a correct solution using this approach.

A correct solution, yes, but also a slow one. The list of cities can be huge —up to a maximum of 200,000—and any solution involving searching a list for matching cities is doomed to be too slow. Let's explore a test case and work out how a dictionary can help.

Here's our test case:

```
12
SCRANTON PA
MANISTEE MI
NASHUA NH
PARKER SC
LAFAYETTE CO
WASHOUGAL WA
MIDDLEBOROUGH MA
MADISON MI
MILFORD MA
MIDDLETON MA
COVINGTON LA
LAKEWOOD CO
```

The first city is SCRANTON PA. To find special pairs involving this city, we need to find other cities whose name starts with PA and whose state is SC. The only other city that meets this description is PARKER SC.

Notice that all we care about for SCRANTON PA is that its name starts with SC and that its state is PA. It could have been called SCMERWIN PA or SCSHOCK PA or SCHRUTE PA; it would still be a special pair with PARKER SC.

Let's refer to the first two characters of a city name followed by the city's state as a *combo*. For example, the combo for SCRANTON PA is SCPA, and the combo for PARKER SC is PASC.

Rather than searching for special pairs of cities, we can now look at special pairs of combos. Let's try this.

There are two cities with the combo MAMI. They happen to be MANISTEE MI and MADISON MI, but all we care about is that there are two of them. The MAMI cities start with MA and are in state MI. To count up the special pairs involving MAMI cities, we need to know the cities that start with MI and have state MA. That is, we need to know the number of MIMA cities. There are three MIMA cities. They happen to be MIDDLEBOROUGH MA, MILFORD MA, and MIDDLETON MA, but all we care is that there are three of them. Okay—so we have two MAMI cities and three MIMA cities. The total special pairs for these combos is therefore $2 * 3 = 6$, because for each of the two MAMI cities, we have a choice of three MIMA cities.

If you're not convinced, here are the six special pairs for these combos:

- MANISTEE MI and MIDDLEBOROUGH MA
- MANISTEE MI and MILFORD MA
- MANISTEE MI and MIDDLETON MA
- MADISON MI and MIDDLEBOROUGH MA
- MADISON MI and MILFORD MA
- MADISON MI and MIDDLETON MA

If we could map combos—SCPA, PASC, MAMI, MIMA, and so on—to the number of occurrences, we could loop through the combos to find the number of special pairs of cities. A dictionary is the perfect tool to store this mapping.

Here's the dictionary that we'd like to create for our test case:

```
{'SCPA': 1, 'MAMI': 2, 'NANH': 1, 'PASC': 1, 'LACO': 2,
 'MIMA': 3, 'COLA': 1}
```

With this dictionary, we can figure out the number of special pairs of cities. Let's work through the process.

The first key is 'SCPA'; its value is 1. To find special pairs of cities involving 'SCPA', we need to look up the value for 'PASC'. That value is also 1. We multiply the two values together, yielding 1 * 1 = 1 special pair of cities involving these combos. We need to carry out this same procedure for each other key in the dictionary.

The next key is 'MAMI'; its value is 2. To find special pairs of cities involving 'MAMI', we need to look up the value for 'MIMA'. That value is 3. We multiply the two values together, yielding 2 * 3 = 6 special pairs of cities involving these combos. With the 1 we found previously, we now have a total of 7.

The next key is 'NANH'; its value is 1. To find special pairs of cities involving 'NANH', we need to look up the value for 'NHNA'. But 'NHNA' isn't a key in the dictionary! There are no special pairs of cities involving these combos. We still have a total of 7.

Pay close attention to this next one. The next key is 'PASC'; its value is 1. To find special pairs of cities involving 'PASC', we need to look up the value for 'SCPA'. That value is also 1. We multiply the two values together, yielding 1 * 1 = 1 special pair of cities involving these combos. But wait: we already accounted for this pair when we processed the key 'SCPA'. If we add 1 here, then we'll end up double-counting this pair. In fact, by processing each key we will double-count *every* special pair of cities. Not to worry, though: we'll make an adjustment later when we're ready to print the final answer. Let's add this 1 in there. With the 7 we found previously, we now have a total of 8.

The next key is 'LACO'; its value is 2. The value for 'COLA' is 1, giving 2 * 1 = 2 special pairs of cities involving these combos. With the 8 we found previously, we now have a total of 10.

There are two keys to go, 'MIMA' and 'COLA'. The first leads us to add 6 to our total; the second leads us to add 2. With the 10 we found previously, we now have a total of 18.

Remember that we've double-counted every special pair of cities. We don't have 18 unique special pairs of cities, then. We have only 18 / 2 = 9 special pairs of cities. All we need to do is divide by 2 to undo the double counting.

If you compare the dictionary we just went through to the cities in the test case, you'll notice that something is missing from the dictionary. It's that city WASHOUGAL WA! Its combo is WAWA, but there's no 'WAWA' key in our dictionary. We're not accounting for this city, and we need to understand why.

The first two characters of WASHOUGAL WA are WA. This means that the only way for WASHOUGAL WA to be part of a special pair of cities is to find another city whose state is WA. Notice that WASHOUGAL WA is in state WA, too. However, the problem specifies that the two cities in a special pair of cities must come from different states. There's therefore no way to find a special pair of cities involving WASHOUGAL WA. To make sure we don't accidentally count fake special pairs, we don't even include WASHOUGAL WA in the dictionary.

Solving the Problem

We're ready to go! We can use a dictionary for a concise, rocket-fast solution to Cities and States. The code is in Listing 8-7.

```
input_file = open('citystate.in', 'r')
output_file = open('citystate.out', 'w')

n = int(input_file.readline())

❶ combo_to_num = {}

for i in range(n):
    lst = input_file.readline().split()
❷  city = lst[0][:2]
    state = lst[1]
❸  if city != state:
        combo = city + state
        if not combo in combo_to_num:
            combo_to_num[combo] = 1
        else:
            combo_to_num[combo] = combo_to_num[combo] + 1

total = 0

❹ for combo in combo_to_num:
❺    other_combo = combo[2:] + combo[:2]
    if other_combo in combo_to_num:
❻        total = total + combo_to_num[combo] * combo_to_num[other_combo]

❼ output_file.write(str(total // 2) + '\n')
```

```
input_file.close()
output_file.close()
```

Listing 8-7: Solving Cities and States

This is a USACO problem where we need to use files rather than standard input and standard output.

The dictionary that we'll build is called `combo_to_num` ❶. It maps from four-character combos, like `'SCPA'`, to the number of cities with that combo.

For each city from the input, we use variables to refer to the first two characters of the name of the city ❷ and its state. Then, if these values are not the same ❸, we combine them and add the combo to the dictionary. If the combo wasn't already in the dictionary, we add it with a value of 1; if it was already there, we increase its value by 1.

The dictionary is now built. We loop through its keys ❹. For each key, we construct the other combo that we need to look up to find special pairs of cities involving this key. If the key is `'SCPA'`, for example, then we want the other combo to be `'PASC'`. To do that, we take the rightmost two characters of the key and follow those by the leftmost two characters ❺. If that other combo is also in the dictionary, then we multiply the two key's values and add that to our total ❻.

All we need to do now is output the total number of special pairs of cities to the output file. As explained in the previous section, we need to divide our total by 2 ❼ to undo the double-counting that results from processing each key in the dictionary.

There we have it: another example of solving a problem with a suitable deployment of a dictionary. Feel free to submit our code!

Summary

In this chapter, we learned about Python sets and dictionaries. A set is a collection of values with no order and no duplicates. A dictionary is a collection of `key:value` pairs. As we saw in this chapter's problems, sometimes these collections are more appropriate than lists. For example, determining whether a value is in a set is ridiculously fast compared to the same operation on a list. If we don't care about the order of values or want to eliminate duplicates, we should seriously consider using a set.

Similarly, a dictionary makes it easy to determine the value mapped to by a key. If we're maintaining a mapping from keys to values, then we should seriously consider using a dictionary.

With sets and dictionaries in the mix, you now have more flexibility for how to store your values. This flexibility, however, means that you need to make a choice. Don't default to using a list anymore! The difference between using one type or another might be the difference between solving the problem or not.

We've reached an important milestone, as we've now covered most of the Python that I'll be teaching you in this book. This doesn't mean that your Python journey is complete. There's a lot more to know about Python beyond what I've included in the book. This does mean, though, that we've reached a point where we can solve a wide variety of problems—in competitive programming or otherwise—with our Python skills.

In the next chapter of the book, we shift gears: from learning new Python features to sharpening our problem-solving ability. We'll focus on one particular type of problem that we can solve by searching through all candidate solutions.

Chapter Exercises

Here are some exercises for you to try. For each, use a set or dictionary. Sometimes, a set or dictionary will help you write code that runs faster; other times, it will help you write code that's more organized and easier to read.

1. DMOJ problem crci06p1, Bard
2. DMOJ problem dmopc19c5p1, Conspicuous Cryptic Checklist
3. DMOJ problem coci15c2p1, Marko
4. DMOJ problem ccc06s2, Attack of the CipherTexts
5. DMOJ problem dmopc19c3p1, Mode Finding
6. DMOJ problem coci14c2p2, Utrka (Try solving this one in three different ways: using a dictionary, using a set, and using lists!)
7. DMOJ problem coci17c2p2, ZigZag (Hint: maintain two dictionaries. The first maps each starting letter to its list of words; the second maps each starting letter to the index of its next word that will be output. That way, we can cycle through the words for each letter without having to explicitly update numbers of occurrences or modify lists.)

Notes

Email Addresses is originally from the 2019 Educational Computing Organization of Ontario Programming Contest, Round 2. Common Words is originally from the 1999 Canadian Computing Olympiad. Cities and States is originally from the USACO 2016 December Silver Contest.

If you'd like to learn more about Python, I recommend *Python Crash Course*, 2nd edition by Eric Matthes (No Starch Press, 2019). When you're ready to take it to the next level, you might like to read *Effective Python*, 2nd edition by Brett Slatkin (Addison-Wesley Professional, 2020), which offers a collection of tips to help you write better Python code.

9

DESIGNING ALGORITHMS WITH COMPLETE SEARCH

An *algorithm* is a sequence of steps that solves a problem. For each problem in this book, we solved it by writing an algorithm in the form of Python code. We'll focus in this chapter on designing algorithms. When faced with a new problem, sometimes it's hard to know what to do to solve it. What algorithm should we write? Fortunately, we don't need to start from scratch each time. Computer scientists and programmers have identified several general types of algorithms, and it's likely that at least one of them can be used to solve our problem.

One type of algorithm is called a *complete search* algorithm; it involves trying all candidate solutions and choosing the best one. For example, if the problem asks us to find a maximum, we try all solutions and choose the largest; if the problem asks us to find a minimum, we try all solutions and choose the smallest. Complete-search algorithms are also known as *brute-force* algorithms, but I'll avoid that term. It's true that the computer is powering its way through, checking solution after solution, but there's nothing brute force about what we're doing as algorithm designers.

We used a complete-search algorithm to solve Village Neighborhood in Chapter 5. We were asked to find the smallest size of the neighborhoods, and we did that by looking at each neighborhood and remembering the size of the smallest one. In this chapter, we'll use complete-search algorithms to solve other problems. We'll see that it can take considerable ingenuity to determine what exactly to search.

We'll solve two problems using complete search: determining which lifeguard to fire and identifying the minimum cost to meet ski training camp requirements. Then we'll see a third problem, counting triples of cows that meet given observations, that requires we go a little further.

Problem #21: Lifeguards

In this problem, we'll need to determine which lifeguard to fire that leaves us with the maximum schedule coverage of a pool. We'll try separately firing each one and observing the results—that's a complete-search algorithm!

This is USACO 2018 January Bronze Contest problem Lifeguards.

The Challenge

Farmer John has purchased a swimming pool for his cows. The pool is open from time 0 to time 1000.

Farmer John hires n lifeguards to monitor the pool. Each lifeguard monitors the pool for a given interval of time. For example, a lifeguard might start at time 2 and end at time 7. I'll denote such an interval as 2–7. The number of units of time covered by an interval is the ending time minus the starting time. For example, the lifeguard whose time interval is 2–7 covers $7 - 2 = 5$ units of time. Those time units are from time 2 to 3, 3 to 4, 4 to 5, 5 to 6, and 6 to 7.

Unfortunately, Farmer John only has enough money to pay for $n - 1$ lifeguards, not n lifeguards, so he must fire one lifeguard.

Determine the maximum number of units of time that can still be covered after firing one lifeguard.

Input

Read input from the file named *lifeguards.in*.

The input consists of the following lines:

- A line containing n, the number of lifeguards who were hired. n is between 1 and 100.

- n lines, one per lifeguard. Each line gives the time when the lifeguard starts, a space, and the time when the lifeguard ends. The start and end times are all integers between 0 and 1,000 and are all distinct.

Output

Write output to the file named *lifeguards.out*.

Output the maximum number of units of time that can be covered by $n - 1$ of the lifeguards.

The time limit for solving each test case is four seconds.

Exploring a Test Case

Let's explore a test case to help justify why a complete-search algorithm makes sense for this problem. Here's the test case:

```
4
5 8
10 15
17 25
9 20
```

One simple rule you might try to use to solve this problem is to fire the lifeguard with the shortest time interval. That makes some intuitive sense, because it seems as though that lifeguard contributes the least to covering the pool.

Does this rule give us a correct algorithm? Let's see. It tells us to fire the 5–8 lifeguard, since that lifeguard has the shortest time interval. That leaves us with the three lifeguards whose time intervals are 10–15, 17–25, and 9–20. These three remaining lifeguards cover exactly the interval 9–25, which consists of 25 − 9 = 16 units of time. Is 16 the correct answer?

Unfortunately, no. It turns out that what we should have done is fire the 10–15 lifeguard. If we do that, then we're left with the three lifeguards whose time intervals are 5–8, 17–25, and 9–20. These three remaining lifeguards cover the intervals 5–8 and 9–25. (Careful: they don't cover the unit of time from 8 to 9.) The first of these intervals covers 8 − 5 = 3 units of time, and the second covers 25 − 9 = 16 units of time, for a total of 19 units of time.

The correct answer is 19, not 16. Firing the lifeguard with the shortest time interval didn't work.

It's not easy to come up with a simple rule that always works to solve this problem. We don't need to worry, though: with a complete-search algorithm, we dodge this requirement entirely.

Here's what our complete-search algorithm will do to solve our test case:

1. First, it will ignore the first lifeguard and determine the number of units of time that the three remaining lifeguards cover. It will obtain an answer of 16. It will remember 16 as the score to beat.

2. Next, it will ignore the second lifeguard and determine the number of units of time that the three remaining lifeguards cover. It will obtain an answer of 19. Since 19 is greater than 16, it will remember 19 as the score to beat.

3. Next, it will ignore the third lifeguard and determine the number of units of time that the three remaining lifeguards cover. It will obtain an answer of 14. The score to beat is still 19.

4. Finally, it will ignore the fourth lifeguard and determine the number of units of time that the three remaining lifeguards cover. It will obtain an answer of 16. The score to beat is still 19.

Having considered the ramifications of firing each lifeguard, the algorithm concludes that 19 is the correct answer. There can be no better answer than this, because we tried every option! We performed a complete search of the possible solutions.

Solving the Problem

To use complete search, it's often helpful to begin by writing a function that solves the problem for a particular candidate solution. We can then call that function many times, once for each candidate solution.

Firing One Lifeguard

Let's write a function to determine the number of time units that are covered when one particular lifeguard is fired. Listing 9-1 shows the code.

```
def num_covered(intervals, fired):
    """

    intervals is a list of lifeguard intervals;
    each interval is a [start, end] list.
    fired is the index of the lifeguard to fire.

    Return the number of time units covered by all lifeguards
    except the one fired.
    """
❶   covered = set()
    for i in range(len(intervals)):
        if i != fired:
            interval = intervals[i]
❷           for j in range(interval[0], interval[1]):
❸               covered.add(j)
    return len(covered)
```

Listing 9-1: Solving when one particular lifeguard is fired

The first parameter is a list of lifeguard time intervals; the second is the index of the lifeguard to fire. Enter the code into the Python shell. Here are two sample calls of the function:

```
>>> num_covered([[5, 8], [10, 15], [9, 20], [17, 25]], 0)
16
```

```
>>> num_covered([[5, 8], [10, 15], [9, 20], [17, 25]], 1)
19
```

These calls confirm that we can cover 16 units of time if we fire lifeguard 0 and can cover 19 units of time if we fire lifeguard 1.

Now let's understand how the function operates. We begin by creating a set that will hold the units of time that are covered ❶. Whenever a unit of time is covered, the code will add the start of that unit of time to the set. For example, if the unit of time from 0 to 1 is covered, then the code will add 0 to the set; if the unit of time from 4 to 5 is covered, it will add 4 to the set.

We loop through the lifeguard time intervals. If a lifeguard isn't fired, then we loop through this lifeguard's time interval ❷ to consider each unit of covered time. We add each of these time units to the set ❸, as promised. Recall that sets don't retain duplicate values; we don't have to worry if we try to add the same unit of time multiple times. We've gone through all of the nonfired lifeguards and added to the set all units of time that are covered. We therefore simply return the number of values in the set.

The Main Program

The main part of our program is in Listing 9-2. It uses the num_covered function to determine the number of units of time that are covered when separately firing each lifeguard. Be sure to enter our num_covered function (Listing 9-1) before this code for a complete solution to the problem.

```
input_file = open('lifeguards.in', 'r')
output_file = open('lifeguards.out', 'w')

n = int(input_file.readline())

intervals = []

for i in range(n):
  ❶ interval = input_file.readline().split()
     interval[0] = int(interval[0])
     interval[1] = int(interval[1])
     intervals.append(interval)

max_covered = 0

❷ for fired in range(n):
  ❸ result = num_covered(intervals, fired)
     if result > max_covered:
         max_covered = result

output_file.write(str(max_covered) + '\n')
```

```
input_file.close()
output_file.close()
```

Listing 9-2: Main program

We're working with files here, not standard input and standard output.

The program begins by reading the number of lifeguards and then uses a range for loop to read each lifeguard's time interval. We read each time interval from the input ❶, convert each of its components to an integer, and append it as a two-value list to our list of intervals.

We use the max_covered variable to track the maximum number of time units that can be covered.

Now we separately fire each lifeguard using a range for loop ❷. We call num_covered ❸ to determine the number of time units that are covered given the firing of one lifeguard. We update max_covered whenever we're able to cover a greater number of time units.

When that loop completes, we'll have checked the number of units of time that can be covered by firing each lifeguard, and we'll have remembered the maximum. We output this maximum to solve the problem.

Feel free to submit our code to the USACO judge. For Python code, this judge uses a time limit per test case of four seconds, but our solution shouldn't come close to that limit. For example, I just ran the code here, and each test case finished in no more than 130 milliseconds.

Efficiency of Our Program

The reason our code is so fast is because there are so few lifeguards—only at most 100 of them. If there were a large number of lifeguards, then our code would no longer solve the problem within the time limit. We'd be fine if there were a few hundred lifeguards. We might squeak through if we had as many as 3,000 or 4,000 lifeguards. Any more than that, though, and our code would be too slow. We probably couldn't make it in time with 5,000 lifeguards, for example. We'd need to design a new algorithm, likely one that uses something faster than complete search.

You might think that 5,000 is a huge number of lifeguards and that it's okay that our algorithm can't go that high. But it's not! Think back to the Email Addresses problem in Chapter 8. There, we had to contend with up to 100,000 email addresses. And think back to the Cities and States problem in the same chapter. There, we had to contend with up to 200,000 cities. By comparison, 5,000 is not a lot of lifeguards.

A complete-search solution often works fine for a small amount of input. Large test cases are often where complete-search solutions break down.

The reason that our complete-search solution for Lifeguards doesn't work well with large test cases is because it does a lot of repeated work. Imagine that we're solving a test case with 5,000 lifeguards. We'll fire lifeguard 0 and call num_covered to determine the number of units of time covered by the remaining lifeguards. Then, we'll fire lifeguard 1 and call num _covered again. Now, what num_covered does this time is similar to what it did on the previous call. After all, things haven't changed much. The only change is that lifeguard 0 is back and lifeguard 1 is fired. The other 4,998 lifeguards are the same as they were! But num_covered doesn't know that. It grinds through all of the lifeguards again. That same thing happens when we fire lifeguard 2, then lifeguard 3, and so on. Each time, num_covered does all of its work from scratch, without learning anything about what it did previously.

Remember that, while useful, complete-search algorithms do have limitations. Given a new problem that we want to solve, a complete-search algorithm is a useful starting point, even if it ultimately turns out to be too inefficient. That's because the act of designing that algorithm may deepen our appreciation of the problem and lead to new ideas for solving it.

In the next section, we'll see another problem where we'll be able to use complete search.

CONCEPT CHECK

Is the following version of num_covered correct?

```
def num_covered(intervals, fired):
    """
    intervals is a list of lifeguard intervals;
    each interval is a [start, end] list.
    fired is the index of the lifeguard to fire.

    Return the number of time units covered by all lifeguards
    except the one fired.
    """
    covered = set()
    intervals.pop(fired)
    for interval in intervals:
        for j in range(interval[0], interval[1]):
            covered.add(j)
    return len(covered)
```

A. Yes

B. No

Answer: B. This function removes the fired lifeguard from the list of lifeguards. That's not allowed, because the docstring doesn't say anything about the function modifying the list. With this version of the function, our program will fail many test cases because lifeguard information is lost over time. For example, when we test firing lifeguard 0, lifeguard 0 is removed from the list. When we later test firing lifeguard 1, lifeguard 0 is unfortunately still gone! If you want to use a version of the function where the fired lifeguard is removed from the list, you need to work with a copy of the list rather than the original.

Sometimes, the problem description makes it clear what we should search through in a complete-search solution. For example, in Lifeguards, we were asked to fire one lifeguard, so it made sense to try firing each one. Other times, we'll have to be more creative to determine what to search through. As you read this next problem, think about what you would search in a complete-search solution.

This is USACO 2014 January Bronze Contest problem Ski Course Design.

The Challenge

Farmer John has n hills on his farm, each with a height between 0 and 100. He would like to register his farm as a ski training camp.

A farm can be registered as a ski training camp only if the difference in height between the highest and lowest hills is 17 or less. Farmer John may therefore need to increase the heights of some of his hills and decrease the heights of others. He is able to change the heights only by integer amounts.

The cost of changing a hill's height by x units is x^2. For example, changing a hill from height 1 to height 4 costs $(4 - 1)^2 = 9$.

Determine the minimum amount that Farmer John will need to pay to change the heights of hills so that he can register his farm as a ski training camp.

Input

Read input from the file named *skidesign.in*.

The input consists of the following lines:

- A line containing integer n, the number of hills on the farm. n is between 1 and 1,000.

- n lines, each of which gives the height of a hill. Each height is an integer between 0 and 100.

Output

Write output to the file named *skidesign.out*.

Output the minimum amount that Farmer John will need to pay to change the heights of hills.

The time limit for solving each test case is four seconds.

Exploring a Test Case

Let's see if we can apply what we learned from Lifeguards to this problem. To solve Lifeguards, we separately fired each lifeguard to figure out the lifeguard that we should fire. To solve Ski Hills, perhaps there's something analogous that we can do with each hill? For example, perhaps we can use each hill's height as the low end in an allowed height range?

We'll give this a try using the following test case:

4
23
40
16
2

The smallest height of these four hills is 2, and the biggest height is 40. The difference between 40 and 2 is 38, greater than 17. Farmer John is going to have to pay to fix these hills!

The first hill is height 23. If we use 23 as the low end of the range, then the high end is $23 + 17 = 40$. We need to calculate the cost to bring all hills into the range 23–40. There are two hills that are out of this range, the ones of heights 16 and 2. Bringing them up to height 23 costs $(23 - 16)^2 + (23 - 2)^2 = 490$. A cost of 490 is the cost to beat.

The second hill is height 40. The high end of this range is $40 + 17 = 57$, so we're looking to get all hills into the range 40–57. The other three hills are out of this range, so each of them contributes to the total cost. That total is $(40 - 23)^2 + (40 - 16)^2 + (40 - 2)^2 = 2,309$. This is greater than 490, our current minimum cost, so 490 is still the cost to beat. (Remember that in this problem we're trying to *minimize* Farmer John's cost, whereas in Lifeguards we were trying to *maximize* coverage.)

The third hill is height 16, which gives us the range 16–33. There are two hills that are out of this range, the ones of heights 40 and 2. The total cost for this range is therefore $(40 - 33)^2 + (16 - 2)^2 = 245$. The new cost to beat is 245!

The fourth hill is height 2, which gives us the range 2–19. If you calculate the cost for this range, you should obtain a cost of 457.

The minimum cost we obtained using that algorithm is 245. Is 245 the answer? Are we done?

No and no! It turns out that the minimum cost is 221. There are two ranges that give us this minimum cost: 12–29 and 13–30. There is no hill whose height is 12. Similarly, there is no hill whose height is 13. We therefore can't use hill heights as the possible low ends of ranges.

Think about what a correct complete-search algorithm could look like, one that's guaranteed not to miss any ranges.

Here's a plan that's guaranteed to get us the correct answer. We start by calculating the cost for range 0–17. Then we calculate the cost for range 1–18. Then 2–19. Then 3–20. Then 4–21, and so on. We test every possible range, one by one, and remember the minimum cost that we obtain. The ranges we test have nothing to do with the heights of the hills. Since we're testing every possible range, there's no way we'll miss finding the best one.

Which ranges should we test? How high should we go? Should we test the range 50–67? Yes. How about the range 71–88? Yes again. How about 115–132? No! Not that one.

The final range that we'll check is 100–117. The reason has to do with the guarantee from the problem description that the height of any hill is at most 100.

Suppose we figure out the cost for range 101–118. Without even knowing the heights of the hills, we know for sure that none of the hills is in this range. The maximum height of a hill, after all, is 100, and our range starts at 101. Now slide our range from 101–118 down to 100–117. This 100–117 range costs less than the 101–118 range! That's because 100 is closer to the hills than 101 is. For example, consider a hill of height 80. This hill would cost us $21^2 = 441$ to raise it to height 101, but only $20^2 = 400$ to raise it to height 100. This shows that 101–118 cannot be the best range to use. There's no point trying it.

Similar logic explains why it's pointless to try any higher range such as 102–119, 103–120, and so on. We can always slide these ranges down to make them cost less.

In summary, we are going to test exactly 101 ranges: 0–17, 1–18, 2–19, and so on, all the way up to 100–117. We'll remember the cost of the best one. Let's do this!

Solving the Problem

We'll take the solution in two steps, just as we did when solving Lifeguards. We'll start with a function to determine the cost of a single range. Then we'll write a main program to call this function once for each range.

Determining the Cost of One Range

Listing 9-3 gives the code for the function that determines the cost of a given range.

```
MAX_DIFFERENCE = 17
MAX_HEIGHT = 100


def cost_for_range(heights, low, high):
    """

    heights is a list of hill heights.
    low is an integer giving the low end of the range.
    high is an integer giving the high end of a range.

    Return the cost of changing all heights of hills to be
    between low and high.
    """
    cost = 0
❶ for height in heights:
    ❷ if height < low:
        ❸ cost = cost + (low - height) ** 2
    ❹ elif height > high:
```

```
❺     cost = cost + (height - high) ** 2
    return cost
```

Listing 9-3: Solving for one particular range

I've included two constants that we'll use later. The MAX_DIFFERENCE constant records the maximum difference allowed between the heights of the highest and lowest hills. The MAX_HEIGHT constant records the maximum height of a hill.

Now let's turn to the cost_for_range function. It takes a list of hill heights and a desired range specified by its low end and high end. It returns the cost of changing hill heights so that all hills are in the desired range. I encourage you to enter the code for the function into the Python shell so that you can try it before continuing.

The function loops through the height of each hill ❶, adding up the cost to bring that hill into the desired range. There are two cases we need to account for. First, the height of the current hill might be out of range by being less than low ❷. The expression low - height gives us the amount of height that we need to add to this hill, and we square that result to get the cost ❸. Second, the height of the current hill might be out of range by being greater than high ❹. The expression height - high gives us the amount of height that we need to subtract from this hill, and we square that result to get the cost ❺. Notice that we don't do anything if the height is already in the low-high range. Once we've gone through all of the heights, we return the total cost.

The Main Program

The main part of our program is in Listing 9-4. It uses the cost_for_range function to determine the cost for each range. Be sure to enter our cost _for_range function (Listing 9-3) before this code for a complete solution to the problem.

```
input_file = open('skidesign.in', 'r')
output_file = open('skidesign.out', 'w')

n = int(input_file.readline())

heights = []

for i in range(n):
    heights.append(int(input_file.readline()))

❶ min_cost = cost_for_range(heights, 0, MAX_DIFFERENCE)

❷ for low in range(1, MAX_HEIGHT + 1):
    result = cost_for_range(heights, low, low + MAX_DIFFERENCE)
    if result < min_cost:
        min_cost = result
```

```
output_file.write(str(min_cost) + '\n')

input_file.close()
output_file.close()
```

Listing 9-4: Main program

We start by reading the number of hills and then read each height into the heights list.

We use the min_cost variable to remember the minimum cost that we've discovered so far. We set min_cost to the cost for range 0–17 ❶. Then, in a range for loop ❷, we try every other range cost, updating min_cost every time we find a smaller cost. When we're done with this loop, we output the minimum cost that we found.

It's time to submit our code to the judge. Our complete-search solution should solve the problem well under the time limit.

In the next problem, we'll see an example where a straight complete-search solution is not efficient enough.

CONCEPT CHECK

Here's a proposed change to the code in Listing 9-4. Take this line:

```
for low in range(1, MAX_HEIGHT + 1):
```

And change it to the following:

```
for low in range(1, MAX_HEIGHT - MAX_DIFFERENCE + 1):
```

Is the code still correct?

A. Yes

B. No

Answer: A. The last range that the code now checks is 83–100, so we have to argue that the ranges we no longer check—84–101, 85–102, and so on—don't matter.

Consider the range 84–101. If we can argue that the range 83–100 is at least as good as 84–101, then we would have no reason to check range 84–101.

The range 84–101 includes height 101. But that's pointless: the highest hill has height 100, so height 101 may as well not even be there. We can remove 101 without making the range worse. If we remove it, we're left with the range 84–100. Aha—but 100–84 is only 16, and we're allowed to have a difference

---

of 17. So we can extend the range by one on the left, giving us a range of 83–100. Surely, making the range bigger like this can't make the range any worse. It might even make the range better, since it's now one unit closer to any hill whose height is 83 or less.

We started with range 84–101 and showed that range 83–100 is at least as good. We can make this same argument for range 85–102, 86–103, and so on. There's no point going any higher than 83–100!

Before continuing, you might like to try solving exercises 1 and 2 from "Chapter Exercises" on page 263.

Problem #23: Cow Baseball

To end this chapter, I've chosen a problem where we'll need to bump up our algorithm design skills beyond complete search. As you read the problem, notice that there's not all that much input. That generally signals the effectiveness of a complete-search algorithm. But not this time, because of the amount of searching that such an algorithm has to do through this input. The difficulty boils down to having too many nested loops. Why do the nested loops bite us here? What can we do about it? Read on!

This is USACO 2013 December Bronze Contest problem Cow Baseball.

The Challenge

Farmer John has n cows. They are standing in a row, each at a distinct integer position. They are having fun throwing a baseball around.

Farmer John is watching the antics. He observes that cow x throws the ball to some cow y to its right, and then that cow y throws the ball to some cow z to its right. He also knows that the distance of the second throw is at least the distance of the first throw and at most twice the distance of the first throw. (For example, if the first throw is distance 5, then the second throw is at least distance 5 and at most distance 10.)

Determine the number of (x, y, z) triples of cows that satisfy Farmer John's observations.

Input

Read input from the file named *baseball.in*.

The input consists of the following lines:

- A line containing n, the number of cows. n is between 3 and 1,000.

- n lines, each of which gives the position of a cow. All positions are unique, and each is between 1 and 100,000,000.

Output

Write output to the file named *baseball.out*.

Output the number of triples of cows that satisfy Farmer John's observations.

The time limit for solving each test case is four seconds.

Using Three Nested Loops

We can use three nested loops to consider all possible triples. We'll start by looking at the code and then discuss its efficiency.

The Code

In "Nesting" in Chapter 3, we learned that we can loop through all pairs of values using two nested loops. Doing so looks like this:

```
>>> lst = [1, 9]
>>> for num1 in lst:
...     for num2 in lst:
...         print(num1, num2)
...
1 1
1 9
9 1
9 9
```

We can similarly loop through all triples of values using three nested loops, like this:

```
>>> for num1 in lst:
...     for num2 in lst:
...         for num3 in lst:
...             print(num1, num2, num3)
...
1 1 1
1 1 9
1 9 1
1 9 9
9 1 1
9 1 9
9 9 1
9 9 9
```

Using three nested loops like this gives us a starting point for solving the Cow Baseball problem. For each triple, we can check whether it matches Farmer John's observations. See Listing 9-5 for the code.

```
input_file = open('baseball.in', 'r')
output_file = open('baseball.out', 'w')

n = int(input_file.readline())

positions = []

for i in range(n):
❶   positions.append(int(input_file.readline()))

total = 0

❷ for position1 in positions:
❸     for position2 in positions:
          first_two_diff = position2 - position1
❹       if first_two_diff > 0:
              low = position2 + first_two_diff
              high = position2 + first_two_diff * 2

❺           for position3 in positions:
                  if position3 >= low and position3 <= high:
                      total = total + 1

output_file.write(str(total) + '\n')

input_file.close()
output_file.close()
```

Listing 9-5: Using three nested for loops

We read all of the cow positions into the positions list ❶. We then loop
over all positions in the list using a for loop ❷. For each of these positions,
we loop through all positions in the list using a nested for loop ❸. At this
point, position1 and position2 refer to two positions from the list. We need a
third nested loop, yes, but not yet. We first need to calculate the difference
between position1 and position2 because that tells us the range of position3s
that we'll be looking for.

We require from the problem description that position2 be on the right
of position1. If it is ❹, then we calculate the low end and high end of the
range for position3 and store them using low and high, respectively. For example, if position1 is 1 and position2 is 6, then we'll calculate 6 + 5 = 11 for
low and 6 + 5 * 2 = 16 for high. Then we loop through the list with a third
nested for loop ❺, looking for positions that are between low and high. For
each such position3, we increase our total by 1.

Following the three nested loops, we have calculated the total number of
triples. We finish up by outputting that number to the output file.

Let's try our program on a small test case to make sure nothing weird is happening. Here it is:

```
7
16
14
23
18
1
6
11
```

The correct answer for this test case is 11. The 11 satisfying triples are as follows:

- 14, 16, 18
- 14, 18, 23
- 1, 6, 16
- 1, 6, 14
- 1, 6, 11
- 1, 11, 23
- 6, 14, 23
- 6, 11, 16
- 6, 11, 18
- 11, 16, 23
- 11, 14, 18

Good news: our program outputs 11 for this test case! It does so because it eventually finds each satisfying triple. For example, at some point, position1 will be 14, position2 will be 16, and position3 will be 18. That triple satisfies the distance requirements, so our program will count it in our total. Don't be worried about what will happen, later, when position1 is 18, position2 is 16, and position3 is 14. We definitely don't want to count that one, because these throws are not going to the right. We're fine, though: the if statement ❹ prevents these triples from being processed.

Our program is correct. But as you'll see if you submit it to the judge, it is not efficient enough. For this problem, and many competitive programming problems, the first few test cases are small—just a few cows, a few lifeguards, or a few ski hills. Our program should be able to solve those in time. The remaining test cases test our program closer and closer to the limit of acceptable input. Our program does not solve those in time. It's too slow.

Efficiency of Our Program

To understand why our program is so slow, it helps to think about the number of triples that it must go through. Think back to the test case we just studied, which had seven cows. How many triples will our program check? Well, for the first cow, there are seven choices: 16, 14, 23, and so on. There are also seven choices for the second cow, and seven choices for the third cow. Multiplying these together, we see that our program checks $7 * 7 * 7 = 343$ triples.

What if we had eight cows instead of seven? Then our program would check $8 * 8 * 8 = 512$ triples.

We can give an expression for the number of triples that works for any number of cows. Let's use n for the number of cows; it could be 7, 8, 50, 1,000, and so on, depending on the test case. Then we can say that the number of triples our program checks is $n * n * n$, or n^3.

We can substitute any number of cows for n to determine the number of triples that we check. For example, we can verify that the number of triples for seven cows is $7^3 = 343$ and that the number of triples for eight cows is $8^3 = 512$. These numbers—343 and 512—are tiny. It would take any computer no more than a few milliseconds to check those many triples. As a conservative guide, you can think of a Python program as being able to check or do about 5,000,000 things per second. The time limit for this problem is four seconds per test case, so we'll be able to check about 20,000,000 triples.

Let's substitute larger numbers for n and see what happens. For 50 cows, we have $50^3 = 125,000$ triples. No big deal: checking 125,000 things is easy for today's computers. For 100 cows, we have $100^3 = 1,000,000$ triples. Again, no problem. We can check a million things in less than a second. For 200 cows, we have $200^3 = 8,000,000$ triples. We're still OK for four seconds, but I hope you're starting to get a little worried. The number of triples is shooting up pretty quickly here, and we're only at 200 cows. Remember that we need to be able to support up to 1,000 cows.

For 400 cows, we have $400^3 = 64,000,000$ triples. That's too many for us to process in four seconds. To add insult to injury, let's try 1,000 cows, the maximum we'll ever get. For 1,000 cows, we have $1,000^3 = 1,000,000,000$ triples. That's one billion. Nope. There's no way we're ever going to be able to check that many triples in four seconds. We'll need to make our program more efficient.

Sorting First

Sorting is helpful here. Let's look at how to use sorting and then discuss the efficiency of our resulting solution.

The Code

Our cow positions can come in any order—there's certainly no guarantee from the problem description that they're sorted. Unfortunately, this leads our program to check many triples that have no chance of satisfying the requirements. For example, checking the triple 18, 16, 14 is pointless, because the numbers aren't in increasing order. If we sorted the cow positions at the outset, then we could avoid ever checking these out-of-order triples.

There's another benefit to sorting. Suppose that position1 refers to some cow position and position2 refers to another. For this pair of positions, we know the smallest value of position3 and largest value of position3 that we care about. We can use the fact that the positions are sorted to cut down on the number of values that we need to check for this range. Before continuing, think about why this is the case. How can we use the fact that the positions are sorted to look at fewer values?

When you're ready, see Listing 9-6 for our code that uses sorting.

```
input_file = open('baseball.in', 'r')
output_file = open('baseball.out', 'w')

n = int(input_file.readline())

positions = []

for i in range(n):
    positions.append(int(input_file.readline()))

❶ positions.sort()

total = 0

❷ for i in range(n):
❸     for j in range(i + 1, n):
            first_two_diff = positions[j] - positions[i]
            low = positions[j] + first_two_diff
            high = positions[j] + first_two_diff * 2

            left = j + 1
❹         while left < n and positions[left] < low:
                left = left + 1

            right = left
❺         while right < n and positions[right] <= high:
                right = right + 1

❻         total = total + right - left

output_file.write(str(total) + '\n')

input_file.close()
output_file.close()
```

Listing 9-6: Using sorting

Before we start looking for triples, we sort the positions ❶.

Our first loop goes through all positions using the loop variable i ❷. It's a range for loop this time, not a for loop, so that we can keep track of which index we're at. That's useful because we can use the value of i + 1 as the starting index for our second loop ❸. The second loop will now never waste time looking at positions that are to the left of the first position.

We next calculate the low and high ends of the range of values for our third position.

Rather than increase total by 1 each time we find a suitable third position, we can instead find the left and right borders of suitable positions and then increase total in one shot. We can only do it this way because the list of positions is sorted. We find each of the borders using a while loop. The first while loop finds the left border ❹. It keeps going as long as the positions are less than low. When it's done, left will be the leftmost index whose position is greater than or equal to low. The second while loop finds the right border ❺. It keeps going as long as the positions are less than or equal to high. When it's done, right is the rightmost index whose position is greater than high. Each of the positions from left up to but not including right can serve as the third position in a triple involving the positions at indices i and j. We add right - left to total to account for these positions ❻.

The two while loops in this program are quite tricky. Let's make sure we know exactly what they're doing by working through an example. We'll use the following list of positions; they're the same as those we used in the previous section, but sorted:

```
[1, 6, 11, 14, 16, 18, 23]
```

Suppose that i is 1 and j is 2 so that the two positions in prospective triples are 6 and 11. For the third position, we're therefore looking for positions greater than or equal to 16 and less than or equal to 21. The first while loop will set left to 4, the leftmost index whose position is greater than or equal to 16. The second while loop will set right to 6, the leftmost index whose position is greater than 21. Subtracting left from right, we obtain 6 − 4 = 2, which means that there are two triples involving positions 6 and 11. Before continuing, I encourage you to convince yourself that these while loops work just fine in "special" cases, such as when there are no suitable third positions or when there is one suitable third position.

We've made strong progress in this section. Our code here is certainly more efficient than the code we gave in Listing 9-5. However, it still isn't efficient enough. If you submit to the judge, you'll see that it doesn't get much further than we got last time. It still times out on most of the test cases.

Efficiency of Our Program

The problem with our program is that finding the third position can still take a long time. Those while loops still have some inefficiency. I can demonstrate this with a new list of positions, namely, the positions from 1 to 32.

```
[1, 2, 3, 4, 5, 6, 7, 8, 9, 10, 11, 12, 13, 14, 15, 16,
 17, 18, 19, 20, 21, 22, 23, 24, 25, 26, 27, 28, 29, 30, 31, 32]
```

Let's focus on when i is 0 and j is 7; these are the positions 1 and 8. For the third position, we're looking for positions that are greater than or equal to 15 and less than or equal to 22. To find the 15, the first while loop scans to the right, one position at a time. It scans the 9, then the 10, then the 11, then the 12, then the 13, then the 14, and finally the 15. Then the second while loop takes over, doing a similarly large amount of scanning, one position at a time, all the way until it finds the 23.

Each while loop implements what's known as a *linear search*. A linear search is a technique that searches through a collection one value at a time. It's a lot of work, scanning through all those values! And there are many other values of i and j that lead to a similar amount of work. For example, try tracing what happens when i is 0 and j is 8, or when i is 1 and j is 11.

How can we improve on this? How can we avoid scanning through a huge chunk of the list, looking for the appropriate left and right indices?

Suppose I give you a book with a thousand sorted integers, one integer per line. I ask you to find me the first integer that's greater or equal to 300. Are you going to look through the numbers one by one? Are you going to look at the 1, then the 3, then the 4, then the 7? Still a long way to go—will you look at the 8, then the 12, then the 17? Probably not! It'd be much faster if you just flipped to the middle of the book. Maybe you find number 450 there. Since 450 is greater than 300, now you know that the number is in the first half of the book. It can't be in the second half, because those numbers are even bigger than 450. You've reduced your work by half by checking only one number! You can now repeat this process on the first half of the book, flipping halfway between the beginning and middle of the book. You might find the number 200 there. Now you know that the 300 is on a later page, somewhere in the second quarter of the book. You can repeat this process until you find 300—and it won't take long at all. This technique—repeatedly dividing the problem in half—is known as *binary search*. It's shockingly fast. It blows away the linear search technique of searching one by one. Python has a binary search function that will put the finishing touches on Cow Baseball. That function, though, is inside of something called a *module*; we'll need to discuss them first.

Python Modules

A *module* is a self-contained collection of Python code. A module generally contains several functions that we can call.

Python comes with a variety of modules that we can use to add functionality to our programs. There are modules for working with random numbers, dates and times, statistics, emails, web pages, audio files, and much more. It would take a separate book to cover them all! There are even modules that you can download should Python not come with the module that you need.

I'll focus in this section on one module—the random module. We'll use it to learn what we need to know about modules. Then we'll be all set for the binary search module in the next section.

Have you ever wondered how people make computer games where things happen at random? Maybe it's a game where you draw cards, where you roll dice, or where enemies spawn unpredictably. The key is the use of random numbers. Python gives us access to random-number generation through its random module.

Before we can use what's in a module, we must *import* it. One way to do this is to import the entire module using the import keyword, like this:

```
>>> import random
```

What's in there? To find out, you can use dir(random):

```
>>> dir(random)
[stuff to ignore
'betavariate', 'choice', 'choices', 'expovariate',
'gammavariate', 'gauss', 'getrandbits', 'getstate',
'lognormvariate', 'normalvariate', 'paretovariate',
'randint', 'random', 'randrange', 'sample', 'seed',
'setstate', 'shuffle', 'triangular', 'uniform',
'vonmisesvariate', 'weibullvariate']
```

One function that's offered by the random module is randint. We pass it the low and high ends of a range, and Python gives us a random integer in the range (including both endpoints).

We can't just call it like a regular function, though. If we try, we get an error:

```
>>> randint(2, 10)
Traceback (most recent call last):
  File "<stdin>", line 1, in <module>
NameError: name 'randint' is not defined
```

We need to tell Python that the randint function is housed in the random module. To do that, we prefix randint with the name of the module and a dot, like this:

```
>>> random.randint(2, 10)
7
>>> random.randint(2, 10)
10
>>> random.randint(2, 10)
6
```

To get help on the randint function, you can type help(random.randint):

```
>>> help(random.randint)
Help on method randint in module random:

randint(a, b) method of random.Random instance
    Return random integer in range [a, b], including both end points.
```

Another useful function in the `random` module is `choice`. We pass it a sequence, and it returns one of its values at random:

```
>>> random.choice(['win', 'lose'])
'lose'
>>> random.choice(['win', 'lose'])
'lose'
>>> random.choice(['win', 'lose'])
'win'
```

If we frequently use a small number of functions from a module, it can be tedious to type the module name and a dot each time. There's another way to import these functions that lets us call them like any other nonmodule function. Here's how we can import only the `randint` function:

```
>>> from random import randint
```

Now we can call `randint` without the `random.` in front:

```
>>> randint(2, 10)
10
```

If we need `randint` and `choice`, we can import them both:

```
>>> from random import randint, choice
```

We won't do so in this book, but we can create our own modules containing whatever functions we like. For example, if we designed a few Python functions related to playing a game, we could place them all in a file named *game_functions.py*. We could then import that module using `import game _functions` and then access the functions within.

The Python programs we've written in this book are not designed to be imported as modules. The reason is that they all read input as soon as they start running. A module shouldn't do that. Rather, a module should wait for its functions to be called before it does anything. The `random` module is an example of a well-behaved module: it only starts giving us random things when we ask for them.

The bisect Module

Now we're ready to play around with binary search. In Listing 9-6, we had two `while` loops. They're slow, so we want to get rid of them. To do that, we're going to replace each one with a call to a binary search function: `bisect_left` for the first `while` loop and `bisect_right` for the second.

Both of these functions are in the `bisect` module. Let's import them:

```
>>> from bisect import bisect_left, bisect_right
```

Let's first discuss `bisect_left`. We call it by providing a list sorted from smallest to largest and a value x. It returns to us the index of the leftmost value in the list that's greater than or equal to x.

If the value is in the list, we get the index of its leftmost occurrence:

```
>>> bisect_left([10, 50, 80, 80, 100], 10)
0
>>> bisect_left([10, 50, 80, 80, 100], 80)
2
```

If the value isn't in the list, then we get the index of the first value that's greater:

```
>>> bisect_left([10, 50, 80, 80, 100], 15)
1
>>> bisect_left([10, 50, 80, 80, 100], 81)
4
```

If we search for something that's greater than every value in the list, we get the list's length:

```
>>> bisect_left([10, 50, 80, 80, 100], 986)
5
```

Let's use `bisect_left` on our list of seven positions from "Sorting First" earlier in this chapter. We'll find the index of the leftmost position that's greater than or equal to 16:

```
>>> positions = [1, 6, 11, 14, 16, 18, 23]
>>> bisect_left(positions, 16)
4
```

Perfect: that's exactly what we need to replace the first `while` loop in Listing 9-6.

To replace the second `while` loop, we'll use `bisect_right` rather than `bisect_left`. We call `bisect_right` just as we called `bisect_left` : with a sorted list and a value x. Rather than returning the index of the leftmost value in the list that's *greater than or equal to* x, it returns the index of the leftmost value that's *greater than* x.

Let's compare `bisect_left` and `bisect_right`. For a value that's in the list, `bisect_right` returns an index greater than that returned by `bisect_left`:

```
>>> bisect_left([10, 50, 80, 80, 100], 10)
0
>>> bisect_right([10, 50, 80, 80, 100], 10)
1
>>> bisect_left([10, 50, 80, 80, 100], 80)
2
```

```
>>> bisect_right([10, 50, 80, 80, 100], 80)
4
```

For a value that isn't in the list, bisect_left and bisect_right return the same index:

```
>>> bisect_left([10, 50, 80, 80, 100], 15)
1
>>> bisect_right([10, 50, 80, 80, 100], 15)
1
>>> bisect_left([10, 50, 80, 80, 100], 81)
4
>>> bisect_right([10, 50, 80, 80, 100], 81)
4
>>> bisect_left([10, 50, 80, 80, 100], 986)
5
>>> bisect_right([10, 50, 80, 80, 100], 986)
5
```

Let's use bisect_right on our list of seven positions from "Sorting First" earlier in this chapter. We'll find the index of the leftmost position that's greater than 21:

```
>>> positions = [1, 6, 11, 14, 16, 18, 23]
>>> bisect_right(positions, 21)
6
```

There we go: that's what we can use to replace the second while loop in Listing 9-6.

The stunning speed of binary search is hard to appreciate using these tiny examples. Time to get real. We'll search one million times for the right-most value in a list of length 1000000. Don't look away when you run this code. You might miss it.

```
>>> lst = list(range(1, 1000001))
>>> for i in range(1000000):
...     where = bisect_left(lst, 1000000)
...
```

On my computer, that takes about a second. You might be wondering what would happen if you replaced the binary search with a call to the list index method. If you try it, you'll literally wait hours for the code to run. That's because index, like the in operator, does a linear search through the list. (See "Efficiency of Searching a List" in Chapter 8 for more on this.) It has no guarantee that the list is sorted, so it can't perform a blazing-fast binary search. It has to go through the values one by one, comparing each of them to the value we're searching for. If you have a sorted list and you want to find values in it, binary search is unstoppable.

Solving the Problem

We're ready to solve Cow Baseball using binary search. See Listing 9-7 for the code.

```
❶ from bisect import bisect_left, bisect_right


  input_file = open('baseball.in', 'r')
  output_file = open('baseball.out', 'w')

  n = int(input_file.readline())

  positions = []

  for i in range(n):
      positions.append(int(input_file.readline()))

  positions.sort()

  total = 0

  for i in range(n):
      for j in range(i + 1, n):
          first_two_diff = positions[j] - positions[i]
          low = positions[j] + first_two_diff
          high = positions[j] + first_two_diff * 2
❷         left = bisect_left(positions, low)
❸         right = bisect_right(positions, high)
          total = total + right - left

  output_file.write(str(total) + '\n')

  input_file.close()
  output_file.close()
```

Listing 9-7: Using binary search

To begin, we import the bisect_left and bisect_right functions from the bisect module so that we can call them ❶. The only other difference compared to Listing 9-6 is that we now use bisect_left ❷ and bisect_right ❸ instead of the while loops.

If you submit our code to the judge now, you should pass all test cases within the time limit.

The arc that we followed in this section is typical of that required to solve hard problems. We might start with a complete-search solution that is correct but, alas, is also too slow, not meeting the judge's time limits. We then make improvements, leading us away from complete search and toward a more refined approach.

Suppose we start with Listing 9-7 and use `bisect_left` in place of `bisect_right`. That is, we take this line:

```
right = bisect_right(positions, high)
```

And we change it to the following:

```
right = bisect_left(positions, high)
```

Does the program still produce the correct answers?

A. It always produces the correct answer, just as before.

B. It sometimes produces the correct answer; it depends on the test case.

C. It never produces the correct answer.

Answer: B. There are test cases for which the modified code does produce the correct answer. Here's one:

```
3
2
4
9
```

The correct answer is 0, and that's what our program produces.

Be careful, though, because there are other test cases for which the modified code produces the wrong answer. Here's one:

```
3
2
4
8
```

The correct answer is 1, but our program produces 0. When i is 0 and j is 1, the program is supposed to set `left` to 2 and set `right` to 3. Unfortunately, using `bisect_left` causes `right` to be set to 2, because the position at index 2 is the leftmost position that's greater than or equal to 8.

Given this counterexample, you might be surprised to know that there *is* a way to use `bisect_left` rather than `bisect_right`. To do it, we need to alter what we search for in the call to `bisect_left`. If you're curious, give it a try!

Summary

In this chapter, we learned about complete-search algorithms, algorithms that search through all options to find the best one. To determine the lifeguard that we should fire, we try firing each lifeguard and choose the best one. To determine the minimum cost to fix ski hills, we try all valid ranges and choose the best one. To determine the number of relevant triples of cows, we check each triple and add the ones that meet the requirements.

Sometimes, complete-search algorithms are efficient enough as they are. We solved the Lifeguards and Ski Hills problems with unadorned complete-search code. Other times, however, we'll need to make our complete-search algorithm more efficient. We did that when solving Cow Baseball by replacing complete-search `while` loops by much faster binary searches.

How do programmers and computer scientists discuss efficiency? How do you know whether an algorithm is going to be efficient enough? And can you avoid implementing algorithms that are simply too slow? Chapter 10 awaits.

Chapter Exercises

Here are some exercises for you to try. For each, use complete search. If your solution is not efficient enough, think about how you can make it more efficient while still producing the right answer.

For each exercise, double-check the judge that the problem comes from: some are on the DMOJ judge, while others are on the USACO judge.

1. USACO 2019 January Bronze Contest problem Shell Game
2. USACO 2016 US Open Bronze Contest problem Diamond Collector
3. DMOJ problem `coci20c1p1`, Patkice
4. DMOJ problem `ccc09j2`, Old Fishin' Hole
5. DMOJ problem `eco016r1p2`, Spindie
6. DMOJ problem `cco96p2`, SafeBreaker
7. USACO 2019 December Bronze Contest problem Where Am I
8. USACO 2016 January Bronze Contest problem Angry Cows
9. USACO 2016 December Silver Contest problem Counting Haybales
10. DMOJ problem `crci06p3`, Firefly

Notes

Lifeguards is originally from the USACO 2018 January Bronze Contest. Ski Hills is originally from the USACO 2014 January Bronze Contest. Cow Baseball is originally from the USACO 2013 December Bronze Contest.

There are other types of algorithms beyond complete search, such as *greedy algorithms* and *dynamic-programming algorithms*. If a problem cannot be solved by complete search, then it's worth thinking through whether it can be solved using one of these other types.

If you're interested in learning more about these and other algorithms topics using Python, I recommend *Python Algorithms*, 2nd edition by Magnus Lie Hetland (Apress, 2014).

I've also written a book about algorithm design: *Algorithmic Thinking: A Problem-Based Introduction* (No Starch Press, 2021). It follows the same problem-based format as this book; as a result, its style and pacing will be familiar to you. However, it uses the C programming language, not the Python programming language, so to make the most of it, you'll want to learn some C beforehand.

In this chapter, we called preexisting Python functions to perform binary searches. If we like, we can write our own binary-search code instead of relying on those functions. The idea of dividing a list in half until we find the value that we want is intuitive, but the code to implement this is surprisingly tricky. Equally surprising is the vast range of problems that can be solved using variations of binary search. My book mentioned earlier, *Algorithmic Thinking*, contains an entire chapter on binary search and what it can do.

10

BIG O AND PROGRAM EFFICIENCY

In the first seven chapters of this book, we focused on writing programs that were correct: for any valid input, we wanted our program to produce the desired output. In addition to correct code, though, we generally want efficient code, code that runs quickly even in the face of huge amounts of input. You may have received the occasional time limit exceeded error when working through the first seven chapters, but our first formal foray into program efficiency wasn't until Chapter 8, when we solved Email Addresses. We saw there that sometimes we need to make our programs more efficient so that they can finish within a given time limit.

In this chapter, we'll first learn how programmers think and communicate about program efficiency. Then, we'll study two problems where we'll need to write efficient code: determining the most desired piece of a scarf and painting a ribbon.

For each problem, we'll see that our initial ideas lead to an algorithm that would not be efficient enough. But we'll keep at it until we design a faster algorithm for the same problem, one that's dramatically more efficient than before. This exemplifies a common workflow for programmers: first, come up with a correct algorithm; then, only if needed, make it faster.

The Problem with Timing

Each competitive programming problem that we solve in this book has a time limit on how long our program will be allowed to run. (I began including time limits in the problem descriptions of Chapter 8, when we started running into programming problems where efficiency is a serious concern.) If our program exceeds the time limit, then the judge terminates our program with a time limit exceeded error. A time limit is designed to prevent solutions that are too slow from passing the test cases. For example, perhaps we come up with a complete-search solution but the author of the problem has worked out a solution that's much faster. That faster solution may be a variation of complete search, as it was when we solved the Cow Baseball problem in Chapter 9, or it may be a different approach entirely. Regardless, the time limit may be set such that our complete-search solution will not finish in time. As such, in addition to being correct, we may need our programs to be fast.

We can run a program to explore whether it is efficient enough. For example, think back to "Efficiency of Searching a List" in Chapter 8 when we tried to solve Email Addresses using a list. We ran code that used bigger and bigger lists to get a sense of the amount of time taken by list operations. This kind of testing can give us some understanding of the efficiency of our programs. If our program is too slow, according to the time limit for the problem, then we know that we need to optimize the current code or find a wholly new approach.

The amount of time taken by a program depends on the computer it is being run on. We don't know what kind of computer the judge is using, but running the program on our own computer is still informative because the judge is probably using a computer that's at least as fast as ours. Say that we run our program on our laptop and it takes 30 seconds on some small test case. If the problem time limit is three seconds, we can be confident that our program is simply not fast enough.

An exclusive focus on time limits, however, is limiting. Think about our first solution to Cow Baseball in Chapter 9. We didn't need to run that code to determine how slow it would be. That's because we were able to characterize the program in terms of the amount of work that it would do if we did run it. For example, in "Efficiency of Our Program" on page 253, we said that for n cows, our program processes n^3 triples of cows. Notice that our focus here is not on the number of seconds our program would take to run, but on how much work it does in terms of the amount of input n.

There are significant advantages to this kind of analysis compared to running our programs and recording execution times. Here are five:

Execution time depends on the computer Timing our program
tells us only how long our program takes on one computer. That's very

specific information, and it gives us little in the way of understanding what to expect when the program is run on other computers. When working through the book, you may have also noticed that the time taken by a program varies from run to run, even on the same computer. For example, you might run a program on a test case and find that it takes three seconds; you might then run it again, on the same test case, and find that it takes two-and-a-half seconds or three-and-a-half seconds. The reason for this difference is that your operating system is managing your computing resources, shunting them around to different tasks as needed. The decisions that your operating system makes influence the runtime of your program.

Execution time depends on the test case   Timing our program on a test case tells us only how long our program takes on that test case. Suppose that our program takes three seconds to run on a small test case. That may seem fast, but here's the truth about small test cases: every reasonable solution for a problem will quickly be able to solve those. If I ask you to tell me the number of unique email addresses among 10 email addresses, or the number of triples of cows among 10 cows, you can quickly do it with the first correct idea that you have. What's interesting, then, are large test cases. They are the ones where algorithmic ingenuity pays off. How long will our program take on a large test case or on a huge test case? We don't know. We'd have to run our program on those test cases, too. Even if we did that, there could be specific kinds of test cases that trigger poorer performance. We may be led to believe that our program is faster than it is.

The program requires implementation   We can't time something that we don't implement. Suppose that we're thinking about a problem and come up with an idea for how to solve it. Is it fast? Although we could implement it to find out, it would be nice to know, in advance, whether or not the idea is likely to lead to a fast program. You would not implement a program that you knew, at the outset, would be incorrect. It would similarly be nice to know, at the outset, that a program would be too slow.

Timing doesn't explain slowness   If we find that our program is too slow, then our next task is to design a faster one. However, simply timing a program gives us no insight into why our program is slow. It just is. Further, if we manage to think up a possible improvement to our program, we'd need to implement it to see whether or not it helps.

Execution time is not easily communicated   For many of the reasons listed, it's difficult to use execution time to talk to other people about the efficiency of algorithms. Execution time is too specific: it depends on the computer, operating system, test case, programming language, and particular implementation that's used. We'd have to provide all of this information to others interested in the efficiency of our algorithm.

Not to worry: computer scientists have devised a notation that addresses these shortcomings of timing. It's independent of the computer, independent of test case, and independent of a particular implementation. It signals why a slow program is slow. It's easily communicated. It's called *big O*, and it's coming right up.

Big O

Big O is a notation that computer scientists use to concisely describe the efficiency of algorithms. The key concept here is the *efficiency class*, which tells you how fast an algorithm is or, equivalently, how much work it does. The faster an algorithm, the less work it does; the slower an algorithm, the more work it does. Each algorithm belongs to an efficiency class; the efficiency class tells you how much work that algorithm does relative to the amount of input that it must process. To understand big O, we need to understand these efficiency classes. We're now going to study seven of the most common ones. We'll see those that do the least amount of work, the ones you'll hope your algorithms fit into. We'll also see those that do considerably more work, the ones whose algorithms will probably give you time limit exceeded errors.

Constant Time

The most desirable algorithms are those that don't do more work as the amount of input increases. No matter the problem instance, such an algorithm takes about the same number of steps. These are called *constant-time* algorithms.

This is hard to believe, right? An algorithm that does about the same amount of work, no matter what? Indeed, solving a problem with such an algorithm is rare. But when you can do it, rejoice: you can't do any better than that.

We've managed to solve a few problems in this book using constant-time algorithms. Think back to the Telemarketers problem in Chapter 2, where we had to determine whether the provided phone number belongs to a telemarketer. I've reproduced our solution from Listing 2-2 here:

```
num1 = int(input())
num2 = int(input())
num3 = int(input())
num4 = int(input())

if ((num1 == 8 or num1 == 9) and
        (num4 == 8 or num4 == 9) and
        (num2 == num3)):
    print('ignore')
else:
    print('answer')
```

Our solution does the same amount of work no matter what the four digits of the phone number are. The code starts by reading the input. Then it makes some comparisons with num1, num2, num3, and num4. If the phone number belongs to a telemarketer, we output something; if it doesn't belong to a telemarketer, we output something else. There's no input that can make our program do more work than this.

Earlier in Chapter 2, we solved Winning Team. Did we solve that one in constant time, too? We did! Here's the solution from Listing 2-1:

```
apple_three = int(input())
apple_two = int(input())
apple_one = int(input())

banana_three = int(input())
banana_two = int(input())
banana_one = int(input())

apple_total = apple_three * 3 + apple_two * 2 + apple_one
banana_total = banana_three * 3 + banana_two * 2 + banana_one

if apple_total > banana_total:
    print('A')
elif banana_total > apple_total:
    print('B')
else:
    print('T')
```

We read the input, compute the total points for the Apples, compute the total points for the Bananas, compare those totals, and output a message. It doesn't matter how many points the Apples or Bananas have—our program always does the same amount of work.

Hold on—what if the Apples scored zillions and zillions of three-point shots? Surely, it takes longer for the computer to work with ginormous numbers than small numbers like 10 or 50? While that's true, we don't have to worry about that here. The problem description states that each team scores at most 100 of each type of play. We're therefore working with small numbers, and it's fair to say that the computer can read or operate on these numbers in a constant number of steps. In general, you can think of numbers up to a few billion as "small."

In big O notation, we say that a constant-time algorithm is $O(1)$. The 1 doesn't mean that you're stuck performing only one step in a constant-time algorithm. If you perform a fixed number of steps, like 10 or even 10,000, it's still constant time. But don't write $O(10)$ or $O(10000)$—all constant-time algorithms are denoted $O(1)$.

Linear Time

Most algorithms are not constant-time algorithms. Instead, they do an amount of work that depends on the amount of input. For example, they do more work to process 1,000 values than they do to process 10 values. What distinguishes these algorithms from each other is the relationship between the amount of input and the amount of work that the algorithm does.

A *linear-time* algorithm is one with a linear relationship between the amount of input and the amount of work done. Suppose we run a linear-time algorithm on an input with 50 values, and then we run it again on an input with 100 values. The algorithm will do about twice as much work on the 100 values compared with on the 50 values.

For an example, let's look at the Three Cups problem from Chapter 3. We solved that problem in Listing 3-1, and I've reproduced our solution here:

```
swaps = input()

ball_location = 1

❶ for swap_type in swaps:
    if swap_type == 'A' and ball_location == 1:
        ball_location = 2
    elif swap_type == 'A' and ball_location == 2:
        ball_location = 1
    elif swap_type == 'B' and ball_location == 2:
        ball_location = 3
    elif swap_type == 'B' and ball_location == 3:
        ball_location = 2
    elif swap_type == 'C' and ball_location == 1:
        ball_location = 3
    elif swap_type == 'C' and ball_location == 3:
        ball_location = 1

print(ball_location)
```

There's a for loop ❶, and the amount of work that it does depends linearly on the amount of input. If there are five swaps to process, then the loop iterates five times. If there are 10 swaps to process, then the loop iterates 10 times. Each iteration of the loop performs a constant number of comparisons and may change what ball_location refers to. Therefore, the amount of work that this algorithm does is directly proportional to the number of swaps.

We typically use n to refer to the amount of input provided to a problem. Here, n is the number of swaps. If there are 5 swaps that we need to perform, then n is 5; if there are 10 swaps that we need to perform, then n is 10.

If there are n swaps, then our program does about n work. That's because the for loop performs n iterations, each of which performs a constant number of steps. We don't care how many steps it performs on each iteration, as long as it's a constant number. Whether the algorithm performs a total of n steps or $10n$ steps or $10,000n$ steps, it's a linear-time algorithm. In big O notation, we say that this algorithm is $O(n)$.

When using big O notation, we don't include numbers in front of n. For example, an algorithm that takes $10n$ steps is written $O(n)$, not $O(10n)$. This helps us focus on the fact that the algorithm is linear time and away from the specifics of the linear relationship.

What if an algorithm takes $2n + 8$ steps—what kind of algorithm is this? This is still linear time! The reason is that the linear term ($2n$) will come to dominate the constant term (8) as soon as n is big enough. For example, if n is 5,000, then $8n$ is 40,000. The number 8 is so small compared to 40,000 that we may as well ignore it. In big O notation, we ignore everything except the dominant terms.

Many Python operations take constant time to do their work. For example, appending to a list, adding to a dictionary, or indexing a sequence or dictionary all take constant time.

But some Python operations take linear time to do their work. Be careful to count them as linear time and not constant time. For example, using the Python input function to read a long string takes linear time, because Python has to read each character on the line of input. Any operation that examines each character of a string or value in a list takes linear time as well.

If an algorithm reads n values and processes each value in a constant number of steps, then it is a linear-time algorithm .

We don't need to go far to see another linear-time algorithm—our solution to Occupied Spaces in Chapter 3 is another such example. I've reproduced our solution from Listing 3-3 here:

```python
n = int(input())
yesterday = input()
today = input()

occupied = 0

for i in range(len(yesterday)):
    if yesterday[i] == 'C' and today[i] == 'C':
        occupied = occupied + 1

print(occupied)
```

We let n be the number of parking spaces. The pattern is the same as for Three Cups: we read the input and then perform a constant number of steps for each parking space.

CONCEPT CHECK

In Listing 1-1, we solved the Word Count problem. Here's the code for that solution.

(continued)

```
line = input()
total_words = line.count(' ') + 1
print(total_words)
```

What is the big O efficiency of our algorithm?

A. O(1)

B. O(n)

Answer: B. It's tempting to think that this algorithm is O(1). After all, there's no loop anywhere, and it looks like the algorithm is performing just three steps: read the input, call count to count the number of words, and output the number of words.

But this algorithm is O(n), where n is the number of characters in the input. It takes linear time for the input function to read the input, because it has to read the input character by character. Using the count method also takes linear time, because it has to process each character of the string to find matches. So this algorithm performs a linear amount of work to read the input and a linear amount of work to count the words. That's a linear amount of work overall.

CONCEPT CHECK

In Listing 1-2, we solved the Cone Volume problem. I've reproduced that solution here:

```
PI = 3.141592653589793

radius = int(input())
height = int(input())

volume = (PI * radius ** 2 * height) / 3

print(volume)
```

What is the big O efficiency of our algorithm? (Recall that the maximum value for the radius and height is 100.)

A. O(1)

B. O(n)

Answer: A. We're dealing with small numbers here, so reading them from the input takes constant time. Calculating the volume takes constant time, too: it's just a few mathematical operations. All we're doing here, then, is a few constant-time steps. That's a constant amount of work overall.

CONCEPT CHECK

In Listing 3-4, we solved the Data Plan problem. I've reproduced that solution here:

```python
monthly_mb = int(input())
n = int(input())

excess = 0

for i in range(n):
    used = int(input())
    excess = excess + monthly_mb - used

print(excess + monthly_mb)
```

What is the big O efficiency of our algorithm?

A. $O(1)$
B. $O(n)$

Answer: B. The pattern for this algorithm is similar to that of our solution to Three Cups or Occupied Spaces, except that it interleaves reading the input with processing it. We let n be the number of monthly megabyte values. The program performs a constant number of steps for each of these n input values. This is therefore an $O(n)$ algorithm.

Quadratic Time

So far we've discussed constant-time algorithms (those that don't do more work as the amount of input increases) and linear-time algorithms (those that do more work linearly as the amount of input increases). Like a linear-time algorithm, a *quadratic-time* algorithm does more work as the amount of input increases; for example, it does more work to process 1,000 values than 10 values. Whereas we can get away with using a linear-time algorithm on relatively large amounts of input, we'll be restricted to much smaller amounts of input on quadratic-time algorithms. We'll see why next.

Typical Form

A typical linear-time algorithm looks like this:

```
for i in range(n):
    <process input i in a constant number of steps>
```

In contrast, a typical quadratic-time algorithm looks like this:

```
for i in range(n):
    for j in range(n):
        <process inputs i and j in a constant number of steps>
```

For an input of n values, how many values does each algorithm process? The linear-time algorithm processes n values, one on each iteration of the for loop. The quadratic-time algorithm, in contrast, processes n values *on each iteration* of the outer for loop.

On the first iteration of the outer for loop, n values are processed (one on each iteration of the inner for loop); on the second iteration of the outer for loop, n more values are processed (one on each iteration of the inner for loop); and so on. As the outer for loop iterates n times, the total number of values that are processed is $n * n$, or n^2. Two nested loops, each of which depends on n, gives rise to a quadratic-time algorithm. In big O notation, we say that a quadratic-time algorithm is $O(n^2)$.

Let's compare the amount of work done by linear-time and quadratic-time algorithms. Suppose that we're processing an input of 1,000 values, meaning that n is 1,000. A linear-time algorithm that takes n steps would take 1,000 steps. A quadratic-time algorithm that takes n^2 steps would take $1,000^2 = 1,000,000$ steps. A million is way more than a thousand. But who cares: computers are really, really fast, right? Well, yes, and for an input of 1,000 values, we're probably okay if we use a quadratic-time algorithm. In "Efficiency of Our Program" on page 253, I gave a conservative rule claiming that we can perform about five million steps per second. A million steps, then, should be doable in all but the strictest time limits.

But any optimism for a quadratic-time algorithm is short-lived. Watch what happens if we crank the number of input values up from 1,000 to 10,000. The linear-time algorithm takes only 10,000 steps. The quadratic-algorithm takes $10,000^2 = 100,000,000$ steps. Hmmm ... if we're using a quadratic-time algorithm, now our computer isn't looking so fast. While the linear-time algorithm still runs in milliseconds, the quadratic-time algorithm will take at least a few seconds. Time limit exceeded there, no question.

CONCEPT CHECK

What is the big O efficiency of the following algorithm?

```
for i in range(10):
    for j in range(n):
        <process inputs i and j in a constant number of steps>
```

A. $O(1)$

B. $O(n)$

C. $O(n^2)$

Answer: B. There are two nested loops here, so your first instinct might be to claim that this is a quadratic-time algorithm. Be careful, though, because the outer for loop iterates only 10 times, independent of the value of n. The total number of steps in this algorithm, therefore, is $10n$. There's no n^2 here; $10n$ is linear, just like n. So, this is a linear-time algorithm, not a quadratic-time algorithm. We'd write its efficiency as $O(n)$.

CONCEPT CHECK

What is the big O efficiency of the following algorithm?

```
for i in range(n):
    <process input i in a constant number of steps>
for j in range(n):
    <process input j in a constant number of steps>
```

A. $O(1)$

B. $O(n)$

C. $O(n^2)$

Answer: B. We have two loops here, and they both depend on n. Isn't this quadratic time, then?

No! These two loops are sequential, not nested. The first loop takes n steps, and the second also takes n steps, for a total of $2n$ steps. This is therefore a linear-time algorithm.

Alternate Form

When you see two nested loops where each depends on n, it's a good bet that you're looking at a quadratic-time algorithm. But it's possible for a quadratic-time algorithm to arise even in the absence of such nested loops. We can find such an example in our first solution to the Email Addresses problem, Listing 8-2. I've reproduced that solution here:

```
# clean function not shown

for dataset in range(10):
    n = int(input())
    addresses = []
    for i in range(n):
        address = input()
❶       address = clean(address)
❷       if not address in addresses:
            addresses.append(address)

    print(len(addresses))
```

We'll let n be the maximum number of email addresses that we see in our 10 test cases. The outer for loop iterates 10 times; the inner for loop iterates at most n times. We're therefore processing at most $10n$ email addresses, which is linear in n.

Cleaning an email address ❶ takes a constant number of steps, so we don't need to worry about that. But this is still *not* a linear-time algorithm, because each iteration of the inner for loop takes more than a constant number of steps. Specifically, checking whether an email address is already in our list ❷ takes work proportional to the number of email addresses already in the list, because Python has to search through the list. That's a linear-time operation on its own! So we're processing $10n$ email addresses, each of which requires n work, for a total of $10n^2$, or quadratic-time, work. This quadratic-time performance is precisely why we received a time limit exceeded error with this code, leading us to use a set rather than a list.

Cubic Time

If one loop can lead to linear time, and two nested loops can lead to quadratic time, then what about three nested loops? Three nested loops, each of which depends on n, leads to a *cubic-time* algorithm. In big O notation, we say that a cubic-time algorithm is $O(n^3)$.

If you thought quadratic-time algorithms were slow, wait till you see how slow cubic-time algorithms are. Suppose that n is 1,000. We already know that a linear-time algorithm will take about 1,000 steps and that a quadratic-time algorithm will take about $1,000^2 = 1,000,000$ steps. A cubic-time algorithm will take $1,000^3 = 1,000,000,000$ steps. A billion steps! But it gets worse. For example, if n is 10,000, which is still a small amount of input, then a cubic-time algorithm will take 1,000,000,000,000 (that's one trillion) steps. One trillion steps would take many minutes of computing time. No joke: a cubic-time algorithm is almost never good enough.

It certainly wasn't good enough when we tried to use a cubic-time algorithm to solve Cow Baseball in Listing 9-5. I've reproduced that solution here:

```
input_file = open('baseball.in', 'r')
output_file = open('baseball.out', 'w')

n = int(input_file.readline())

positions = []

for i in range(n):
    positions.append(int(input_file.readline()))

total = 0

❶ for position1 in positions:
  ❷ for position2 in positions:
        first_two_diff = position2 - position1
        if first_two_diff > 0:
            low = position2 + first_two_diff
            high = position2 + first_two_diff * 2

          ❸ for position3 in positions:
                if position3 >= low and position3 <= high:
                    total = total + 1

output_file.write(str(total) + '\n')

input_file.close()
output_file.close()
```

You'll see the telltale of cubic time in this code: three nested loops ❶ ❷ ❸, each of which depends on the amount of input. As you'll recall, the time limit for that problem was four seconds, and we could have up to 1,000 cows. A cubic-time algorithm, processing a billion triples, is way too slow.

Multiple Variables

In Chapter 5, we solved the Baker Bonus problem. I've reproduced our solution from Listing 5-6 here:

```
for dataset in range(10):
    lst = input().split()
    franchisees = int(lst[0])
    days = int(lst[1])

    grid = []
```

```
❶ for i in range(days):
        row = input().split()
        for j in range(franchisees):
            row[j] = int(row[j])
        grid.append(row)

    bonuses = 0

❷ for row in grid:
        total = sum(row)
        if total % 13 == 0:
            bonuses = bonuses + total // 13

❸ for col_index in range(franchisees):
        total = 0
        for row_index in range(days):
            total = total + grid[row_index][col_index]
        if total % 13 == 0:
            bonuses = bonuses + total // 13

    print(bonuses)
```

What is the big O efficiency of this algorithm? There are some nested loops in here, so a first guess is that this algorithm is $O(n^2)$. But what is n?

In the problems we've discussed to this point in the chapter, we used the single variable n to represent the amount of input: n could be the number of swaps or the number of parking spaces or the number of email addresses or the number of cows. But in the Baker Bonus problem, we're dealing with two-dimensional input, so we need *two* variables to represent its amount. We'll call the first variable d, the number of days; we'll call the second f, the number of franchisees. More formally, because there are multiple test cases per input, we'll let d be the maximum number of days and f the maximum number of franchisees. We need to give the big O efficiency in terms of *both* d and f.

Our algorithm consists of three major components: reading the input, calculating the number of bonuses from the rows, and calculating the number of bonuses from the columns. Let's take a look at each of these.

To read the input ❶, we perform d iterations of the outer loop. On each of these iterations we read a row and call split, which takes about f steps. We take another f steps to loop through the values and convert them to integers. In total, then, each of the d iterations performs a number of steps proportional to f. Reading the input therefore takes $O(df)$ time.

Now for the row bonuses ❷. The outer loop here loops d times. Each of these iterations calls sum, which takes f steps because it has to add up f values. Like reading the input, then, this part of the algorithm is $O(df)$.

Finally, let's look at the code for the column bonuses ❸. The outer loop loops f times. Each of those iterations leads to the inner loop iterating d times. The total here, again, is $O(df)$.

Each component of this algorithm is $O(df)$. Adding three $O(df)$ components together yields an $O(df)$ algorithm overall.

CONCEPT CHECK

What is the big O efficiency of the following algorithm?

```
for i in range(m):
    <do something that takes one step>
for j in range(n):
    <do something that takes one step>
```

A. $O(1)$

B. $O(n)$

C. $O(n^2)$

D. $O(m+n)$

E. $O(mn)$

Answer: D. The first loop depends on m, and the second depends on n. The loops are sequential, not nested, so their work is added rather than multiplied.

Log Time

In "Efficiency of Our Program" on page 255, we discussed the difference between linear search and binary search. A linear search finds a value in a list by searching the list from beginning to end. That's an $O(n)$ algorithm. It works whether or not the list is sorted. A binary search, by contrast, works only on a sorted list. But if you have a sorted list, then binary search is blazingly fast.

Binary search works by comparing the value we're searching for to the value at the middle of the list. If the value at the middle of the list is larger than the value we're searching for, we continue searching in the left half of the list. If the value at the middle of the list is smaller than the value we're searching for, we continue searching in the right half of the list. We keep doing this, ignoring half of the list each time, until we find the value that we're looking for.

Suppose we use binary search to find a value in a list of 512 values. How many steps does it take? Well, after one step, we've ignored half the list, so we're left with about 512 / 2 = 256 values. (It doesn't matter whether our value is larger than half of the values in the list or smaller than half the values in the list; in each case, we ignore one half of the list.) After two steps, we're left with $256 / 2 = 128$ values. After three steps, we're left with $128 / 2 = 64$ values. Continuing, after four steps we have 32 values, after five steps we have 16 values, after six steps we have 8 values, after seven steps we have 4 values, after eight steps we have 2 values, and after nine steps we have only 1 value.

Nine steps—that's it! That's way better than taking up to 512 steps using linear search. Binary search does far less work than a linear-time algorithm. But what kind of algorithm is it? It's not constant time: while it takes very few steps, the number of steps does increase a little as the amount of input increases.

Binary search is an example of a *logarithmic-time* or *log-time* algorithm. In big O notation, we say that a logarithmic-time algorithm is $O(\log n)$.

Logarithmic-time refers to the logarithm function in mathematics. Given a number, this function tells you the number of times you have to divide that number by a base to get to 1 or less. The base we typically use in computer science is 2, so we're looking for the number of times you have to divide a number by 2 to get to 1 or less. For example, it takes 9 divisions by 2 to take 512 down to 1. We write this as $\log_2 512 = 9$.

The logarithm function is the inverse of the exponential function, the latter of which may be more familiar to you. Another way to calculate $\log_2 512$ is to find the power p so that $2^p = 512$. Since $2^9 = 512$, we confirm that $\log_2 512 = 9$.

It's shocking how slowly the logarithm function grows. For example, consider a list of one million values. How many steps would binary search take to search that? It takes $\log_2 1{,}000{,}000$ steps, which is only about 20. Logarithmic-time is much closer to constant-time than it is to linear-time. It's a huge win any time you can replace a linear-time algorithm by a logarithmic-time one.

n log n Time

In Chapter 5, we solved the Village Neighborhood problem. I've reproduced our solution from Listing 5-1 here:

```
n = int(input())

positions = []

❶ for i in range(n):
      positions.append(int(input()))

❷ positions.sort()

left = (positions[1] - positions[0]) / 2
right = (positions[2] - positions[1]) / 2
min_size = left + right
```

```
❸ for i in range(2, n - 1):
      left = (positions[i] - positions[i - 1]) / 2
      right = (positions[i + 1] - positions[i]) / 2
      size = left + right
      if size < min_size:
          min_size = size

  print(min_size)
```

Looks like a linear-time algorithm, eh? I mean, there's a linear-time loop to read the input ❶ and another linear-time loop to find the minimum size ❸. Is this code $O(n)$, then?

It's too early to tell! The reason is that we haven't yet taken into account that we sort the positions ❷. We can't just ignore that; we need to know about the efficiency of sorting. As we'll see, sorting is slower than linear time. So, since sorting is the slowest step here, whatever the efficiency is of sorting will be the efficiency overall.

Programmers and computer scientists have devised many sorting algorithms, and these algorithms can roughly be divided into two groups. The first group consists of algorithms that take $O(n^2)$ time. The three most famous of these sorting algorithms are bubble sort, selection sort, and insertion sort. You can learn more about these sorting algorithms on your own if you like, but we won't need to know anything about them to continue here. All we have to keep in mind is that $O(n^2)$ can be quite slow. For example, to sort a list of 10,000 values, an $O(n^2)$ sorting algorithm would take about $10,000^2$ = 100,000,000 steps. As we know, this would take any computer at least a few seconds. That's pretty disappointing: sorting 10,000 values feels like something computers should be able to do almost instantly.

Enter the second group of sorting algorithms. This group consists of algorithms that take only $O(n \log n)$ time. There are two famous sorting algorithms in this group: quick sort and merge sort. Again, you're free to look them up if you like, but we don't need the details here.

What does $O(n \log n)$ mean? Don't let the notation confuse you. It's just the multiplication of n by $\log n$. Let's try this out on a list of 10,000 values. Here, we have $10,000 * \log 10,000$ steps, which is only about 132,877. This is a very small number of steps, especially compared to the 100,000,000 steps taken by the $O(n^2)$ sorting algorithms.

Now we can ask the question we really care about: what sorting algorithm is Python using when we ask it to sort a list? Answer: an $O(n \log n)$ one! (It's called Timsort. If you'd like to learn more, start with merge sort, because Timsort is a souped-up merge sort.) No slow $O(n^2)$ sorting here. In general, sorting is so fast—so close to linear time—that we can use it without affecting our efficiency too much.

Returning to Village Neighborhood, now we see that its efficiency is not $O(n)$ but, because of the sort, $O(n \log n)$. In practice, an $O(n \log n)$ algorithm only does a little more work than an $O(n)$ algorithm and far less than an $O(n^2)$ algorithm. If your goal is to design an $O(n)$ algorithm, designing one that's $O(n \log n)$ is probably good enough.

Handling Function Calls

Starting in Chapter 6, we wrote our own functions to help us design larger programs. In our big O analysis, we need to be careful to include the work done when we call these functions.

Let's revisit the Card Game problem from Chapter 6. We solved it in Listing 6-1, and part of our solution involved calling our no_high function. I've reproduced that solution here:

```
NUM_CARDS = 52


❶ def no_high(lst):
      """
      lst is a list of strings representing cards.

      Return True if there are no high cards in lst, False otherwise.
      """
      if 'jack' in lst:
          return False
      if 'queen' in lst:
          return False
      if 'king' in lst:
          return False
      if 'ace' in lst:
          return False
      return True


  deck = []

❷ for i in range(NUM_CARDS):
      deck.append(input())

  score_a = 0
  score_b = 0
  player = 'A'

❸ for i in range(NUM_CARDS):
      card = deck[i]
      points = 0
      remaining = NUM_CARDS - i - 1
      if card == 'jack' and remaining >= 1 and no_high(deck[i+1:i+2]):
          points = 1
      elif card == 'queen' and remaining >= 2 and no_high(deck[i+1:i+3]):
          points = 2
      elif card == 'king' and remaining >= 3 and no_high(deck[i+1:i+4]):
          points = 3
```

```
    elif card == 'ace' and remaining >= 4 and no_high(deck[i+1:i+5]):
        points = 4

    if points > 0:
        print(f'Player {player} scores {points} point(s).')

    if player == 'A':
        score_a = score_a + points
        player = 'B'
    else:
        score_b = score_b + points
        player = 'A'

print(f'Player A: {score_a} point(s).')
print(f'Player B: {score_b} point(s).')
```

We'll use n to represent the number of cards. The no_high function ❶ takes a list and uses in on it, so we might conclude that it is $O(n)$ time. (in may have to search the whole list to find what it's looking for, after all.) However, we only ever call no_high with lists of constant size—maximum four cards—so we can treat each call of no_high as $O(1)$ time.

Now that we understand the efficiency of no_high, we can determine the big O efficiency of the complete program. We begin with a loop that takes $O(n)$ time to read the cards ❷. We then enter another loop that iterates n times ❸. Each iteration takes just a constant number of steps, possibly including a call of no_high that takes a constant number of steps. This loop, then, takes $O(n)$ time. The program therefore consists of two $O(n)$ pieces, so it is $O(n)$ overall.

Be careful to accurately judge the amount of work performed when a function is called. As you just saw with no_high, this may involve looking at both the function itself and the context in which it is called.

CONCEPT CHECK

What is the big O efficiency of the following algorithm?

```
def f(lst):
    for i in range(len(lst)):
        lst[i] = lst[i] + 1


# Assume that lst refers to a list of numbers
for i in range(len(lst)):
    f(lst)
```

(continued)

A. $O(1)$

B. $O(n)$

C. $O(n^2)$

Answer: C. The loop in the main program iterates n times. On each iteration, we call function f, which itself has a loop that iterates n times.

Summary

The algorithms that do the least work are $O(1)$, followed by $O(\log n)$, followed by $O(n)$, followed by $O(n \log n)$. Have you solved a problem using one of these four? If so, you're probably done. If not, then depending on the time limit, you may have more work to do.

We're now going to look at two problems where a straightforward solution will not be efficient enough—it won't run within the time limit. Using what we just learned about big O, we'll be able to predict this inefficiency even without implementing the code! We'll then work on a faster solution and implement it to solve the problem within the time limit.

Problem #24: Longest Scarf

In this problem, we'll determine the longest desired scarf that we can produce by cutting an initial scarf. After reading the following description, pause: how would you solve it? Can you come up with multiple algorithms whose efficiency you'd like to investigate?

This is DMOJ problem dmopc20c2p2.

The Challenge

You have a scarf whose length is n feet, and each foot has a specific color.

You also have m relatives. Each relative indicates what their desired scarf looks like by specifying the color of its first foot and last foot.

Your goal is to cut your original scarf in such a way as to produce the longest desired scarf for one of your relatives.

Input

The input consists of the following lines:

- A line containing the integer scarf length n and integer number of relatives m, separated by a space. n and m are each between 1 and 100,000.

- A line containing n integers separated by spaces. Each integer specifies the color of one foot of scarf in order from the first foot to the last foot. Each integer is between 1 and 1,000,000.

- m lines, one per relative, containing two integers separated by a space. These numbers describe the relative's desired scarf: the first integer is the desired color of the first foot, and the second integer is the desired color of the last foot.

Output

Output the length of the longest desired scarf that can be produced by cutting your original scarf.

The time limit for solving the test cases is 0.4 seconds.

Exploring a Test Case

Let's make sure we know exactly what is being asked by working through a small test case. Here it is:

```
6 3
18 4 4 2 1 2
1 2
4 2
18 4
```

We have a scarf that's 6 feet long and three relatives. The color of each foot of the scarf is 18, 4, 4, 2, 1, and 2. What's the longest desired scarf we can make?

The first relative wants a scarf whose first foot is color 1 and whose last foot is color 2. The best we can do is give this relative a 2-foot scarf: the 2 feet (colors 1 and 2) at the end of the scarf.

The second relative wants a scarf whose first foot is color 4 and whose last foot is color 2. We can give them a 5-foot scarf: 4, 4, 2, 1, 2.

The third relative wants a scarf whose first foot is color 18 and whose last foot is color 4. We can give them a 3-foot scarf: 18, 4, 4.

The maximum length of a desired scarf that we can make is 5, so that's the answer for this test case.

Algorithm 1

The way we just processed that test case might immediately suggest to you an algorithm that we can use to solve this problem. Namely, we should be able to go through the relatives and figure out the maximum length of a desired scarf for each one. For example, the maximum length for the first relative might be 2, so we remember that. The maximum length for the second relative might be 5. That's longer than 2, so we remember the 5. The maximum length for the third relative might be 3. This isn't greater than 5—no change here. If this reminds you of a complete-search algorithm (Chapter 9): good, because it is one!

There are m relatives. If we knew how long it would take us to process each relative, then we'd be able to work out the big O efficiency we'd be dealing with.

Here's an idea: for each relative, let's find the leftmost index of the color of the first foot and the rightmost index of the color of the last foot. Once we had these indices, then no matter how long the scarf, we could use these indices to quickly determine the length of the longest desired scarf for this relative. For example, if the leftmost index of the color of the first foot is 100 and the rightmost index of the color of the last foot is 110, then their longest desired scarf is $110 - 100 + 1 = 11$.

Depending on how we try to find these indices, we might be lucky and find them quickly. For example, we might scan from the left for the leftmost index of the color of the first foot and scan from the right for the rightmost index of the color of the last foot. Then, if the color of the first foot is near the beginning of the scarf and the color of the last foot is near the end, we'll discover these indices very quickly.

We might not be lucky, though. Finding one or both of the indices could take up to n steps. For example, suppose that a relative wants a scarf whose first foot is a color that shows up right at the end of the scarf or that doesn't show up in the scarf at all. We will have to check the entire n feet of the scarf, one foot at a time, to figure this out.

So, about n steps per relative. That's linear time, and we know that linear time is fast. Are we good? No, because in this case the linear-time work is far more menacing than it may appear. Remember that we'd be doing this $O(n)$ work for each of the m relatives. We therefore have an $O(mn)$ algorithm overall. m and n can be as big as 100,000. So, mn can be as big as 100,000 $* 100,000 = 10,000,000,000$. That's 10 billion! Given that we can do about five million operations per second and that our time limit is 0.4 seconds ... yeah, we're not even close. There's no need to implement this algorithm. We're certain that it will time out on large test cases. We may as well move on and spend our time implementing something else. (If you're nevertheless curious about the code, please see the online resources associated with the book. Just remember that without even looking at the code, we already figured out that it would be too slow. The power of big O analysis is in helping us understand whether an algorithm is doomed even before we implement it.)

Algorithm 2

We're going to have to somehow process each of the relatives—there's no getting around that. What we'll focus on optimizing, then, is the amount of work that we do per relative. Unfortunately, processing a relative in the way we did in the previous section may cause us to check over a huge portion of the scarf. It's this searching through the scarf, once per relative, that's crushing us. We need to get that searching under control.

Suppose that we could look through the scarf only once, up-front, before we knew anything about what the relatives wanted. We could remember two things about each color in the scarf: its leftmost index and its rightmost index. Then, no matter what each relative wants, we could figure out the maximum length of their desired scarf using the left and right indices that we had already stored.

For example, assume we have this scarf:

18 4 4 2 1 2

We would store the following information for it:

Color	Leftmost index	Rightmost index
1	4	4
2	3	5
4	1	2
18	0	0

Suppose that a relative wants a scarf whose first foot is color 1 and whose last foot is color 2. We look up the leftmost index for color 1, which is 4, and the rightmost index for color 2, which is 5. We then calculate 5 − 4 + 1 = 2, and that's the length of the longest desired scarf for this relative.

Amazing: no matter how long the scarf, we can just do a quick calculation for each relative. No more running through the scarf over and over. The only tricky thing here is how to calculate all the leftmost and rightmost indices for the colors and to do so by looking through the scarf only once.

The code is presented in Listing 10-1. Try to figure out how the `leftmost_index` and `rightmost_index` dictionaries are constructed before you continue reading my explanation that follows.

```
lst = input().split()
n = int(lst[0])
m = int(lst[1])

scarf = input().split()
for i in range(n):
    scarf[i] = int(scarf[i])
```

❶ `leftmost_index = {}`
❷ `rightmost_index = {}`

❸ `for i in range(n):`
    `color = scarf[i]`
   ❹ `if not color in leftmost_index:`
        `leftmost_index[color] = i`
        `rightmost_index[color] = i`
   ❺ `else:`

```
        rightmost_index[color] = i

max_length = 0

for i in range(m):
    relative = input().split()
    first = int(relative[0])
    last = int(relative[1])
    if first in leftmost_index and last in leftmost_index:
      ❻ length = rightmost_index[last] - leftmost_index[first] + 1
        if length > max_length:
            max_length = length

print(max_length)
```

Listing 10-1: Solving Longest Scarf, algorithm 2

This solution uses two dictionaries: one to keep track of the leftmost index for each color ❶ and one to keep track of the rightmost index for each color ❷.

As promised, we look at each foot of the scarf just once ❸. Here's how we keep the leftmost_index and rightmost_index dictionaries up-to-date:

- If the color of the current foot has never been seen before ❹, then the current index serves as both the leftmost and rightmost index for this color.

- Otherwise, the color of the current foot has been seen before ❺. We don't want to update the leftmost index for this color, because the current index is to the right of the old one. We *do* want to update the rightmost index, though, because we have found an index to the right of the old one.

Now for the payoff: for each relative, we can simply look up the leftmost and rightmost indices from these dictionaries ❻. The maximum length of the desired scarf is the rightmost index of the color of the last foot, minus the leftmost index of the color of the first foot, plus one.

As I'll argue now, this algorithm is far better than algorithm 1. Reading the scarf takes $O(n)$ time, as does processing the scarf's feet. That's $O(n)$ time so far. We then take a constant number of steps to process each relative (not n steps like before!), so that's $O(m)$ time. In total, we have an $O(m + n)$ algorithm, rather than an $O(mn)$ algorithm. Given that m and n can be at most 100,000, we're doing only about 100,000 + 100,000 = 200,000 steps, easily done within the time limit. You can submit our code to the judge to prove it!

Problem #25: Ribbon Painting

Here's another problem where the first algorithm that we might come up with is too slow. We won't waste much time on that algorithm, though, because our big O analysis will tell us all we need to know before we consider implementing the code. We'll then spend our time designing a faster algorithm.

This is DMOJ problem `dmopc17c4p1`.

The Challenge

You have a purple ribbon whose length is n units. The first unit goes from position 0 up to but not including position 1, the second unit goes from position 1 up to but not including position 2, and so on. You then carry out q paint strokes, each of which colors a segment of the ribbon blue.

Your goal is to determine the number of units of the ribbon that are still purple and the number of units of the ribbon that are now blue.

Input

The input consists of the following lines:

- A line containing the integer ribbon length n and integer number of paint strokes q, separated by a space. n and q are each between 1 and 100,000.

- q lines, one per paint stroke, containing two integers separated by a space. The first integer gives the starting position of the paint stroke; the second gives the ending position of the paint stroke. The starting position is guaranteed to be less than the ending position; each integer is between 0 and n. The paint stroke goes from the starting position up to but not including the ending position. As a quick example here, if a paint stroke has a starting position of 5 and an ending position of 12, then the stroke paints the ribbon from position 5 up to but not including position 12.

Output

Output the number of units of the ribbon that are still purple, a space, and the number of units of the ribbon that are now blue.

The time limit for solving the test cases is 2 seconds.

Exploring a Test Case

Let's look at a small test case. This test case will not only ensure that we've interpreted the problem correctly but also highlight the perils of a naive algorithm. Here it is:

```
20 4
18 19
4 16
4 14
5 12
```

Our ribbon's length is 20, and there are four paint strokes. How much of the ribbon do our paint strokes turn blue?

The first paint stroke paints one unit blue, the one that starts at position 18.

The second paint stroke paints the units of ribbon starting at positions 4, 5, 6, 7, and so on, all the way up to position 15. That's 12 units painted blue by this stroke, and 13 blue units in total.

The third paint stroke paints 10 units blue. But all of those units are already blue from the second paint stroke! It would be a colossal waste of time indeed if we spent time "painting" anything with this paint stroke. Whatever algorithm we come up with better not fall into this time-wasting trap.

The fourth paint stroke paints 7 units blue. But again: all of these units are already blue!

Now we're done painting, and we have 13 blue units. There are 20 − 13 = 7 remaining purple units, so the correct output for this test case is:

---

7 13

Solving the Problem

The maximum length of the ribbon is 100,000, and the maximum number of paint strokes is 100,000. Recall algorithm 1 from when we solved Longest Scarf, where we learned that an $O(mn)$ algorithm was too slow with these bounds. Similarly, here, an $O(nq)$ algorithm would be inadequate, as it would not finish within the time limit on large test cases.

This means that we cannot afford to process each unit that is painted by each paint stroke. It would be nice if we could more easily focus on only the *new* units that are painted blue by a paint stroke. Then we could go through each paint stroke and add up the number of blue units that it contributes.

Fair enough, but how can we determine the contribution of each paint stroke? That's tricky, because bits and pieces of the next paint stroke may have already been painted blue by previous paint strokes.

This situation is made much simpler, however, if we sort the paint strokes first. Remember from "n log n Time" earlier in this chapter that sorting is extremely fast, taking only $O(n \log n)$ time. There's no efficiency concern in using sorting, so let's understand why sorting helps us here.

Sorting the paint strokes from the test case in the prior section gives us the following list of paint strokes:

---

4 14
4 16
5 12
18 19

Now that the paint strokes are sorted, we can efficiently process them. As we do so, we'll store the rightmost position of any paint stroke that we've processed so far. We'll start this rightmost position off at 0 to indicate that we haven't painted anything.

Our first paint stroke paints 14 − 4 = 10 units blue. Now our stored rightmost position is 14.

Our second paint stroke paints 12 units blue, yes, but how many of those 12 does it turn from purple to blue? After all, it overlaps the previous paint stroke, so some of these units were blue already. We can calculate the number of new blue units by subtracting 14, our stored rightmost position, from 16, the ending position of the current paint stroke. This is how we ignore the units already painted blue by previous paint strokes. So, there are 16 − 14 = 2 new blue units and 12 blue units in total. Crucially, we just figured this out without processing the individual units of this paint stroke. Before we continue, don't forget to update our stored rightmost position to 16.

Our third paint stroke is like the second in that it starts prior to our stored rightmost position. Unlike the second paint stroke, however, its ending position does not extend past our stored rightmost position at all. So, this paint stroke adds no new blue units, and our stored rightmost position is still 16. Again, we figured this out without grinding through each of this paint stroke's positions!

Be careful with the fourth paint stroke. It does *not* add 19 − 16 = 3 new blue units. We have to treat this paint stroke differently because its starting position is to the right of our stored rightmost position. In this case, we don't use the stored rightmost position at all, calculating instead 19 − 18 = 1 new blue unit, and 13 blue units in total. We also update our stored rightmost position to 19.

The only question is how we sort the paint strokes in our Python code. We need to sort them by their starting position; if multiple paint strokes have the same starting position, then we want to sort those by their ending position.

That is, we want to take a list like this:

```
[[18, 19], [4, 16], [4, 14], [5, 12]]
```

and produce this:

```
[[4, 14], [4, 16], [5, 12], [18, 19]]
```

Happily, as we discovered in "Task 4: Sort Boxes" in Chapter 6, the list sort method works in exactly this way. When given a list of lists, sort sorts using the first values in each list; when those values are tied, the lists are further sorted using the second values. Check it out:

```
>>> strokes = [[18, 19], [4, 16], [4, 14], [5, 12]]
>>> strokes.sort()
>>> strokes
[[4, 14], [4, 16], [5, 12], [18, 19]]
```

Algorithm: check. Sorting: check. We're in great shape! Just one more thing we'd like to know before we see the code: what will be its big O efficiency? We need to read the q queries; that takes $O(q)$ time. Then we need to sort the queries; that takes $O(q \log q)$ time. Finally, we need to process the queries; that takes $O(q)$ time. The slowest of these is the $O(q \log q)$ time for the sorting, so that's our overall big O efficiency.

Now we have everything we need for a speedy solution. Check it out in Listing 10-2.

```
lst = input().split()
n = int(lst[0])
q = int(lst[1])

strokes = []

for i in range(q):
    stroke = input().split()
❶   strokes.append([int(stroke[0]), int(stroke[1])])

❷ strokes.sort()

rightmost_position = 0

blue = 0

for stroke in strokes:
    stroke_start = stroke[0]
    stroke_end = stroke[1]
❸   if stroke_start <= rightmost_position:
        if stroke_end > rightmost_position:
❹           blue = blue + stroke_end - rightmost_position
            rightmost_position = stroke_end
❺   else:
❻       blue = blue + stroke_end - stroke_start
        rightmost_position = stroke_end

print(n - blue, blue)
```

Listing 10-2: Solving Ribbon Painting

We read each paint stroke, appending it as a list of two values to our strokes list ❶. We then sort all of the paint strokes ❷.

We next need to process each paint stroke from left to right. There are two key variables that drive this processing: variable rightmost_position stores the rightmost position that we have painted so far, and variable blue stores the number of units that we have painted blue so far.

To process a paint stroke, we need to know whether it starts before or after our stored rightmost position. Let's think about each of these cases in turn.

First: what do we do when the paint stroke starts before our stored right-most position ❸? This paint stroke might give us some new blue units, but only if it extends past our stored rightmost position. If it does, then the new blue units are those between the stored rightmost position and the ending position of the paint stroke ❹.

Second: what do we do when the paint stroke starts after our stored rightmost position ❺? This time, the paint stroke is completely separate from the painting we have done so far; this entire paint stroke is a new blue segment. As such, the new blue units are those between the ending position and starting position of this paint stroke ❻.

Notice in each case that we also correctly update our stored rightmost position so that we're ready to process any further paint strokes.

That's a wrap! Guided by our big O analysis, we were able to dismiss an algorithm whose implementation we knew would be too slow. We then thought about a second algorithm—and before implementing it, we knew it would be plenty fast. It's time to submit our code to the judge and bask in our success.

Summary

In this chapter, we learned about big O analysis. Big O is an important efficiency building block for further study of algorithm design. You'll see it everywhere: in tutorials, in books, probably in your next job interview!

We also solved two problems where we needed to design very efficient algorithms. Not only were we able to do that, but we were also able to use big O to obtain a satisfying understanding of exactly why our code was so efficient.

Chapter Exercises

Here are some exercises for you to try. For each, use big O to determine whether your proposed algorithm is efficient enough to solve the problem within the time limit. You might also like to implement algorithms that you know are going to be too slow. That would give you extra practice solidifying your Python knowledge and confirm that your big O analysis was spot-on!

Some of these problems are quite challenging. There are two reasons. First, you might agree based on your work throughout the book that coming up with *any* algorithm can be tough. Coming up with a faster algorithm can be even tougher. Second, this is the end of our time together, but only the beginning of the study of algorithms. I hope that these problems both help you appreciate what you've accomplished and offer evidence that there's a lot more beyond this book if you want it.

1. DMOJ problem `dmopc17c1p1`, Fujo Neko (The problem talks about using fast input/output. Don't ignore that!)

2. DMOJ problem `coci10c1p2`, Profesor

3. DMOJ problem `coci19c4p1`, Pod starim krovovima (Hint: to maximize the number of empty glasses, you want to put as much liquid as possible in the biggest glasses.)

4. DMOJ problem `dmopc20c1p2`, Victor's Moral Dilemma

5. DMOJ problem `avocadotrees`, Avocado Trees!

6. DMOJ problem `coci11c5p2`, Eko (Hint: the maximum number of trees is far fewer than the maximum number of heights. Consider each tree from tallest to shortest.)

7. DMOJ problem `wac6p2`, Cheap Christmas Lights (Hint: don't try flipping a switch each second—how would you know which one to flip? Instead, store them up, and use them all as soon as you can shut off all the lights that are on.)

8. DMOJ problem `ioi98p3`, Party Lamps (Hint: all that matters for each button is whether it is pressed an even or odd number of times.)

Notes

Longest Scarf is originally from the DMOPC '14 March Contest. Ribbon Painting is originally from the DMOPC '20 November Contest.

AFTERWORD

Before you jump into whatever is next, I'd like to take a minute to congratulate you on what you've accomplished to this point. It's possible that you hadn't done any programming before picking up this book. Or maybe you had done a little programming and wanted to improve your problem-solving ability. Regardless, if you've made it through the book and spent the necessary time grinding through the exercises, you now know how to solve problems using a computer. You learned how to understand a problem description, design a solution, and write that solution in code. You learned about if statements, loops, lists, functions, files, sets, dictionaries, complete-search algorithms, and big O analysis. These are the core tools of programming, and the tools that you'll turn to again and again. You can also now call yourself a Python programmer!

Perhaps your next step is to learn more about Python. If that's the case, see the notes at the end of Chapter 8.

Perhaps your next step is to learn another programming language. One of my personal favorites is C. Compared to Python, it brings you much closer to what's actually going on inside your computer when programs are running. If you'd like to learn C, there's no better book than *C Programming: A Modern Approach*, 2nd edition, by K. N. King (W. W. Norton & Company, 2008). I think you're well positioned to read that book at this point. You might also consider learning a language such as C++, Java, Go, or Rust, depending on the types of programs you want to write (or simply because of what you've heard about these languages).

Perhaps your next step is to learn more about designing algorithms. If that's the case, see the notes at the end of Chapter 9.

Perhaps your next step is to take a break from this. To do something else. To solve other kinds of problems that may or may not have anything to do with computing.

Happy problem solving!

PROBLEM CREDITS

I'm grateful for the time and expertise offered by everyone who helps people learn through competitive programming. For each problem in this book, I have sought to identify its author and where the problem came from. If you have additional information or credits for any of the following problems, please let me know. Updates will be posted on the book's website.

Here are the abbreviations that are used in the following table:

CCC: Canadian Computing Competition

CCO: Canadian Computing Olympiad

COCI: Croatian Open Competition in Informatics

DMOPC: DMOJ Monthly Open Programming Competition

ECOO: Educational Computing Organization of Ontario Programming Contest

Ural: Ural School Programming Contest

USACO: USA Computing Olympiad

Chapter	Section	Original title	Competition/author
1	Word Count	Not a Wall of Text	2015 DMOPC/ FatalEagle
1	Cone Volume	Core Drill	2014 DMOPC/ FatalEagle
2	Winning Team	Winning Score	2019 CCC
2	Telemarketers	Telemarketer or Not?	2018 CCC
3	Three Cups	Trik	2006/2007 COCI
3	Occupied Spaces	Occupy Parking	2018 CCC
3	Data Plan	Tarifa	2016/2017 COCI
4	Slot Machines	Slot Machines	2000 CCC
4	Song Playlist	Do the Shuffle	2008 CCC
4	Secret Sentence	Kemija	2008/2009 COCI
5	Village Neighborhood	Voronoi Villages	2018 CCC
5	School Trip	Munch 'n' Brunch	2017 ECOO/ Andrew Seidel Reyno Tilikaynen
5	Baker Bonus	Baker Brie	2017 ECOO/ Andrew Seidel Reyno Tilikaynen
6	Card Game	Card Game	1999 CCC
6	Action Figures	Cleaning the Room	2019 Ural/ Ivan Smirnov
7	Essay Formatting	Word Processor	2020 USACO/ Nathan Pinsker
7	Farm Seeding	The Great Revegetation	2019 USACO/ Dhruv Rohatgi Brian Dean
8	Email Addresses	Email	2019 ECOO/ Andrew Seidel Reyno Tilikaynen Tongbo Sui
8	Common Words	Common Words	1999 CCO
8	Cities and States	Cities and States	2016 USACO/ Brian Dean
9	Lifeguards	Lifeguards	2018 USACO/ Brian Dean
9	Ski Hills	Ski Course Design	2014 USACO/ Brian Dean
9	Cow Baseball	Cow Baseball	2013 USACO/ Brian Dean
10	Longest Scarf	Lousy Christmas Presents	2020 DMOPC/ Roger Fu
10	Ribbon Painting	Ribbon Colouring Fun	2017 DMOPC/ Jiayi Zhang

CCC and CCO problems are owned by the Centre for Education in Mathematics and Computing (CEMC) at the University of Waterloo.

INDEX

Boolean expression, if statement, 31
Boolean expression, while loop, 73
Boolean operators, 37, 38, 78
  and, 39
  not, 40
  or, 38
Boolean type, 27, 28
Boolean values, 28
break, 96
brute-force algorithms. *See*
        complete-search algorithms
bug, 55

C

C Programming: A Modern Approach,
      2nd edition (King), 296
calling a method, 8
Card Game problem, 137, 169
  challenge, 138
  defining and calling functions, 140
    functions with arguments, 141
    functions without arguments, 141
    keyword arguments, 143
    local variables, 144
    mutable parameters, 145
    return values, 147
  function documentation, 149
  high card, 138
  input, 138
  output, 138
  problem solving, 150
  rules, 138
  types of cards, 138
cd command, 4
center method, 109
char, 50
choice function, 258
Cities and States problem, 231
  challenge, 231
  input, 231
  output, 231
  problem solving, 234
cleaning an email address, 205
closing files, 179
code duplication, avoiding, 116, 137
  huge size, 116
  list of sizes, building, 117
comment lines, 43

comments, 42, 43
Common Words problem, 215
  challenge, 215
  dictionaries, 218
  indexing dictionaries, 220
  input, 216
  inverting dictionaries, 225
  looping through dictionaries, 222
  output, 216
  problem solving, 227
    code, 227
    kth most common words, 229
    main program, 230
    suffix, adding, 229
complete-search algorithms, 237–239,
    245
  Cow Baseball problem, 249
  Lifeguards problem, 238
  Ski Hills problem, 244
Computers and the World of the Future
    (Greenberger), 201
conditional execution, 27
Cone Volume problem, 1, 18
  challenge, 19
  input, 19
  math in Python, 19
    exponents, 19
    pi, 19
  output, 19
  problem solving, 22
  strings and integers, converting, 20
constant-time algorithms, 268, 269
continue, 96, 98
count method, 8, 9, 109
Cow Baseball problem, 249
  bisect module, 258
  challenge, 249
  input, 249
  nested loops, 250
    code, 250
    program efficiency, 252
  output, 250
  problem solving, 261
  Python modules, 256
  sorting first, 253
    code, 253
    program efficiency, 255
cubic-time algorithm, 277
curly brackets, 85, 210, 211, 218

find method, 206
float function, 121
floating-point numbers, 9–14, 20
for loops, 49–52, 56, 57, 69, 72, 87,
    176, 226, 270
  block, 51
  if statement inside, 51
  iteration, 65
  limitations, 72, 92
  range, 72
  variables, 49
for statement, 49
functions, 15, 137, 140
  Action Figures problem, 153
  Card Game problem, 137
  choice, 258
  define and create, 141
  dir, 108, 109
  documentation, 149–150
  exponential, 280
  float, 121
  help, 109
  input, 15, 140, 171, 174
  int, 21
  invert_dictionary, 226
  keyword arguments, 143
  len, 50, 211, 219
  list, 61
  local variables, 144
  logarithm, 280
  max, 117
  min, 117
  mutable parameters, 145
  nonmodule, 258
  open, 173
  parameter, 142
  print, 16, 31, 32, 44, 51, 85, 140, 171
  randint, 257, 258
  range, 59
  return values, 147
  search, 213, 214
  str, 22
  sum, 126, 130
  type, 27
  with arguments, 141
  without arguments, 141

G

get method, 221
Gmail address, 204. *See also* Email
    Addresses problem
grid variables, 133

H

help function, 109
high card, 138, 139

I

if statements, 25, 27, 30, 31, 49, 78,
    141
  block of, 31, 32
  for loops, inside, 51
  if by itself, 31
  if with elif, 32
  if with else, 33
  isupper in, 52
  logic, 43, 49
in operator, 96, 208, 213, 215, 260
indefinite loops, 51. *See also* while
    loops
  Secret Sentence problem, 91
  Slot Machines problem, 69
  Song Playlist problem, 86
index error, 89
index method, 126, 260
indexing, 57–59, 89, 93, 105, 107
  dictionaries, 220
  range for loops, 61
infinite loops, 74
input function, 15, 140, 171, 174
input redirection, 44
input-process-output model, 2
insert method, 112
int function, 21
integer interpretation, 183
integers, 9–14
interactive programs, 2
intersection method, 213
invert_dictionary function, 226
isupper method, 52, 109
items method, 224
iteration of loops, 50

W

w, mode of, 173

while loops, 69, 73, 80, 87, 90, 91
  Boolean expression, 73, 74, 87, 96
  indefinite loops, 73
  through indices, 93
  using, 73
    Boolean operators, 78
    nesting loops in loops, 77
  variables, 73

while statement, 73

Winning Team problem, 25
  Boolean type, 27
  challenge, 26
  conditional execution, 26, 27
  if statements, 25, 27, 30
    if by itself, 31
    if with elif, 32
    if with else, 33
  input, 26, 35
  output, 26, 35
  problem solving, 35
  relational operators, 28

Word Count problem, 1, 2, 5
  challenge, 5
  input, 5
  input-process-output model, 2
  integer and floating-point numbers, 9
    assignment statement, 11
    changing variable values, 13
    variables, 11
  output, 6
  problem solving, 16
    judge, submitting to, 18
    program, 17
    running the program, 17
    text editor, launching, 16, 17
  reading input, 15
  strings, 6
    methods, 8
    operators, 7
    representation, 6
  variable, using, 14
  writing output, 15

write method, 177–179

RESOURCES

Visit *https://nostarch.com/learn-code-solving-problems/* for errata and more information.

More no-nonsense books from **NO STARCH PRESS**

BEYOND THE BASIC STUFF WITH PYTHON
Best Practices for Writing Clean Code
BY AL SWEIGART
384 PP., $34.95
ISBN 978-1-59327-966-0

REAL-WORLD PYTHON
A Hacker's Guide to Solving Problems with Code
BY LEE VAUGHAN
360 PP., $34.95
ISBN 978-1-7185-0062-4

HOW COMPUTERS REALLY WORK
A Hands-On Guide to the Inner Workings of the Machine
BY MATTHEW JUSTICE
392 PP., $39.95
ISBN 978-1-7185-0066-2

ALGORITHMIC THINKING
A Problem-Based Introduction
BY DANIEL ZINGARO
408 PP., $49.95
ISBN 978-1-7185-0080-8

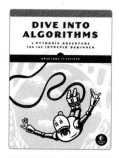

DIVE INTO ALGORITHMS
A Pythonic Adventure for the Intrepid Beginner
BY BRADFORD TUCKFIELD
248 PP., $39.95
ISBN 978-1-7185-0068-6

EFFECTIVE C
An Introduction to Professional C Programming
BY ROBERT C. SEACORD
272 PP., $49.95
ISBN 978-1-7185-0104-1

PHONE:
800.420.7240 OR
415.863.9900

EMAIL:
SALES@NOSTARCH.COM

WEB:
WWW.NOSTARCH.COM